Special thanks to the authors, editors, art directors,
copyeditors, and other staff members of *Fine Homebuilding*
who contributed to the development of the articles in this book.

CONTENTS

BUILDING DECKS

FROM THE EDITORS OF Fine Homebuilding

The Taunton Press

The Taunton Press
Inspiration for hands-on living®

The Taunton Press Inc., 63 South Main St., PO Box 5506, Newtown, CT 06470-5506
e-mail: tp@taunton.com

Editor: Alex Giannini
Copy editor: Seth Reichgott
Indexer: Jay Kreider
Cover Design: Alexander Isley, Inc.
Interior Design: Cathy Cassidy
Layout: Susan Lampe-Wilson
Front cover photographer: John Ross, courtesy *Fine Homebuilding*, © The Taunton Press, Inc.
Back cover photographer: Daniel S. Morrison, courtesy *Fine Homebuilding* © The Taunton Press, Inc.

Taunton's For Pros By Pros® is a trademark of The Taunton Press, Inc.,
registered in the U.S. Patent and Trademark Office.

Library of Congress Cataloging-Publication-Data

Building decks / author, from the editors of Fine homebuilding.

   p. cm.

 Includes index.

 ISBN 978-1-60085-355-5

 1. Decks (Architecture, Domestic) I. Taunton Press. II. Fine homebuilding.

 TH4970.B8523 2011

 690'.893--dc22

                    2010042429

Printed in the United States of America
10 9 8 7 6 5 4 3 2 1

The following manufacturers/names appearing in *Building Decks* are trademarks: Accoya®, Alcoa®, Armor-Rail®, Azek®, Bear Board™, Bigfoot Systems®, Biowash®, Bostich®, Cambia®, Cepco Bowrench®, Certainteed®, Concealoc®, CorrectDeck®, CrossTimbers®, Cuprinol®, CWF-UV®, Deck Clip™, DeckIt™, Dec-Klip®, Deck Lok™, Deckmaster®, Deck-Mate®, DeckProtector®, Deck Spacers™, Deck-Tie®, EB-TY®, EcoLife®, Eliminator™, Eon®, Evercote®, Equator®, EverGrain®, Fasco®, Fastenator®, FastenMaster®, Feeney®, Fein®, Fiberon®, Frisbee®, Fypon®, GeoDeck®, Gossen®, Grace®, Grace Ice and Water Shield®, GuardDog®, Headcote®, Highpoint®, Hinkley®, Hitachi®, Invisi-Fast™, Ipe Clip®, Ipe Clip Extreme™, Kichler®, Kleenex®, Latitudes®, Latitudes Intrepid®, LedgerLok®, Lexan®, Live Cylinder™, Lumber Loc®, Maine Deck Brackets®, Makita®, MicroPro®, Milwaukee®, MoistureShield®, Monarch®, Muro®, NailScrews®, Novaline®, Osmose®, PAM®, Paslode®, Positive Placement®, Penofin®, Porter-Cable®, PosiSquare™, PureWood®, Quik Drive®, Razorback®, Redibase®, Rhino Deck®, Rockler®, Scrail®, Sea Gull Lighting®, Sabre™, Senco®, Shadoe®, Sherwin-Williams® Woodscapes®, Sikkens®, Simpson®, Simpson Strong-Tie®, Speed® Square, Square-Driv®, Square Foot®, Stabila®, Stanley®, Stripex®, Sundeck®, TerraDek®, Thompson's Water Seal®, Tiger Claw®, TimberLok®, TimberSIL®, TimberTech®, Titebond®, Titen®, TrapEase®, Trex®, Ultra-Tec®, Vaughan Bowjak®, VEKAdeck®, Vycor®, Wolmanized®, WoodLife®, Xerox®, YorkWrap™.

About Your Safety: Homebuilding is inherently dangerous. From accidents with power tools to falls from ladders, scaffolds, and roofs, builders risk serious injury and even death. We try to promote safe work habits through our articles. But what is safe for one person under certain circumstances may not be safe for you under different circumstances. So don't try anything you learn about here (or elsewhere) unless you're certain that it is safe for you. Please be careful.

Building methods change and building codes vary by region and are constantly evolving, so please check with your local building department.

PART 3: RAILINGS AND STAIRS

PART 4: DETAILS AND DESIGN

PART 5: BUILDING A DECK

INTRODUCTION

When I bought my house, a fixer-upper, the deck was relatively new. The framing, decking, and railings were all built with pressure-treated lumber. The ledger seemed to be flashed properly and showed no signs of rot. The deck stood on four, 8-in. concrete piers that seemed to be spaced appropriately. The decking was laid in a nice diagonal pattern. But the builders didn't pull a permit for the project—the 9-in. baluster spacing was a dead giveaway. They also didn't use any metal connectors on the project. I bought the house anyway and figured someday, when I completed the dozens of more urgent projects, I'd do some upgrades on the deck, fix the widely spaced balusters, and retrofit joist hangers and post bases and caps.

What I didn't notice at the time was that the piers were starting to lean with the sloping grade of my backyard. But within the first couple of years that I owned the house, this situation grew more problematic. As the piers settled down-hill, the joists began to pull away from the ledger. The deck quickly rose to the top of my to-do list. After a weekend of digging, hunched over beneath my deck, I finally pulled the existing piers out of the ground and found that they were only 3 ft. deep. That's about a foot short of the frost line and the building code where I live.

A well-built deck can be a valuable upgrade to your home and to your life, while a poorly built deck will be nothing but a headache, or worse a safety hazard. That's why we cover this topic so often in *Fine Homebuilding* magazine and why the codes are so protective over this area of our homes. If you're considering tackling a deck project this year, I highly recommend this collection of articles from some of the best builders from across the country. The first story, by Rick Arnold, on page 4 helped me get my new piers right. Now I'm getting ready to turn my attention to the chapter on railings. And if you're wondering if you should pull a permit for your project, the answer is yes. Your building inspector can help you sort out the details, and any prospective buyer should demand to see it.

—Brian Pontolilo, editor, *Fine Homebuilding*

A Solid Deck Begins with Concrete Piers

■ BY RICK ARNOLD

Dig a hole and fill it with concrete. How hard can that be? I've seen old decks built on top of little more than a shovelful of concrete, cinder blocks up on end, and even 8-in. by 12-in. patio blocks. I've also seen old decks—not to mention a couple of new ones—sink and pull away from a house, heave up with the same results, and even both sink and heave from one end to the other.

An insufficient design or a bad installation of this simple foundation system can have disastrous consequences in terms of safety, aesthetics, and a builder's reputation. That's why I approach piers with the same care as I do a house or addition foundation.

Soil Conditions and Load Requirements Determine Pier Size and Spacing

Because piers perform the same job for the deck that the foundation does for the house, it's critical to size and space them properly (see the sidebar on p. 9).

I begin by figuring out how many piers are needed. This decision depends mostly on deck design. For this project, I was building a simple 12-ft. deep by 16-ft. wide rectangular deck with a double rim joist to act as a beam. The beam could span about 8 ft. between posts, but I prefer to space posts about 6 ft. apart for greater support and to minimize the diameter of the piers. To calculate the number of piers, I divided the 16-ft. rim beam by whole numbers until I got a figure of 6 ft. or less. Here, I found that dividing the beam into three sections gave me a span of roughly 5 ft. 4 in., which came out to four piers in total; one at each end and two along the length.

After calculating the number of piers I need, I determine the size they need to be. The size of builder's tube dictates the size of the bottom of the pier, which is the area that will be in contact with soil at the bottom of the excavation. To figure this out, I calculate the maximum weight each

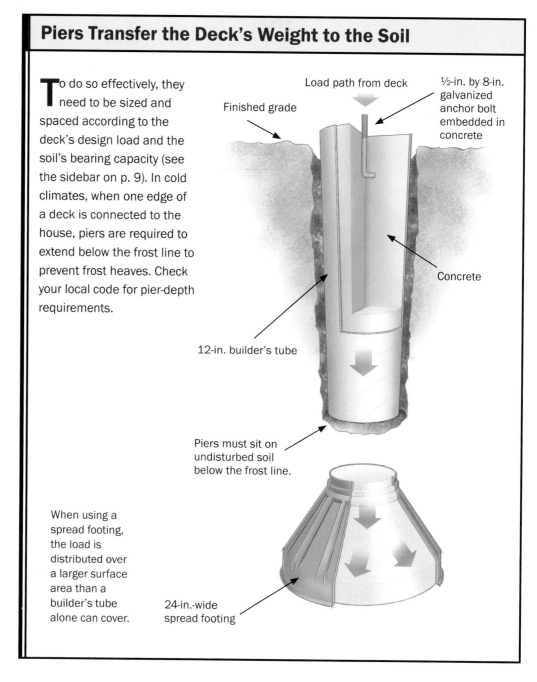

Piers Transfer the Deck's Weight to the Soil

To do so effectively, they need to be sized and spaced according to the deck's design load and the soil's bearing capacity (see the sidebar on p. 9). In cold climates, when one edge of a deck is connected to the house, piers are required to extend below the frost line to prevent frost heaves. Check your local code for pier-depth requirements.

Load path from deck

Finished grade

½-in. by 8-in. galvanized anchor bolt embedded in concrete

Concrete

12-in. builder's tube

Piers must sit on undisturbed soil below the frost line.

When using a spread footing, the load is distributed over a larger surface area than a builder's tube alone can cover.

24-in.-wide spread footing

pier must be designed to bear (by code). For the deck in this chapter, I figured a 1,600-lb. load on each of the two inside piers (see the sidebar on p. 9). Then I compared that to the bearing capacity of the soil at the bottom of the hole. I was building on hard-packed gravel which, according to the IRC table 401.4.1, has a load-bearing value of 3,000 lb. per sq. ft. (psf).

The bearing capacity of a 10-in.-dia. tube in 3,000 psf soil is 1,650 psf (0.55 × 3,000). The design load of each inside pier is 1,600 lb., so a 10-in. tube will work. However, by jumping up to a 12-in. tube, the bearing capacity becomes 2,370 psf (0.79 × 3,000), which can carry the 1,600-lb. load more easily. For just a bit more concrete, I ensure the pier is well designed. I typically ignore the pier weight because there is enough fat in these calculations to justify this simplification.

The two outside-corner piers are required to bear only half the weight, but to simplify the work process, I use the same size tubes for all four of the piers.

The depth you set the piers at depends a lot on the region of the country you're working in. In climates where frost is an issue, the minimum depth is established by code. For this project, the bottoms of the piers have to be 36 in. below finished grade.

Wherever you live, it is important to dig past soil that contains organic matter (topsoil) and any uncompacted fill. Organic matter decomposes over time and settles; loose fill also settles over time. In most cases, the depth of undisturbed soil is not known until the excavation is well underway.

Everything You Need

A few tools, even fewer materials, and a little sweat will get most deck foundations out of the ground in less than a day.

- Builder's tubes
- 80-lb. bags of ready-mix concrete
- Garden hose
- Foundation spikes
- Batterboards
- ½-in. by 8-in. anchor bolts, nuts, and washers
- Adjustable post bases
- Post-hole digger
- Digging bar
- Electric concrete mixer
- Stabila® plate level

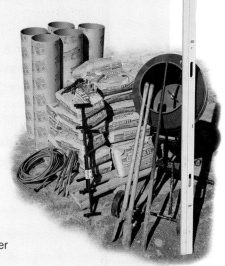

Footings Spread the Weight over a Larger Area

If the piers will be used in soil with poor bearing capacity or if the deck has a heavy design load, use a spread footing to distribute the load over a greater surface area. The more expensive, labor-intensive way to do this requires a relatively large excavation for each pier. After forming and pouring the footings, you have to install the tubes and backfill around them, then complete a second pour for the piers. But plastic footing forms bring this process down to just one pour.

For most of these systems, a builder's tube is fastened to the top of the form; then the assembly is lowered into the hole, backfilled, and poured in one shot. See the manufacturer's Web site for sizing and load requirements.

BigFoot Systems®
www.bigfootsystems.com
Available from 20 in.
to 36 in. dia.

Square Foot®
www.sqfoot.com
Available from 22 in.
to 32 in. dia.

Redibase®
www.redibase-form.com
Available in 24 in. dia.

The Footing Tube
www.foottube.com
A builder's tube and spread footing in one. Top diameter sizes range from 6 in. to 12 in.

Begin Layout with Deck Dimensions

Once I know the size and the number of piers I'm going to use, the next step is to lay them out on site. If the deck details aren't drawn on the plans, I sketch the outside deck framing to determine exactly where the center of the supporting posts are in relation to the outside dimensions of the deck. Then I use those locations to form a layout rectangle. I use batterboards and string to locate the exact center of the post, which is also the location for the anchor bolts that hold the post hardware in place.

Once the post locations are identified and marked with surveyor's paint, I remove the strings and dig the pier holes. When the holes are deep enough, I rough-cut the builder's tubes, drop them in, and replace the stringlines. I keep the tubes centered on the strings while they are backfilled, and I double-check the measurements with a tape measure.

Rather than try to cut tubes to exact height, I leave them long and pour concrete to the desired height inside the tube. In most cases, I like the pour to come a couple of inches above the finished grade. If the piers are on a pitched elevation, the tops of the piers won't be level with each other. On this job, the finished grade was level, so I used a long level to carry the elevation across the piers.

After marking each pier with a small nail pushed through at the right height, I again remove the strings so that I can pour the concrete into the tubes. Once they're filled to the right height, I float the concrete smooth with a scrap of wood. Then I replace the string, and using a slight up-and-down motion to prevent air from becoming trapped, I insert the anchor bolts in their proper locations.

Rick Arnold is a contributing editor to Fine Home-building. Technical assistance by Rob Munach, P.E.

How Much Concrete Do I Need?

To pour the piers for an average-size deck, I use 80-lb. bags of concrete and an electric mixer, which rents for about $45 a day or sells for $250 or so. For major pours, I have a concrete truck deliver a 2,500-lb. mix. Either way, the basic formulas below will help you to estimate the number of bags or cubic yards of concrete required based on pier size and depth.

EXAMPLE
Size of tubes: 8 in.
Number of tubes: 8
Average depth
  per tube: 4 ft.
0.53 (8 x 4) = 17 bags

Tube size	Number of 80-lb. bags per foot	Cubic yards per foot
8 in.	0.53 bag	0.013 cu. yd.
10 in.	0.8 bag	0.02 cu. yd.
12 in.	1.2 bags	0.03 cu. yd.
14 in.	1.6 bags	0.04 cu. yd.

Three things affect the number and the size of piers you use: the way you frame the deck, the weight the deck is designed for, and the load-bearing capacity of the soil. For the deck I'm building, I chose to support the double rim joist with piers instead of a cantilevered approach that uses piers beneath a beam. I use the International Residential Code's (IRC) design load for decks, which is 50 lb. psf (40 psf live load, 10 psf dead load). Different soils have different bearing capacities (measured in psf); consult table 401.4.1 of the IRC (www.iccsafe.org) for the bearing capacities of different soil types or check with your local building official.

Step 1. Space piers evenly beneath the double rim joist

Because I'm using a double rim joist to support the floor joists, I use four piers to support this 16-ft. deck.

Step 2. Distribute the deck's weight onto the piers

A 12-ft. by 16-ft. deck is 192 sq. ft. Multiply by 50 psf to determine the design load, 9,600 lb. Half of that weight (4,800 lb.) is carried by the ledger; the other half is carried by the piers. Because the corner piers carry only half the weight that the inside piers carry, dividing 4,800 lb. by 3 tells me the two inside piers must each bear 1,600 lb.

Step 3. Transfer the weight to the soil

For this project, I was working in hard-packed gravel, which I estimate to have a bearing capacity of 3,000 psf. Using the table above, I multiply the square-foot equivalent of each tube by 3,000 psf to find one that will work in this soil. A 10-in. tube will bear 1,650 psf, which is close, but I chose to bump up to 12-in. piers for peace of mind. To keep things simple, I made the corner piers the same size.

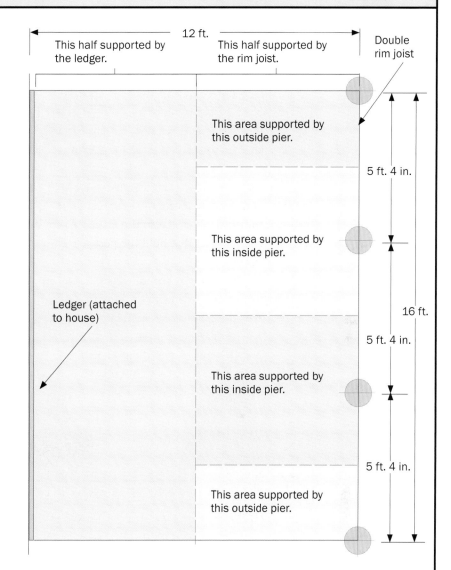

This half supported by the ledger.

This half supported by the rim joist.

12 ft.

Double rim joist

This area supported by this outside pier.

5 ft. 4 in.

This area supported by this inside pier.

Ledger (attached to house)

16 ft.

5 ft. 4 in.

This area supported by this inside pier.

5 ft. 4 in.

This area supported by this outside pier.

Tube dia.	8 in.	10 in.	12 in.	14 in.
Sq. ft.	0.35	0.55	0.79	1.1

Use Two Lines for a Dead-On Layout

With the ledger location transferred to grade level, I can measure out from the house foundation and run a stringline to represent the centerpoint of the piers. A single line parallel to the house intersecting a line perpendicular to the house locates the center of the far-corner pier. Measurements for the rest of the piers are taken from this intersecting point. Batterboards help to set the lines accurately (see the "Tip," below).

Plumb down from a high ledger. With a Stabila plate level (www.stabila.com), I carry one end of the ledger down to the grade. I drive a stake into the ground here to anchor a line that will run perpendicular to the house.

TIP

Rousseau makes a reusable batterboard system that is easy to install with foundation spikes and allows for horizontal, vertical, rough, and precision adjustments of the string with a couple of thumbscrews (www.rousseauco.com).

Batterboards and a stringline locate the piers. Use a tape measure to find the approximate centerline of the piers. I set the batterboards a couple of feet beyond the corner-pier locations so that the boards won't be disturbed when holes are dug.

$A^2 + B^2 = C^2$. To make sure I'm measuring square from the foundation, I use a tape measure to create a right triangle. If A (the pier distance from the house) equals B (the same distance measured along the foundation), then $A^2 + B^2 = C^2$ (the diagonal measurement I'm looking for with my tape). A helper moves the line for accurate pier placement.

TIP

If excavating multiple holes, consider renting a gas-powered auger.

Mark piers with paint. Measure the remaining piers from the far-corner pier. A dot marks the centerpoint, and a rough circle highlights where to dig. Pull the stringlines and prepare to dig, but keep the batterboards in place.

The best holes have no rocks. But just in case you encounter a few, make sure to have a long digging bar in addition to a post-hole digger. Take care not to disturb the batterboards or their settings because you'll have to reattach the strings later. Dig down deep enough so that the bottom of the pier rests on undisturbed soil below the frost line.

Fine-Tune Layout before and after the Pour

Once the holes are dug, put the stringlines back on the batterboards. When setting each builder's tube, use the lines and a tape measure to center them according to layout, adjusting the hole locations as needed. Take the time to check the tube locations often as you backfill to keep them on layout. After all the fill is in place and the final layout check is made, fill the tubes with concrete, and insert the anchor bolts.

Double-check the corners. I spend a little extra time checking the location of the final corner pier to make sure that it's in the right spot, because I won't get a chance to move it once the concrete is poured. Use a nail to mark the finished height of the piers, keeping it a couple of inches above the finished grade. If you need to have piers all at the same height, use a long level or a transit to locate their finished height.

Backfill with a measuring tape and a shovel. I cut the builder's tubes so that they stick out a few inches above grade when placed in the hole. To make sure a tube is placed precisely, I hold it on its layout while a helper backfills. Pack the soil around the tube every so often as you go.

A shovel makes up for bad aim. Fill the tubes with concrete until it reaches the nail. The concrete should be just slightly on the wet side, about the consistency of thick oatmeal. As the concrete is poured into the tube, a helper uses a shovel to agitate the mix every 8 in. to 10 in. to work out air pockets.

TIP

A mixer does the most difficult work of mixing the concrete. Just dump in the mix, turn it on, then add water.

Place anchor bolts accurately. Once all the piers are poured, I go back and insert anchor bolts in the center of the piers. I measure from the line running perpendicular to the house to set anchor bolts accurately. Be sure to leave the threads high enough so that a post base, washer, and nut can be added later.

Adjustable post bases allow for final tweaks. After the concrete is cured completely, I attach adjustable post bases. I like to use Simpson® ABA-style bases because they allow me to fine-tune the post location after the post is attached.

Get Your Deck Off to a Good Start

■ BY SCOTT GRICE

Whether it's used for barbecuing or for relaxing in a hot tub, the deck, by my estimation, is the best room of the house. If built the wrong way, though, this asset quickly can become a liability. More often than not, the catalyst for this transformation is a poorly detailed ledger board, usually in the form of bad flashing.

Proper detailing requires two things: selecting the right hardware to attach the ledger to the house; and adequately weatherproofing the house/ledger connection.

A Ledger Supports and Stabilizes a Deck

Because it supports floor joists, the ledger carries much of the deck's load. Its connection to the house transfers this load to the foundation while providing stability. Because the connection is usually a shear load, the fasteners must be strong and well anchored to the house.

Through bolts, such as hex or carriage bolts, are the best choice for anchoring

the ledger because they won't strip out of the wood as lag screws might. But often, due to inaccessible framing, lag screws must be used. As long as they're installed with care (see the top drawing on p. 17), lag screws work fine. You may want to talk with the building inspector, though. The International Residential Code says, "Where positive connection to the primary building structure cannot be verified during inspection, decks shall be self-supporting."

Regardless of which fasteners you use, be sure that they provide a suitable amount of corrosion resistance to the new arsenic-free pressure-treated wood.

Don't Let the Ledger Rot the Walls

In Portland, Oregon, we receive an average of 37 in. of rain every year; the rain here is persistent. If there's a hole in the siding, rainwater gets into it. Once in the house, water gets to and rots the framing. Flashing, gravity, and sealants are critical to keeping out water.

Because the thought of leaks disrupts my sleep, I use backups when detailing a ledger. Sloping the deck, caulking the vulnerable joints, and flashing properly should prevent water from getting in at the ledger board. Felt paper above the ledger directs any water that has made its way behind the siding to the 2×2 flashing and out. And if water somehow does make it behind the ledger, there's another layer of paper to protect the house and a space for that water to drain. As with any security program, redundancy is superfluous only when not needed.

Scott Grice is a builder in Portland, Oregon.

The pressure-treated ledger is larger than the joists, in this case to compensate for peculiar floor framing. The top row of fasteners is lag screws attached to floor framing, and the bottom row is bolts running through a beam. In the West, pressure-treated wood (hem-fir) often is stained brown to blend with cedar and redwood and must be incised to allow adequate penetration of the treatment chemicals.

Use Bolts, Flashing, and an Airspace

Through bolts are the best choice for fastening the ledger, but they'll do no good if they're fastened to rotten wood. Meticulous water detailing stops rot before it starts. **Note:** If you live in a cold climate, you can step the deck down to avoid water problems caused by melting snow. The International Residential Code allows up to an 8-in. step.

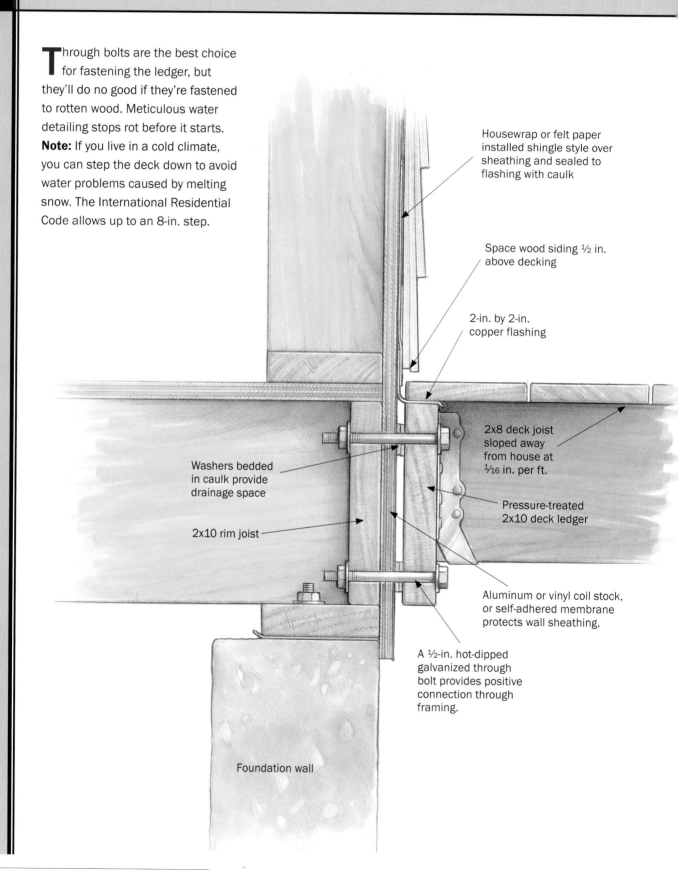

Housewrap or felt paper installed shingle style over sheathing and sealed to flashing with caulk

Space wood siding ½ in. above decking

2-in. by 2-in. copper flashing

2x8 deck joist sloped away from house at ¹⁄₁₆ in. per ft.

Pressure-treated 2x10 deck ledger

Washers bedded in caulk provide drainage space

2x10 rim joist

Aluminum or vinyl coil stock, or self-adhered membrane protects wall sheathing.

A ½-in. hot-dipped galvanized through bolt provides positive connection through framing.

Foundation wall

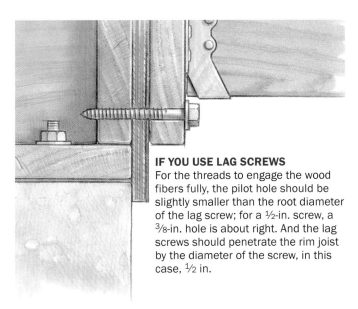

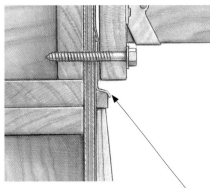

IF YOU USE LAG SCREWS
For the threads to engage the wood fibers fully, the pilot hole should be slightly smaller than the root diameter of the lag screw; for a ½-in. screw, a ⅜-in. hole is about right. And the lag screws should penetrate the rim joist by the diameter of the screw, in this case, ½ in.

IF YOU HAVE SIDING BELOW THE DECK
Add a drip-cap flashing above the siding, and tuck it behind the housewrap. The detail will match that of the flashing above the ledger.

JOIST SPAN DRIVES FASTENER SPACING

Longer floor joists require tighter fastener spacing. Table R502.2.2.1 of the 2009 IRC prescribes maximum fastener spacing for ½ in. lag screws, ½ in. bolts, and ½ in. bolts with ½ in. of stacked washers.

Fastener spacing accurate for the following conditions:
• Combined live and dead load of 50 lb. per sq. ft.
• Spruce-pine-fir rim joist or minimum of 1 in. x 9½ in. Douglas Fir LVL rim board.
• Southern pine or hem-fir deck ledger.

Check with your local building official for different load requirements or when fastening into other rim joist materials.

½ in. lag screw
½ in. bolt
½ in. bolt with ½ in. stacked washers

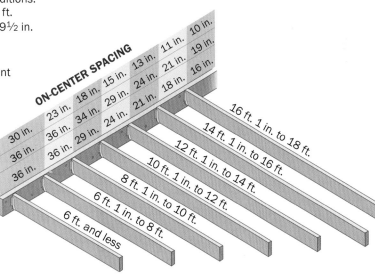

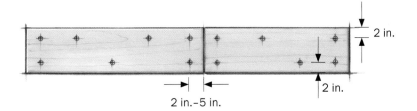

2 in.

2 in.

2 in.–5 in.

Stagger fasteners 2 in. down from the top and up from the bottom of the ledger. Install two fasteners between 2 in. and 5 in. at the ends of ledger sections.

Smart Deck-Framing Strategies

■ BY MIKE GUERTIN

I love building decks. If I had to pick one part of the house that I enjoy building the most, it's the deck. There's no rush to dry it in so that other subs can work, it's a straightforward outdoor project, and we're heroes when the job is finished. Lately, my decks have been getting better as I find better ways to use new products and techniques that extend the life of the deck and its host structure.

Design a Layout That's Strong and Relatively Simple

There are numerous ways to design and frame a deck structure, which typically consists of the footings, the posts, the beams, the ledger, and the joists. I like to use framing layouts that suit the deck design and simplify the framing as much as possible. This project consisted of a 900-sq.-ft. wraparound deck that began 8 ft. above the walkout portion of a finished basement and patio and ended at grade level at the back door.

Instead of building a deck frame cantilevered over a carrying beam, I incorporated the load-bearing characteristics into a rim beam made of a doubled 2×12 to maximize the headroom and to reduce the need for a forest of support posts. The wider rim also would later help to conceal a deck drainage system that I would install before the decking went down.

Mike Guertin is a remodeling contractor in East Greenwich, Rhode Island, and editorial adviser to Fine Homebuilding. His Web site is www.mikeguertin.com.

Beefy Brackets Separate the Ledger from the Wall

Challenge

Maine Deck Brackets (www.deckbracket.com)

The first challenge in any deck project is mounting and flashing the ledger to the building. Ledgers conventionally bolted to the wall framing usually demand a flashed break in the siding, a time-consuming method that's often not weathertight or rot-resistant.

Strategy

On this deck, I used heavy-duty aluminum brackets from Maine Deck Brackets®; I find them ideal for shingle siding. The beam-shaped sections are bolted directly to the house's rim joist. In turn, the deck ledger is bolted to the bracket's outer flange. To make the bracket's point of attachment as solid and as waterproof as possible, I first strip back five courses of shingles to create a space about a foot wide. I then lift up a flap of building paper and cut a rectangle in the sheathing. I line the back of the sheathing cutout with a self-sealing flashing tape like Grace's Vycor® DeckProtector® (www.na.graceconstruction.com). After the flange is mounted, I surround and lap onto the sides of the web with flashing tape for an effective seal. The tape directs water to the top lap of the shingle course beneath. Once the head flap of builder's felt is back in place, the seal is water-resistant. An additional bead of caulk can be applied between the siding and the bracket's web.

My associate, Mac, and I spaced the deck brackets on approximate 40-in. centers so that we could use a single 2x8 to span between them. To keep the bolt holes away from the ledger butt joints, we positioned joints between brackets and used LedgerLok® screws (www.fastenmaster.com) to connect a 3-ft.-long splice board on the back side of the primary ledger.

Create a space for the bracket flange. After stripping back the shingles and a flap of builder's felt, I mark and cut out a section of sheathing directly over the rim joist.

Brackets demand through bolts, not lags. After drilling the pilot holes, I flash the cutout and bolt the bracket, which requires access to the other side of the rim joist.

Redundant overlaps are the best waterproofing. Considering the consequences, it's best to flash and to counterflash behind, around, and over the brackets.

Labeling simplifies reassembly. I number each shingle with its course and position as I remove it, which makes reinstallation easier.

Use a spare bracket for bolt layout. Once the brackets are in place, we can transfer their locations to the ledger, drill pilot holes, and bolt the 2x into place. Any gaps around the exposed bracket web can be caulked (inset photo).

Challenge

Manufacturers of pressure-treating chemicals have modified ACQ treatments or come up with new formulas that are less corrosive, and hardware manufacturers have improved their protective coatings. However, the potential for accelerated corrosion still exists.

Strategy

Choosing stainless-steel hardware or applying isolation membranes where hardware contacts wood can help a deck to last longer. Peel-and-stick flashing, staple-on plastic ribbon like YorkWrap™ (www.yorkmfg.com), or even strips of #30 builder's felt can be used as isolation membranes. We isolated each ledger bracket by wrapping its outer flange. We also positioned 4-in.-wide strips on the rim joist and ledger at each hanger location, then wrapped the joist ends.

Just to be sure. Strips of peel-and-stick flashing are either stapled (below) or adhered to the places where a framing connector comes into contact with pressure-treated framing lumber.

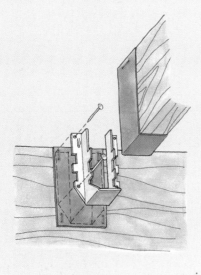

Joist-Hanger Setup Saves Time

Challenge

We had about 120 joist hangers on this project, so installing them as quickly and accurately as possible was crucial. Joist hangers can be attached to joist ends first, to the ledger and the rim joist first, or after the joists are tacked in position. I prefer to fasten the hangers to the ledger and the rim joist so that the joists can be dropped in quickly. There's less struggling to hold joists flush before nailing, an important consideration when working off scaffolding.

Strategy

Commercial versions are available, but I find that a simple T-jig takes 10 minutes to make and works best. Because we wrapped the joist ends with membrane, we needed a slightly wider-than-standard space between the sides of the hangers, so we ripped the leg of the T from ¾-in. stock $1^{11}/_{16}$ in. wide. The 2x4 top registers against the top of the ledger. The leg's bottom has eased corners to match the hanger profile; the hanger is seated tight and flat to the bottom of the leg.

We used a new metal-connector pneumatic nailer from Bostitch® (www.bostitch.com) to drive the more than 750 1½-in. or 2½-in. nails and 500 3-in. nails needed to mount the hangers. These nailers pinpoint the holes stamped in the hardware and sink the nails precisely. They saved us more than eight hours of tedious hammer work and paid for themselves twice on this job alone. To keep the joist tops flush, we checked the width of all the joists and pulled any that were ⅛ in. more or less than the average. (If we'd just pulled stock off the pile, narrower joists would be lower and wider ones higher because the hangers are all at the same level.)

When there are a lot of out-of-tolerance joists, we group them in like-size order and set their associated hanger heights so that the tops are flush. We lucked out on this job. The unit of 2x8s delivered had only two out-of-tolerance joists.

Keep the drudgery to a minimum. A jig to locate hangers and a dedicated nail gun save a day's worth of labor.

Establish a Straight Rim Beam on Temporary Supports

Challenge

The rim beam—a load-bearing rim joist—must be set in position, level and parallel to the house, before the posts can be installed. There always seems to be room for debate regarding the benefit of a deck's slope away from the house. Spaces between deck boards should permit water to drain so that there's little chance for it to flow toward the building. But on decks with tight deck boards, a slope away from the building is a wise move. This deck frame will eventually have a drainage system installed beneath that slopes toward the outside, and the deck boards won't be tight. In this case, I opted to set the deck itself dead level.

Strategy

Before the deck went up, Mac and I laid out the joist positions on the inside face of a 2x12 rim beam and applied strips of isolation membrane (see the bottom right photo on p. 22). We used A-frame scaffolds to support the beam during assembly.

After aligning the ends of the rim, we used a stringline and gauge blocks to straighten the beam. Then we ran 1x3 furring strips between the ledger and the rim beam at each post position to keep it straight and parallel. A laser set on the ledger established a level reference for us as we raised or lowered the beam. To speed the leveling process, I placed a target block on the beam at each post location, marked to the height of the laser line above the ledger. Adjustable jacks dial in the finish height and support the beam until permanent posts are installed. In the past, we've used an adjustable A-frame support made of 2x4s. Nailed together at the apex, the 2xs are spread on a wider 2x. By knocking the legs in or out, we raise or lower the beam; stop blocks fix the legs' final position (see the bottom right photo on the facing page).

Establish a parallel rim first. With the rim beam temporarily supported, we use long lengths of strapping to set a constant distance from the house to the outside edge.

Go by the string. To establish a straight rim, we put guide blocks on each end, run a string between, and adjust the distance by renailing the strapping.

Laser perfect. To gauge the height of the rim relative to the house, I set a laser level on the ledger and read the results on a marked target block.

Temporary but Adjustable Posts

I found some tall screw jacks (Post Shores; www.gostepup.com) to set the height of the rim beam on decks. In the past, we've also used a simple 2x A-frame (see the photo below right) whose legs can be adjusted to raise or lower the beam.

Install the Posts in the Right Place

Challenge

You can't install the posts until the height and position of the rim beam are established.

Strategy

With the rim beam straightened and braced, we squared up the frame and installed the end rim boards. We used adjustable wall braces to lock the frame in position, then plumbed down from the beam to the slab at each post position (about 8 ft. on center, spaced equally along the perimeter). After marking for the post bases, we drilled into the slab and used 5-in. by ½-in. wedge-type anchors to bolt down the bases. Post ends were wrapped with isolation membrane, then attached to the beam with galvanized connectors.

Locate post bases. Plumbing down from the rim, I mark and drill holes for the post-base anchor bolts, then install the bases. With the post ends wrapped in isolation membrane, I set the posts in place.

Footing Forms Stay Sturdy Until You're Ready to Pour

According to my engineer, 12-in.-dia. footings would have sufficed for this soil type and deck load, but I chose plastic footing forms from Square Foot® (www.sqfoot.com) to give the deck broader support. These forms provide more than four times the footing area of 12-in.-dia. footings. Also, because I knew it would be several weeks between the time I set the forms and the time we poured, I used 8-in.-dia. galvanized-steel ducts salvaged from a renovation project. I knew the steel wouldn't soften or crush in the interim as cardboard tubes might. We poured a 6-in.-deep concrete slab beneath the deck area and tied the perimeter reinforcing rod and wire mesh to the vertical rods in each footing. Where the deck turned the corner, the footings were closer together, so I used only the salvaged ducts as tube forms without the larger footings.

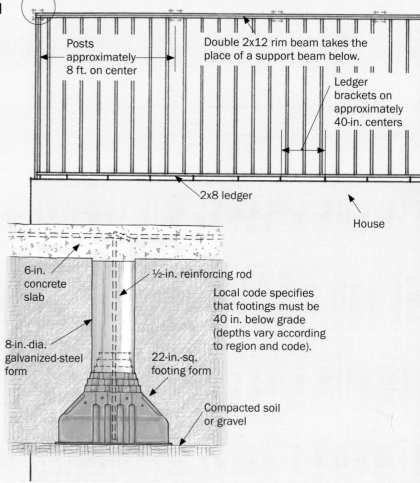

Posts approximately 8 ft. on center

Double 2x12 rim beam takes the place of a support beam below.

Ledger brackets on approximately 40-in. centers

2x8 ledger

House

6-in. concrete slab

½-in. reinforcing rod

Local code specifies that footings must be 40 in. below grade (depths vary according to region and code).

8-in.-dia. galvanized-steel form

22-in.-sq. footing form

Compacted soil or gravel

Work Safer in the Air

Challenge

Deck framing is easier when the deck is close to the ground. When the deck is 8 ft. high and you have nearly 60 joists to install, it's a big job to get this framing done efficiently without compromising safety.

Strategy

We trimmed the joists $\frac{1}{8}$ in. to $\frac{1}{2}$ in. shorter than the span, which helped us to drop them in place without ripping the isolation membrane. There is a limit, however; joist ends can have no more than a $\frac{1}{8}$-in. gap, according to the joist-hanger manufacturer. We set up planks between A-frame scaffolds to walk on and stacked enough joists to fill a plank-size section. With one crew member at each end, we dropped in the joists and drove in the diagonal nails through the hangers before moving the scaffold down for the next section. Once the joists were all nailed off, we cleaned up and got ready to run decking.

Framing approximately 16 in. on center

2x8 joists

Work a section at a time. After setting up staging, we laid out and dropped the joists into the hangers, nailing them off as we went.

Because the deck is level, not sloped, the ledger can continue out to the rim beam. If the deck were sloped, a diagonal brace would be installed to handle the transition around the corner.

Integrate the Old With the New

Around the corner, where the deck was close to grade level, the old but sound concrete back steps interfered with several joists. We scribe-fit the joist ends to rest on the landing and added full-width support with a 2x4 sleeper. Fastened to the lower step with wedge-type anchors, the sleeper also acts as a base for toenailing joists.

Better Ways to Frame a Deck

■ BY JOHN SPIER

The wood frame of a deck leads a hard life. Without the protection of roof or walls, a deck frame is completely exposed to the weather. Though subjected to heavy loads, a wood deck is supported by just a few posts or piers instead of a solid foundation. And it's a rare homeowner who gives a second thought to maintaining a deck once it has been built. In spite of all this, a deck is expected to be safe and attractive, and to last as long as the house that it's attached to.

These goals aren't unreasonable if you pay attention to the details and materials that I'll explain in this chapter. Although the deck featured here is framed against a new addition, these details work equally well when a new deck is added to an existing house.

Waterproof First

Adhesive-backed membrane applied to the wall sheathing protects the house by isolating the deck ledger. The membrane backing is scored carefully; a narrow strip left in place allows the housewrap to tuck underneath the membrane later (see the photo at right).

The floor of the house determines the level of the deck, so one person measures down to the floor on the inside while another measures to the top of the framing (see the bottom right photo). A snapped line guides ledger placement.

A Good Start Is Essential

After the piers and their metal post bases are installed (see "A Solid Deck Begins with Concrete Piers," pp. 4–13), I can begin preparations to frame the deck.

I've been building houses on Block Island, Rhode Island, for almost 20 years, and unless otherwise requested, I frame decks with pressure-treated lumber, which stands up well to the rigors of weather. I use straight material free of major defects. For fasteners, I prefer hot-dipped galvanized nails driven by hand. The deck ledgers attach with galvanized bolts and lags. I use gun-driven nails only to tack framing in place until permanent fasteners are installed, such as when nailing the spacers to the ledger.

Waterproof, Then Frame

Before the ledger goes on, I waterproof the house sheathing with an adhesive-backed membrane. I like to use Grace Ice & Water Shield® (W.R. Grace & Co.; www.graceathome.com; 800-354-5414). The membrane goes on well above the top of the deck ledger and runs 6 in. or so past the end.

Above the deck, the housewrap has to overlap the membrane and flashing, but below the ledger, the membrane must overlap the housewrap. If the housewrap hasn't been installed (as in this case), I score the membrane's peel-off backing and leave about 3 in. along the bottom of the membrane so that the housewrap can be tucked under at a later date (see the top photo on the facing page). A combination of careful detailing and high-quality flashing materials completes the waterproofing measures (see the drawing at right).

Two Ledgers Protect House and Frame

The actual deck framing starts with a ledger securely fastened to the house. For decks less than 8 ft. wide, a single ledger may suffice, but for most decks, I prefer a double ledger that's fastened to the house with through-bolts and lag screws. The two-ledger system lets me attach the deck board nearest the house without perforating the flashing. Check with your local building official before utilizing this double ledger design.

I establish a level line for the ledger based on the floor inside the house. Installing the deck 3 in. to 4 in. below the floor level keeps water and debris away from the door threshold and makes a comfortable step into the house. Holding a level in the window openings near each end of the deck, I measure down, make marks on the membrane (see the bottom right photo on the facing page), and then snap a chalkline for the top of the primary ledger. A few nails hold this ledger in place until the bolts and the lags can be installed.

Pressure-treated plywood spacers separate the two ledgers (see the photos on p. 32). I make the spacers about 3 in. wide and ½ in. shorter than the width of the ledger (9-in. spacers for 9½-in.-wide 2×10 ledgers). The top of each spacer is pointed to shed water. I install the spacers 32 in. on center. Because the spacer layout is also the layout for the bolts and lags, I plan for the spacers to fall between the deck joists and between the floor joists in the house. I tack the spacers to the first ledger with a couple of nails in opposite corners where I won't drill into them later.

The secondary ledger is laid out for both the bolts and the deck joists. Before the ledger goes up, I counterbore each through

bolt and lag location so that the washer and bolt stay below the surface of the ledger and away from any water running off the deck. The secondary ledger then nails to the first at every spacer, with just enough strategically placed nails to hold it in place until the bolts can be installed. At this point, I drill and insert one bolt in every other layout location to keep the ledgers in place while the rest of the framing process continues.

Anatomy of a Double Ledger

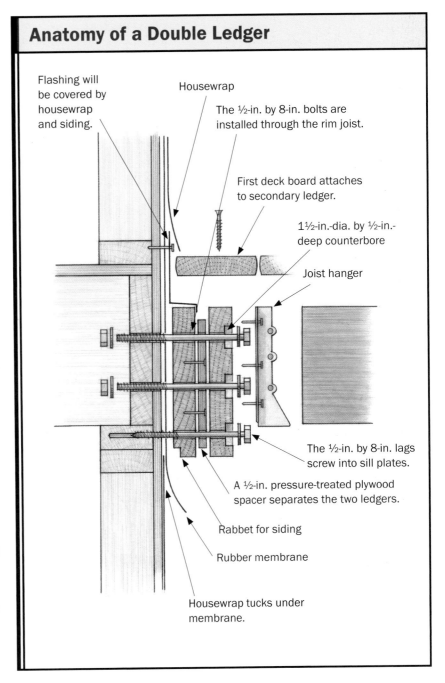

Flashing will be covered by housewrap and siding.

Housewrap

The ½-in. by 8-in. bolts are installed through the rim joist.

First deck board attaches to secondary ledger.

1½-in.-dia. by ½-in.-deep counterbore

Joist hanger

The ½-in. by 8-in. lags screw into sill plates.

A ½-in. pressure-treated plywood spacer separates the two ledgers.

Rabbet for siding

Rubber membrane

Housewrap tucks under membrane.

6x6 Posts and a Double Rim Joist Add Strength

Once the ledgers are installed, I turn to the posts that support the opposite side of the deck. The posts fit into metal post bases bolted to the piers. On occasion, I've used custom-fabricated stainless-steel bases, but I usually use Simpson Strong-Tie® ABU66 post bases (www.strongtie.com; 800-999-5099). The bases provide a secure connection, so the piers hold the deck down as well as up.

A common choice for deck posts is 4×4 stock, but I prefer 6×6s, which can be notched to hold a double rim joist and help support the deck guardrail (see the drawing on p. 34); but to be safe, always check with your building official before notching guardrail posts. To get the length of the first

Install a Double Ledger

A double ledger allows for a strong frame and an impenetrable flashing system that protects the house (see the drawing on p. 31). Nails hold the first ledger in place until the bolts and lags are installed later. The plywood spacers come next, made with pointed tips to shed water (photo 1). Before the secondary ledger is installed, counter-bore holes for two bolts and a lag screw are drilled at each spacer location (photo 2). With the secondary ledger held in place by nails, one person bores through the framing members, and bolts attach the ledger assembly to the house (photo 3).

post, I level over from the top of the ledger and measure down to the post base (see the photos at right).

After squaring the bottom of the post, I transfer the measurement to locate the notch. Corner posts are notched on two adjacent sides, while the notch runs along only one side of intermediate posts. I first cut the top and bottom of each notch at the proper depth. Then I plunge-cut the edges of the notch. A rap with a framing hammer knocks out the waste, and I clean up the corners with a sharp chisel.

While the posts are resting on sawhorses, I cut the tops, using the railing, trim, and framing details to establish the length. Because 6×6 posts tend to look massive, I often soften the edges with routed chamfers.

Inner rim joists are installed first. Before setting the first post in place, I cut the inner rim joist for that end of the deck. The rim joist attaches to the double ledger at the house and slips into the notch on the corner post (see the photos on p. 34). After starting a few nails to hold the rim joist in place, I adjust the post base until the post is plumb in both directions. When I'm satisfied, I drive the nails home. Then I square the rim joist to the ledger using a large measured triangle, such as a 6-8-10, and brace it in position.

With the first post braced plumb and square, I move to the post on the opposite corner of the deck. I connect the first corner post to the opposite corner post with a long 2×10 for the inner rim joist. This rim joist holds the post plumb in one direction, while a regular joist keeps it plumb in the other.

This is a good place to explain that this deck wraps around the addition with 45-degree corners, so instead of framing for a 90-degree corner with a single post, I used two posts to form the 45-degree angle. I modified the notches for these posts to hold the 45-degree rim joist.

For the intermediate post between the corner posts, I simply measure down from the rim joist to the post base for the height of the notch. If the distance between posts

Prep the Posts

Leveling over from the ledger determines the length of the posts (photo 1). Instead of rolling each post to square the bottom, line up the framing square underneath the post and draw the line with the pencil out of sight (photo 2). Cut the top and bottom of the notch first, then plunge-cut along the edges (photo 3). A routed chamfer softens the edges of the 6×6 posts (photo 4).

Longer level. I use this handy level in all phases of house framing. For deck framing, the level extends up to 13 ft., making it useful for plumbing tall posts or for leveling over from a ledger to a pier. **Extendable level by Plumb-It** (www.plumb-it.com; 800-759-9925).

Bigger saw. My brother-in-law is a timber framer who works on our crew frequently. His big circular saw cuts to a 3¾-in. depth, which lets me work on 6×6 posts without having to dig out my handsaw. **Milwaukee® 10¼-in. circular saw** (Model 6460; www.milwaukeetool.com; 800-729-3878).

Square the Corners

Notches in the 6×6 posts keep the double rim joists flush with the outside of the posts (see the drawing at right). The first rim joist connects the corner post to the ledger and holds the post plumb (photo 1). After the joist is checked for level (photo 2), it is held square while a diagonal brace is nailed into place. Another rim joist helps to establish the opposite corner (photo 3), which is checked for square with a diagonal measurement and secured temporarily with a 2×4 brace (photo 4).

Corner Details

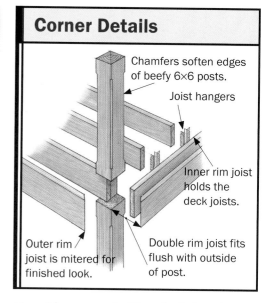

Chamfers soften edges of beefy 6×6 posts.

Joist hangers

Inner rim joist holds the deck joists.

Outer rim joist is mitered for finished look.

Double rim joist fits flush with outside of post.

cannot be spanned with a single length of framing, I stretch a taut string between the posts and measure down. As each intermediate post slips into place, I install a regular joist nearby to hold the rim joist straight and the post plumb.

Joists Are Nailed Twice

If the outside walls of the house are relatively straight and the corner posts are the same distance from the house, I cut all the deck joists to the same length. I reject stock that's excessively crowned or bowed. I mark crowns on all the joists and set them where they can be accessed easily.

Joists have to be installed with proper hangers, and in an ideal world, you would set the hangers first, drop in the joists, and nail them off. But even the best grades of framing material vary too much in width for this approach. So I nail the joists in place first and then install the hangers. Following those steps keeps the tops of the joists aligned properly with the tops of the ledger and rim joists. With just the inner rim joist in place, I can drive nails directly into the joists to secure them. A toenail on each side holds each joist in place at the ledger end.

Once the joists are in place, I check the posts with a level, casting an eye along the perimeter to make sure everything is

Finish the Frame

1

2

With the inner rim joist set around the perimeter, the tops of the deck joists align with the rim and nails through the rim hold them in place until the hangers can be installed (photo 1). The ledger end of each joist is toenailed. For this deck, the outer rim joist is the finished face, so the best-looking stock is used. Mitered corners create a more finished look (photo 2).

Accurate nailer. The most tedious part of deck building is putting in joist hangers. On the first job, the Positive Placement® nailer paid for itself in time saved. Boredom relief was a bonus. (Model F250S-PP; www.paslode.com; 800-222-6990).

Faster wrench. Whenever I have a lot of lags to drive, my impact wrench comes to the rescue of my bruised knuckles. Porter-Cable® 1/2-in. pneumatic impact wrench (Model PT502; www.deltaportercable.com; 800-321-9443).

straight. Then one crew member tacks the hangers in place with the integral tabs on them; another follows with a pneumatic positive-placement nailer. We finish installing the ledger by drilling and driving through bolts and lags. If the deck is large, I break out an automotive pneumatic nut driver, which makes quick work of the bolts and lags.

The last step is installing the outer rim joist. For the strongest assembly, I offset any butt joints from the joints in the inner rim joist. On this deck, the outer rim joist was also the finished surface, so I chose the nicest-looking stock and mitered the corners for a more finished look (see the top right photo above).

Although the frame is now ready for the decking, I often cover the joists with plywood while the project is underway. As with the finished floors inside, I try to install the decking after the heaviest work has been done to keep it looking nice.

John Spier and his wife, Kerri, own Spier Construction, a custom-home building company on Block Island, Rhode Island.

In Pursuit of the Perfect Plank

■ BY JEFFERSON KOLLE

You might think deck boards have it easy: endless relaxation, center stage at parties and barbecues, hours spent doing nothing but soaking up the sun. But that would be forgetting the high heels, the scraping lawn chairs, and the energetic retriever dragging his Frisbee®. It also would be forgetting how destructive the sun gets hour after hour, its relentless heat and light making even the toughest deck boards fade, twist, cup, check, and try to pull themselves free of the fasteners that hold them to the joists. Nevermind the rain and the snow, and the days and the months when everyone goes inside except the deck boards. Or the worst kind of deck party, where the guests include mold and mildew and really, really hungry insects.

Considering the abuse heaped on the average deck, it's worth the time to choose the most durable and long-lasting planks out there. As recently as 2008, almost 85 percent of all deck boards sold were made from real wood, but that number is expected to drop to 77 percent by 2011 as man-made decking gains market share. But the battle is far from over. Wood-treatment processes continue to evolve, improving the durability of decking made from trees while addressing concerns about toxicity and hardware corrosion. At the same time, synthetic-decking manufacturers have fine-tuned the look of their products while correcting early problems with fading and decomposition.

Wood Loses Its Edge, Then Makes Some Gains

In California, where the deck craze started more than a half-century ago, redwood was the top choice for decking because it was beautiful, plentiful, and insect- and rot-resistant. As other areas of the country realized how cool it was to hang around outside, green-tinted, pressure-treated yellow pine deck boards were nailed down everywhere. Both woods proved problematic.

Old-growth redwood was in short supply, and conservationists started asking loudly whether it was right to harvest some of the oldest living things on Earth just to keep homeowners' feet out of the crabgrass while they grilled their veggie burgers. Second-growth redwood, though, proved not as durable as the old lumber, mainly due to the amount of sapwood and knots, and an inner heartwood that wasn't nearly as insect- and weather-resistant. Other naturally durable wood decking, such as cedar and Douglas fir, had similar deficiencies, which required lots of maintenance.

Pressure-treating wood wasn't the perfect answer, either. Early formulas were infused with a potentially toxic cocktail of copper, arsenic, and chromium. These treatments were phased out of the residential market at the end of 2003. And while pressure-treating does prevent decay, wetting and drying cycles affect pressure-treated decking just like any wood, causing the boards to cup, check, and splinter. Assorted solutions of liquid deck preservatives—oils, varnishes, and soaps—can slow the effects of insects and weather, but most people want a deck to relax on, not work on.

Synthetics Have Their Shortcomings

Man-made decking planks for residential use hit the market in the early 1990s. Using re-cycled plastics and waste-wood fiber ground into wood "flour," these products appeared to be the answer for homeowners who had an increasing environmental awareness and an anathema for maintenance. But the early wood and plastic composite products (known as WPCs) looked as much like real wood as a milk jug looks like a cow. Plus, the rot, mold, and mildew that lunched on solid wood also liked to eat the wood flour in the wood-plastic composites (the other ingredient in WPCs are thermoplastics—polyethylene, polypropylene, and polyvinyl chloride—meaning they can be heated and molded or extruded to retain a shape).

Other manufacturers made planking products from a variety of solid plastics with no added organic material. Some used recycled materials, but others didn't, claiming that utilizing virgin plastics solved some of the flaws associated with the mixture of materials from post-consumer plastics.

The Manufacturer–Contractor Connection

You'll probably spend some time deciding what type of decking to buy. You'll do your research, and after making your decision, you'll probably call a contractor.

There's a chance that when he pulls up in his truck, you'll see emblazoned on the side a big logo for TimberLook (or some other decking brand). During your conversation, you'll tell him you'd like to use Fauxwood GrainRight decking because you've read up on all the choices and that seems to be the best for your deck.

"I use TimberLook," he says, pulling out full-color brochures of amazing-looking decks. His company name, incidentally, is printed at the top of the brochure, and just then you notice that his business card also has the TimberLook logo.

"Why TimberLook?" you ask.

"It's all we ever use," he says. "It's the best."

For him, definitely. For you, probably definitely.

Most of the large synthetic-decking manufacturers have contractor-rewards programs, aka loyalty programs. Before this makes you cry foul, know that these programs can benefit you, too.

Manufacturers offer a variety of perks to contractors who use their products. Along with personalized product literature, deck builders can qualify for discounts, signage, sponsorships at local home shows, even the chance for discount tools or NASCAR tickets. And many manufacturers' Web sites will list preferred deck builders on a searchable, find-a-contractor menu tab.

So how does it benefit the consumer if his deck board disintegrates while his contractor is sitting in the VIP seats at the Daytona 500? First, any good contractor wants to avoid callbacks more than anything. That means regardless of the swag he's

getting from the manufacturer, he isn't going to install a fail-prone product.

Second, along with the fishing gear he's gotten from TimberLook, it's likely he's also gotten installation training and technical updates, either at the manufacturer's facility or in the field from a factory rep. You also can be assured that if a contractor is standing behind a product, the manufacturer is standing behind the contractor.

Of course, you'll also want to ask to visit a contractor's recent job, because all decks look great on a Web site or on the back of a digital camera. Finally, don't make a color choice based on a 3×5 board sample; find a real deck or a large sample flooring section you can look at in person.

Woods

RED CEDAR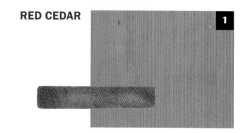

COPPER AZOLE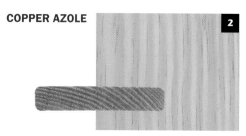

WOLMANIZED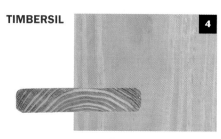

TIMBERSIL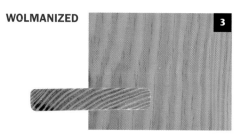

ACCOYA

THERMOFOREST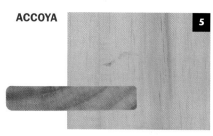

WONDER WOODS AND SUPER SYNTHETICS

WOODS	COST	WARRANTY
1. Naturally weather-resistant domestic woods Redwood White cedar Red cedar Alaskan yellow cedar	$ to $$$	None stated
2. Metallic pressure-treated wood MCA (micronized copper azole) ACQ (alkaline copper quaternary) CA (copper azole) MCQ (micronized copper quaternary)	$	Limited lifetime
3. Nonmetallic pressure-treated wood Wolmanized® L3 www.wolmanized.com EcoLife® www.treatedwood.com/ecolife	$ to $$	Varies, depending on product
4. Silicate-infused wood TimberSIL® www.timbersilwood.com	$ to $$	40 years against rot and decay
5. Acetylated wood Accoya® www.accoya.com	$$$	50 years above ground
6. Thermally modified wood Bay Tree Technologies www.purewoodproducts.com Cambia® www.cambiawood.com EcoVantage www.ecoprem.com ThermoForest Products www.superiorthermowood.com	$$ to $$$$	Limited for 20 to 25 years, depending on manufacturer
7. Tropical hardwoods Ipé Tigerwood Cumara Garapa Red meranti	$$ to $$$	Depends on importer or distributor; 35 years for some
8. Bamboo Cali Bamboo www.calibamboo.com Pacific Western Wood Products www.pacificwesternwood-products.com Sundeck® www.sundeckamericas.com	$$$ to $$$$	Up to 25 years, depending on manufacturer

SYNTHETICS	COST	WARRANTY
9. Wood-plastic composites (WPCs) MoistureShield® www.moistureshield.com TimberTech® www.timbertech.com GeoDeck® www.geodeck.com Trex® www.trex.com Fiberon® www.fiberondecking.com Rhino Deck® www.rhinodeck.com Latitudes Intrepid® www.latitudesdecking.com	$$ to $$$	15 to 25 years; may be transferable if you sell your house
10. PVC Azek® www.azek.com Fiberon Outdoor Flooring www.fiberondecking.com VEKAdeck® www.vekadeck.com Trex Escapes www.trex.com Gossen® www.gossencorp.com	$$$$	20 to 25 years; may be transferable if you sell your house
11. Capstock Trex Transcend www.trex.com Fiberon Horizon www.fiberondecking.com Latitudes Capricorn www.latitudesdecking.com TimberTech XLM www.timbertech.com	$$$ to $$$$	20 to 25 years; may be transferable if you sell your house

PROS/CONS	MAINTENANCE
Pros: Real-wood look; low cost; widely available **Cons:** Soft, subject to scratches and scrapes; more expensive heartwoods are more resistant to insects and rot than second-growth sapwoods; some species may be more popular in certain areas of the country	Requires diligent cleaning to prevent microbe growth and sealing to prevent checking and to maintain color
Pros: Inexpensive and long lasting; insect- and microbe-resistant; can be stained to change color; widely available **Cons:** May require expensive coated or stainless-steel hardware; weathers quickly, rough looking; dimensionally unstable—has a tendency to split, crack, and warp	Requires annual cleaning and periodic resealing to prevent checking, cracking, and warping
Pros: Noncorrosive to fasteners; contains no copper that can leach into groundwater and soil; more stable than metallic pressure-treated wood; can be painted and stained; widely available **Cons:** Plain looking; may need to be stained	Soap and water cleanup to remove dirt
Pros: Nontoxic; noncorrosive to fasteners; more stable than untreated wood; fire resistant; indigestible to insects and microbes **Cons:** Limited availability	Periodic cleaning and sealing
Pros: Indigestible to insects and microbes; stable, paintable, stainable **Cons:** Limited availability; expensive	Periodic cleaning and sealing
Pros: Wood is 70% more stable after treating; domestic, sustainable, and available as FSC-certified; pleasant, toasted color; insect- and microbe-resistant **Cons:** Limited availability	Periodic cleaning and sealing
Pros: Real wood appearance with stunning grain patterns; insect-, microbe-, and fire-resistant; widely available **Cons:** Sealing required to retain color; environmental concerns over jungle deforestation; FSC certification adds to cost	Requires periodic cleaning
Pros: Insect- and microbe-resistant; qualifies for LEED credit (rapidly renewal material) **Cons:** Factory-applied finish cannot be sanded; limited availability, but online ordering possible; expensive	Cleaning and sealing recommended

PROS/CONS	MAINTENANCE
Pros: Insect-, splinter-, and weather-resistant; durable, but can scratch; many contain recycled materials; low maintenance; wood-grain patterns mimic natural woods **Cons:** May fade	Requires cleaning to remove dirt and debris, which can foster mold and mildew growth on wood fibers
Pros: Lighter weight than wood or composites; insect-, splinter-, stain-, and fade-resistant; low maintenance **Cons:** Mostly limited to pale colors; some look like plastic; environmental concerns; expensive	Soap and water cleanup to remove dirt
Pros: Combines the best features of composites and PVC decking; wood-grain patterns mimic different woods **Cons:** Expensive	Soap and water cleanup to remove dirt

Woods (continued)

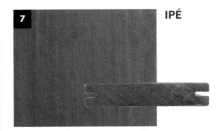

IPÉ

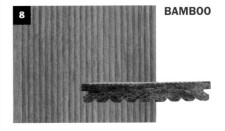

BAMBOO

Synthetics

RHINO DECK

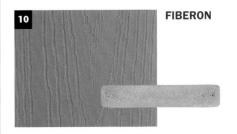

FIBERON

TREX TRANSCEND

Lots of homeowners were happy with their early synthetic decks, but there were also reports of planks fading, expanding excessively, and sagging between joists. Barbecue sauce, suntan lotion, and red wine also left permanent stains on many of the synthetic products. Unexplained disintegration beset some synthetics. One contractor I spoke with told me that an early product failure resulted in decking that "resembled a crumbling graham cracker."

Class-action suits popped up like mushrooms. Synthetic-decking manufacturers backpedaled, altering promises of no maintenance to ones of low maintenance. Sealers and cleaners for synthetic products came on the market, and the companies that made these products offered advice about maintenance. One anonymous company rep asked me this rhetorical question: "You don't have to wash your car, but aren't you going to if you want it to last longer and look nice? Same thing with your deck, right?"

Wrong, said many consumers.

Synthetics Offer Solutions

Synthetic-deck manufacturers didn't take consumer complaints lying down, and they steadily improved their products as more and more players entered the market.

Companies introduced matching deck-railing systems to complement their boards, along with proprietary hidden-fastener systems and grooved boards that allow the planks to be held in place invisibly. Wood-grain embossing and richer, fade-resistant colors with variegated striations made the composites look more like real wood.

But more important than accessories and aesthetics is the attention put on improving the boards' performance. WPC makers fussed with the chemistry of their boards to make them more resistant to stains and to the sun's UV-rays. New ways of encapsulating the organic materials

(including not only wood waste but also rice hulls) improved rot-resistance and discouraged microbe growth.

Meanwhile, decking made from cellular polyvinyl chlorides (PVC) gained a foothold in the market. Lightweight as well as scratch- and stain-resistant, the PVC boards clean up with soap and water and contain no organic material to support mold growth. Similar to vinyl siding in composition and characteristics, PVC decking was initially available only in lighter, almost pastel colors. It could fade and had high expansion and contraction rates due to temperature swings—enough, even, to shear the screws that held it in place.

Many manufacturers now make several types of decking. For instance, Trex—the Kleenex® of synthetic decking thanks to its early entry in the business and its huge marketing and advertising budgets—sells six different lines of decking. Some are WPC, and some are PVC. Fiberon, a synthetic-decking company started by one-time lumber pressure-treater Doug Mancosh, also makes both composite and PVC decking. Asked why the company makes so many products, Edie Kello, director of marketing at Fiberon, says, "This young industry is evolving and creating products that outperform their predecessors. Each line provides different solutions."

Bobby Parks is the owner of Peachtree Decks and Porches in Atlanta, and since working on his first deck in 1989, he has been involved in the design and building of more than $30 million worth of decks. "Synthetic decking has really evolved since I started," he said. "Composites have always had a better look but were marginal performers. And PVC decking had great performance with marginal looks." But he concludes, "This is all changing with the new products."

> *One contractor I spoke with told me that an early product failure resulted in decking that "resembled a crumbling graham cracker."*

Synthetic's Latest Advance

The latest solution for Trex, Fiberon, Azek, TimberTech, and some other manufacturers is to cover their boards—both WPC and PVC—with a protective layer of plastic polymer. In the industry, these coated planks are referred to as capstock.

The coatings, most available with slip-resistant, wood-grain embossing and in very dark colors, are harder than the material they cover and are stain-, scratch-, and fade-resistant. None of the manufacturers I spoke with would reveal what was in their proprietary polymer. Fiberon says its capstock covering is similar to "the covering on a golf ball." Trex says, cryptically, that its includes "nine elements," and Azek describes its as an "alloy blend."

They all have certain characteristics in common: The caps are expensive, which could be the reason why manufacturers use the material to cover only the exterior of the plank, rather than making solid boards out of it. Trex's coated decking line, called Transcend, is covered only on three sides so that "the underside breathes to avoid surface separation."

Capstock decking boards carry the highest price of all synthetic products, and manufacturers are bolstering their hopes for these new products with long-term, materials-only warranties. Fiberon's Kello says that capstock decking solves all the problems previously associated with synthetic-decking products and that in the next few years, "all the lower-end composites will go away."

Tropical Options

As synthetic manufacturers have improved their products—including making them look more like real wood—the real-wood folks have been busy making better wood.

Among this new generation of wood for decking are tropical hardwoods, the best

Ipé decking

known being ipé, which are milled from Central and South American trees. These woods are very dense, so much so that some of them won't float, and they resist chemical infusion through pressure-treating. They are extremely weather-, rot-, and insect-resistant, not to mention beautiful. Rich, almost surreal grain patterns and colors make dazzling decks, which, if they are to retain their colors, need periodic sealing. Left unsealed, tropical hardwoods won't rot, but like all woods, they will fade or turn gray over time.

Tropical hardwoods have an excellent track record for longevity and low maintenance—one reason the city of New York has used them on over 12 miles of coastal walkways. This type of widespread use over the past decade, however, has raised lots of concerns about illegal harvesting and deforestation in the jungles of Central and South America.

The Forest Stewardship Council (FSC), a nonprofit organization, certifies wood that has been harvested responsibly. According to Dan Ivancic at Advantage Trim & Lumber, a direct importer of ipé and other tropical hardwoods since 1992, FSC certification

Tropical hardwoods have an excellent track record for longevity and low maintenance—one reason the city of New York has used them on over 12 miles of coastal walkways.

adds a premium of about 25 percent to 50 percent to the cost of the lumber.

Bamboo flooring for indoor use has been all the rage for several years, and now several companies have introduced bamboo decking for exterior use. One of them, Cali Bamboo, is understandably tight-lipped about how it makes its product, other than to say it's strand-woven in "an incredibly unique process of compressing and intertwining the fibers," which are held together with a glue free of added urea formaldehyde.

Making Domestic Wood Better

While tropical woods flooded the high-end market, the pressure-treating industry changed to alternate formulas to replace chromated copper arsenate (CCA), the most common being alkaline copper quaternary (ACQ) and copper azole (CA). While less toxic, these preservatives aren't so kind to galvanized nails, screws, and joist hangers, requiring the use of specially coated or stainless-steel fasteners, which adds to the cost of a decking project.

But the new generation of pressure-treating offers products, both metallic and nonmetallic, that are less corrosive and more environmentally benign. Among them is wood treated in a process that uses sodium silicates—aka glass—to make the wood structurally more stable and strong. Wood treated in this way is indigestible to bugs and microbes, is paintable, and won't corrode galvanized fasteners. Marketed as TimberSIL, it's fast building nationwide distribution.

Pickled Pine and Cooked Wood

Meanwhile, other guys in lab coats have come up with some unique processes to make wood better for decking and exterior use.

One of the most impressive, considering its 50-year exterior-use warranty, is Accoya, a brand name for radiata pine from New Zealand that goes through a process called acetylation, which alters the cell structure of the wood so that it will no longer absorb water or be digestible by insects, mold, or mildew. According to Chris Fiaccone, marketing manager at Titan Wood, the company that sells Accoya, the wood's stability increases about 70 percent during acetylation, a process similar to pickling. He said the wood is 10 percent harder after treatment and totally nontoxic. "When you cut it," says Fiaccone, "what you essentially get is food-grade sawdust." Accoya sells for about the same price as ipé and is available through an increasing number of North American distributors.

Another wood-altering process, thermal modification, has been used in Europe for a long time and is heating up the decking business on this continent. Thermally modifying wood involves baking it at temperatures up to 500°F. Different wood species require a variety of recipes (some involving steam) and cooking times, but the transformation is similar: The high heat bakes the wood's sugars, making them insoluble in water and indigestible to microbes and to insects. Stability and weather resistance are also increased. Thermal modification gives woods a pleasing baked color, similar to a slice of toast.

Several companies sell thermal wood, and others license the technology to wood processors that want to get cooking.

Here's the ultimate deal: All decking—real wood or wood wannabe—is going to require some attention, sometime. You vacuum your house, so why shouldn't you have to clean your outdoor floor? The new and seemingly impervious high-end capstock deck boards should require only periodic cleaning with soap and water. Real wood decks also need cleaning and will need sealing if they are to remain new-looking (see the chart on pp. 40–41 for care of specific decking types).

Aluminum Decking: Cooler Than You Think

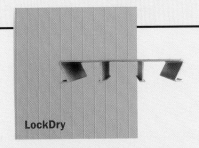

LockDry

What if you could find a decking material that had a lifetime warranty; was impervious to insects, mold, mildew, and rot; was fire-resistant, waterproof, and cool underfoot; and didn't pretend to look anything like wood? Would you buy it in a heartbeat? If so, then aluminum decking is for you.

If you can get around the aesthetics, however, it's difficult to argue with the attributes. Aluminum decking has a nonslip surface from powder-coating or an application of polyurea (the same stuff used for spray-on pickup-truck bed liners). Color choices range from white to a flat terra-cotta red to gray and brown. Not the widest palette, true, but I warned you about the aesthetics.

Aluminum deck planks lock together and can be fastened to wood joists with common screws. The cross sections of manufacturers' products differ, but all have a small internal gutter that drains any water that might make its way through the deck surface. The benefit of a waterproof deck surface is that it can be used to protect a room or storage area below. Because water doesn't drain through the deck surface, manufacturers recommend framing an aluminum deck so that it slopes slightly away from the house to allow water to run off. Aluminum decking, available with matching railing systems, is cool underfoot in hot weather. Its ribbed profile is designed to dissipate heat like the fins on an air-cooled lawnmower engine.

Once you get around the fact that this decking looks a little different from what you're used to, what's not to like? For one thing, at $4 to $5 a lineal ft., it's expensive. And some people don't like the pinging sound aluminum decking makes when you walk across or drop something on it. Maybe they prefer the sound they hear when they knock on wood. Or is that just a superstition to prevent their wood deck from rotting?

Aluminum decking

Rather than expect (and pay dearly for) the perfect plank, it may make more sense to accept that your deck, like every other part of your house, requires some looking after. That may mean getting down on your hands and knees and doing a little work once or twice a year. But then get out the guacamole and the tiki torches—it's party time.

Jefferson Kolle is a freelance writer and former Fine Homebuilding *editor.*

Deck Boards Done Right

■ BY MIKE GUERTIN

On the face of it, building a deck looks like an easy project, and for the most part it is. There are lots of ways to plan and install deck boards, and it seems as if I've tried most of them. Over the years, I've refined a process that works for me. Depending on the deck, I might vary the process a bit, but for the most part, I follow the same practice: Order deck boards, manage joint layout, lay down boards with correct spacing, and attach the decking with neatly aligned screws. At each step, I try to work efficiently because it's easy to get bogged down if you're not careful.

First, Protect the Joists

I used to assume that pressure-treated deck joists would last forever, but they can rot, especially boards made of incised hem-fir or Douglas fir whose treatment penetration doesn't reach the core of the lumber. Deck fasteners act as wedges and split the joist tops. This splitting might not occur initially if the joists are still wet, but it's inevitable that over repeated drying and wetting cycles, the joist tops will crack. Capillary action draws moisture between the deck boards and the joist tops, and that moisture settles into the cracks. Add bits of debris into

the mix, and it's just a matter of time before decay takes hold like a cavity in a candy lover's tooth.

One simple way to help the joists resist water damage is to protect the tops with a strip of builder's paper or roofing membrane cut at least a half-inch wider than the joist. The material sheds water that gets between the deck boards away from the joist. I first saw this technique when dismantling an old porch floor. Even though the decking had reached the end of service, the 80-year-old Douglas-fir joists were in nearly perfect condition; each was capped with a 3-in.-wide strip of #30 tar paper. Where the tar paper had failed, the joists were rotted. Many manufacturers sell plastic, rubber, and self-adhesive strips just for this purpose. Instead of buying material, I often cut my own joist caps from roll ends of tar paper and synthetic roof underlayment that I've saved. With the joists protected, I can start installing the decking, using the layout I planned.

Board Lengths Should Reflect Deck Size

When a deck is short enough, I order boards to span the full length. This works well for decks that are 12 ft., 16 ft., and even 20 ft. if you can find long boards. When I'm framing

Stringline gives you a reference to keep decking straight.

Leave enough overhang for a clean trim cut.

1. Plan 'em Out

It's easier to maintain a straight run of decking if the joints are staggered. I like to separate butt joints on adjacent boards by at least three joists, and I don't repeat a butt joint on the same joist for at least four courses.

2. Line 'em Up

To deck efficiently and still allow for adjustments, I work the boards in groups. I place four or five boards, then insert spacers at every fourth joist. After I run a stringline, I check the alignment of the last board and the distance between the stringline and the house.

3. Tack 'em Down

I tack-screw only the last board, which locks the rest of the group in place. Then I recheck the line and finish fastening the last board. I continue laying groups of boards along those same courses all the way to the end, then go back and screw down the field.

MITERED DECKS NEED EXTRA BLOCKING Where the framing changed direction, I added blocking to support the last few feet of decking.

One-by blocking provides support along the miter and is held 2 in. apart to allow drainage.

Joists run perpendicular to the house.

One-by cross-blocking on 16-in. centers supports decking.

the deck, I often downsize it slightly (15 ft. 10 in. instead of 16 ft., for example) so that a full-length board will have enough overhang at the ends for a clean trim cut.

When a deck is greater than stock lengths can span, I plan for the joints to fall in a sequence at least 4 ft. apart (see the drawing on the facing page). The decking looks better, and it's easier to keep decking straight when joints are spread throughout the field of boards. I also avoid boards shorter than 4 ft. at the ends for appearance's sake. Rather than just ordering a mountain of single-length boards and cutting them as needed, I select a combination of lengths to match the overall deck length. For a 22-ft. deck, I might order 16-ft. and 12-ft. boards (half a 12-footer is the makeup); on a 42-ft. deck, I would work with 16-ft. and 10-ft. boards.

The L-shape of the 58-ft.-long deck shown here leaves a variety of cutoffs that I could use to finish one course or to start the next. The trick is managing those pieces to avoid waste. I worked with 16-ft. boards as my primary stock. Starters were 16 ft., 12 ft., 8 ft., and 4 ft. I ran out the courses with 16-ft. boards and used the cutoffs as starter stock. Boards sometimes have snipe near the ends that creates a narrower or wider spot within 18 in. of the butts. Offsetting the joints by 4 ft. spreads out these differences in width through the field.

Start at the Rim, and Work to the House

Many builders start the decking from the house and work toward the rim. This sequence is fine provided that you plan the course spacing or design the deck frame so that you don't end up with a narrow board at the outside edge. Narrow boards (less than half a board's width) at the perimeter are hard to fasten, limit the overhang, often loosen, and look funny. I work from the rim toward the house so that I can start with a full-width board at the posts.

Create the 100-Year Joist

To keep water from invading the joists through splits caused by deck fasteners, staple a 2-in. strip of builder's paper or roofing membrane on the tops of all joists.

(1) **Vycor** (www.grace.com)
(2) **YorkWrap** (www.yorkmfg.com)
(3) **Synthetic roof underlayment**
(4) **#30 builder's paper**

Notching accurately around the posts is critical to getting a straight start for the decking. After the first board is established, I select a bunch of straight, uniform boards and lay down three to four courses. Spacers placed every 4 ft. to 6 ft. help me to gauge the gap between the deck boards. (On this project, I used decking that was kiln-dried after treatment, so I needed to establish uniform gaps between the boards.)

When I'm driving deck screws or nails without pilot holes, I skip the board ends and return later to drill the pilot holes for stainless-steel trim screws. I'm less likely to split boards using that technique.

Decking doesn't always run precisely parallel to the building. This can be due to the rim and building being out of parallel or to the deck boards going out of alignment during installation. There are a couple of

Start with a Straight Run and Clean Notches

1 I align the first board by pulling a string from one end of the deck to the other to represent the inside edge of the board. Keep in mind that this board will overhang the rim ¾ in. (photo 1). I measure the distance between the string and the post, and transfer that measurement to the board, marking the depth of the notch (photo 2). I use a Speed® Square to locate and transfer the locations of the post sides (photo 3). When cutting the notch, I aim for a notch that's ¹⁄₁₆ in. to ⅛ in. bigger than the post (photo 4). The gaps permit water to drain through rather than be drawn into a tight joint between decking and post. Posts are likely to swell and shrink with moisture changes, too, so the gap allows seasonal movement of the post that won't split the board.

The First Straight Run Sets the Standard

1

To establish the first straight board at the posts, I drive a screw into every fourth joist (photo 1). After using a stringline to check that the board is straight, I adjust as needed and drive the rest of the screws. Decking looks better when the fasteners are installed neatly. To this end, I make a low-tech jig from a piece of thin plywood marked for each screw position (photo 2). I orient the guide along the joist edge viewed between the deck boards, and I use my foot to hold it while driving screws from an auto-feed gun. My goal isn't precise screw location, just close alignment that doesn't catch the eye.

2

Screw guns that save your back and knees

An auto-feed screw gun isn't as fast as a pneumatic nail gun, but it does allow you to work upright rather than on all fours. And screws have much better holding power. I'm a fan of auto-feed screw guns with either a handle or shaft extension. Once you develop a rhythm, you can drive screws with near-pinpoint accuracy. One key to driving consistently is to follow through the drive with even, determined pressure until the driver has finished setting the screw.

PAM® (www.pamfast.com), Makita® (www.makita.com), Muro® (www.muro.com), Senco® (www.senco.com), Quik Drive® (www.quikdrive.com), and other manufacturers offer complete auto-feed screw-gun kits or accessory extensions.

If you use screws, match them to the decking

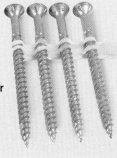

Wood decking screws have ribs (or wings) on the underside of the screw head or wings that open a countersink or press the deck board into the decking.

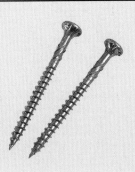

Screws made for composite and plastic decking have wings or reverse threads under the head to cut a pilot hole for the head to seat.

Spacers Keep the Gaps Consistent

I save scraps of thin plywood and cut U-shaped spacers that straddle the joist to stay in place (photo 1). The spacers I made for this job were about ⁵⁄₁₆ in. thick. There are also commercial plastic devices made in different thicknesses and styles (see below). As the decking courses near the house, I make sure that the last board isn't too narrow (not less than half a board) and that the gap between the house and the board is about ¾ in. wide (photo 2). Here, to close the space at the house, I padded the plywood spacers with plastic coil stock on the last five courses; the incremental gain added up to ⁵⁄₁₆ in., just enough to bring the gap at the house within tolerances (photo 3). I levered a flat bar against the house to tighten the last few courses; a scrap of decking protects the siding. Spacers also keep miters open and dry (photo 4). After using a rip guide to cut the 45-degree angles in place on one side

of the deck's miter, I could cut the mating pieces on a miter saw first and screw them down. To keep joints at a uniform space that would drain properly, I used a strip of plastic coil stock as a gauge.

Ready-Made Deck Spacers

Deck Spacers™ are stay-in-place spacers that cap the joists and help to shed water and debris (www.strongtie.com).

Deck-Mate® is a spacer and a screw-layout jig in one (www.johnsonlevel.com).

Deckit™ spacers are meant to be used repeatedly as a gauge, like my plywood versions (www.woodpileproducts.com).

ways to deal with out-of-parallel decking: A couple of boards in the last set of decking can be ripped with a taper, or the joint spacing can be adjusted. Minute adjustments in board width or joint spacing spread out over several courses won't catch the eye. Using one of these microadjustments avoids a severe taper rip of the last board next to the house, where it can be seen easily.

I always leave a ½-in. to ¾-in. space between the last deck board and the house. Water and any debris falling into the area will be flushed out rather than become trapped against the flashing, where it can fester and accelerate corrosion of metal flashing or rot the deck board. On this project, the last set of deck boards ended 1⅛ in. shy of the building, which is a bigger space than I prefer. To close the gap, I added 1/16 in. to the last five spaces by inserting a couple of shims made of plastic coil stock at each plywood spacer. The resulting space to the building was a strong ¾ in.

When the Decking Changes Direction, Don't Forget the Blocking

The framing of this L-shaped deck ran perpendicular to the building. The decking met at the corner in a 17-ft.-long miter. From the corner of the house to the corner of the deck, I added diagonal blocking between the joists to pick up the 45-degree cuts (see the drawing on p. 48). Rather than a single line of blocking, I added two rows of diagonal blocking spaced about 2 in. apart along the 45-degree cutline. The space lets water drain through the butt joints and moves the screw location farther from the end to reduce the chance of splitting the boards.

I also had to cross-block joists parallel to the deck boards from the bottom of the L. Blocking is screwed to the joists and is

cleated beneath the drainage membrane for additional support.

I ran the first section of decking beyond the 45-degree cutline. Then I snapped a chalkline and used a plywood straightedge to guide a perfect cut. I cut 45-degree ends on the adjoining boards with a miter saw, then ran the rest of the deck pieces in each course toward the end of the deck. I trimmed the butt ends overhanging the deck after all the decking was laid.

Mike Guertin is a remodeling contractor in East Greenwich, Rhode Island, and editorial adviser to Fine Homebuilding. His Web site is www.mikeguertin.com.

Tools Tame Wild Wood

Pressure-treated deck boards are often warped, but there's no reason to discard them—just tame them with a board straightener. Years ago, I'd screw a cleat to a joist and drive a wedge-shaped block between the unruly board and the cleat to straighten the board. Now, there are tools to straighten boards efficiently.

CEPCO BOWRENCH®

www.cepcotool.com
Operation: Joist gripping pins and lever arm.
Pro: Good leverage. Low cost.
Con: Can dent soft decking.

VAUGHAN BOWJAK®

www.hammernet.com
Operation: Pin secures tool to joist top; lever pushed board.
Pro: Compact; easy to use. Low cost.
Con: Pin tears joist tape. Weak leverage.

STANLEY® BOARD BENDER

www.stanleytools.com
Operation: Joist gripping knuckle and lever arm.
Pro: Good leverage. Can be foot-activated.
Con: Awkward positioning; short range of movement against board.

Deck Fastener Options

■ BY JUSTIN FINK

Fasteners used to be a minor cost in the large scheme of building a deck. Buried beneath the price of concrete footings, framing lumber, top-notch planks, and a high-quality stain or sealer, galvanized nails were the standard choice, almost an afterthought. With the average deck costing several thousand dollars, a few boxes of nails were just a drop in the bucket.

Things have changed over the past decade. The preservatives used for pressure-treated lumber have been altered, hardwood and synthetic decking have swept the nation, and decks have become very popular across the country. These changes have created a market in which deck fasteners are as important—and sometimes as expensive—as the planks they secure.

The affordable galvanized nails of the past are competing with specialized screws and hidden fasteners designed for premium-level projects. Today, there are three basic fastener categories to choose from: top down, edge mount, and undermount.

The Total Cost Might Surprise You

Modern fasteners are anything but cheap. Let's say you have a 20-ft. by 40-ft. (800 sq. ft.) deck with joists spaced 16 in. on center and plan to fasten 2×6 planks with screws; you will need roughly 3,000 fasteners. With the average deck screw ranging in price from 5¢ to 17¢ apiece, using top-down fasteners will cost you from $150 to $510.

If you install an edge-mount deck fastener such as EB-TY®, Ipe Clip®, or Tiger Claw®, you aren't just buying screws. You often are investing in a complete kit that includes hardware, compatible driver bits, and wooden plugs to hide the screw holes in the first board. For the same 800-sq.-ft. deck, an edge-mount kit costs from $336 to $952.

Undermount systems like Invisi-Fast™ or Deckmaster® typically cost even more because you're paying for larger pieces of metal. Prices range from $448 to $1,864 to cover the same area.

Making Sense of Corrosion, Compatibility, and Fastener Coatings

Corrosion resistance is important whether you choose to secure decking with nails, screws, or hidden fasteners. Even the seemingly innocuous plastic hidden fasteners such as EB-TY and Ipe Clip require the use of metal screws.

Lumber manufacturers have discontinued the old CCA (chromated-copper arsenate) wood-preservative treatment and have replaced it with arsenic-free treatments such as CA (copper azole), ACQ (alkaline copper quaternary), MCQ (micronized copper quaternary), and others.

Although these new compounds pose less of a health hazard, some have high copper content (about 6 times more than CCA) that can accelerate corrosion in fasteners and hardware made of brass, lead, mild steel, aluminum, or zinc.

This has added a new wrinkle to choosing all fasteners on a deck, from lag bolts to joist hangers to deck fasteners. Unless there is a protective coating or a physical separation, the fasteners will deteriorate.

For joist hangers, stainless steel is the best option. Hot-dipped galvanized is the next-best choice. These fasteners are graded by the weight of their protective coating such that G-60 means that there's 0.60 oz. of zinc per sq. ft. of metal. Choose G-185 for your fasteners.

Top Downs: Fast but Visible

Driving nails or screws straight through decking boards and into joists is the old-fashioned approach to laying down a deck. But there's been plenty of innovation in top-down fasteners. Stainless-steel and durable coatings stand up to the weather and to the more corrosive chemicals used in today's pressure-treated wood. Auger points and special threads make screws easier to drive, reduce the chances of splitting the wood, and (depending on the type of decking) eliminate the need for pilot holes. Some screws even have heads designed to make countersinking easy or to eliminate the unsightly "mushrooming" that can occur when fastening down synthetic decking. If budget and installation speed are priorities and if you like the ability to remove fasteners easily should a board need replacing, this family of fasteners is your best bet.

Stainless Steel

Galvanized

Razorback® & Woodpecker

A good choice for hardwood decking, these screws have coarse, square-shaped threads that cut into the wood as they spin. Razorback screws (9¢ apiece) have an auger point to improve self-drilling performance and come with either a square or star-drive head. Swan Secure's Woodpecker (13¢ per screw) relies on a small ridge running along the shank to make driving easier. Both screws are available with or without color-coated heads.
www.starbornindustries.com; www.swansecure.com

Razorback

Woodpecker

Nails

Old-timers and penny-pinchers aren't the only people still fastening decks with nails. These fasteners still are used more than any other type. If you go this route, building codes require hot-dipped galvanized fasteners—available at any hardware store for about 2¢ apiece. Stainless-steel nails are the premium choice and typically cost about 5¢ apiece. Opt for spiral or ring-shank versions to minimize nail pops. **www.mazenails.com; www.mcfeelys.com; www.manasquanfasteners.com**

SplitStop™

Available in stainless steel (15¢) and both synthetic (6¢) and ACQ-rated finishes (5¢), these screws are compatible with all types of decking. An auger point eliminates the need for a pilot hole, and knurled shoulders above the threaded section of the shank are designed to reduce splitting. Nibs under the head aid in countersinking the screw. With square-drive or star-drive heads, these screws are pretty versatile. **www.splitstop.com**

SplitStop

TrapEase

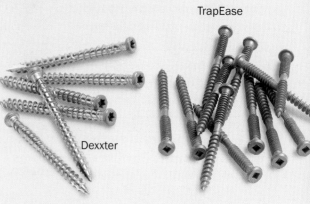

Dexxter

No-Co-Rode

Recommended for use with wood decking but not synthetics, these screws are affordable (5¢ apiece) but don't have the self-drilling and split-resistant characteristics of other types. Mechanical galvanizing creates a rough surface texture and makes it necessary to use an undersize square driver ($1).
www.mcfeelys.com

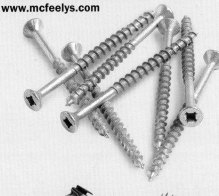

Production-style fastening. If you have a large area to cover—or if you're concerned about hammer tracks on the deck surface—consider using pneumatic nailers or collated screw guns in lieu of manual fastening. These options are fast and help to minimize labor costs. The model shown above is Hitachi's® new SuperDrive W6V4SD.
www.hitachipowertools.com

TrapEase® & Dexxter

Both of these screws use changing thread patterns and an undercut head to eliminate the common problem of mushrooming in synthetic materials (see the detail photo at left). The epoxy-coated zinc TrapEase screws are available in four colors, at about 8¢ apiece. Swan Secure's stainless-steel Dexxter costs about 17¢ apiece. **www.fastenmaster.com; www.swansecure.com**

Headcote® & Scrudini

Headcote stainless-steel screws (10¢ apiece) are designed to blend with most conventionally used deck materials, including cedar, mahogany, ipé, and a wide range of colored synthetics. Make sure to match the head with the color the deck will fade to, rather than the color of the planks when they are new. Swan Secure also offers a colored head coating for any of its deck screws sold under the brand name Scrudini. **www.starbornindustries.com; www.swansecure.com**

Scrudini

Headcote

Deck-Mate with Evercote®

These nationally available screws are very cost effective at just 7¢ apiece. The corrosion-resistant coating is green or tan, and the Square-Driv® head can accept a #3 Phillips bit and a #2 square driver, or (for best results) the special combination bit that's included with a box of screws. Expect to drill a pilot hole when screwing down hardwood decking.
www.deckmatescrews.com

GuardDog®

These screws are available in a range of lengths from 1⅝ in. to 3½ in. and have guaranteed corrosion resistance for the life of the deck. The PosiSquare™ heads also take a #2 square driver and Phillips bits. Screws cost about 7¢ each. **www.fastenmaster.com**

Edge Mounts: Fussy but Inconspicuous

Some edge-mount fasteners get their holding power from prongs driven into board edges, but most have flanges that fit in slots. Integral spacers establish a uniform distance between deck planks, and there's a hole for a screw that anchors the fastener to deck joists. Manufacturers typically recommend using a router or a biscuit joiner to cut a slot in the plank over each joist, but many decking boards are now available with grooved edges to accept hidden fasteners.

Whichever edge-mount fastener you use, trouble-free installation depends on boards that are flat and straight. Most synthetic decking comes this way, but the same can't be said for solid wood. A cupped or curved board must be forced into place and held there to get slots aligned properly for fastener installation.

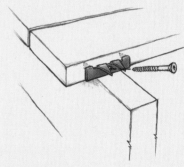

1. Tiger Claw

Tiger Claw fasteners are available in hardened- or stainless steel—both with black-oxide coatings—and are offered in three varieties, making them compatible with all types of decking. To drive claws into the edges of a board, you hammer against a proprietary installation block (included in every box of fasteners). The oncoming board is driven onto the fastener claws with a mallet or decking clamp. Cost per sq. ft.: 48¢ to 85¢ depending on decking type. **www.deckfastener.com**

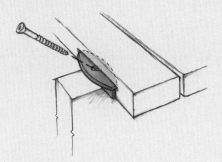

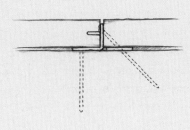

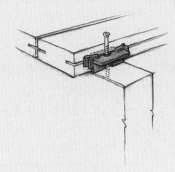

2. EB-TY

These polypropylene fasteners are available in ³⁄₃₂-in. or ¼-in. board spacing, with or without Live Cylinder™, which allows for board expansion and contraction. To avoid squeaks, decking should be secured to joists with construction adhesive. Cost per sq. ft.: $1. www.ebty.com

3. Dec-Klip®

The Klip's thick point may be a good choice for softwoods, but it doesn't penetrate easily in dense hardwoods or composite decking. With a tall upright leg, the fasteners are best suited to 2× decking rather than more common 5/4 in. thick stock. Cost per sq. ft.: 45¢. www.dec-klip.com

4. Lumber Loc®

Made from UV-resistant polypropylene, these fasteners work with exotic hardwoods, composite, and plastic decking. Each has spring-like spacers that maintain a constant pressure against deck planks as the wood expands and contracts seasonally. Cost per sq. ft.: 63¢. www.lumberloc.com

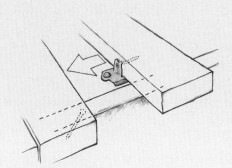

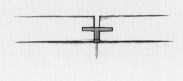

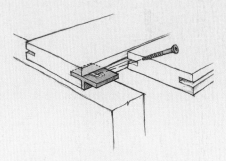

5. Deck-Tie®

Designed to be used with all types of decking, Simpson's galvanized-zinc fastener is secured between deck boards with a single 10d by 1½-in. nail. Cost per sq. ft.: 42¢. www.strongtie.com

6. Deck Clip™

The Deck Clip is designed for use in hardwoods. When installed properly, a ⅛-in. gap separates the marine-grade aluminum fastener from underlying pressure-treated framing to prevent corrosion. This product is not compatible for direct contact with pressure-treated decking. Cost per sq. ft.: 90¢. www.deckclip.com

7. Ipe Clip Extreme™

Available in gray, brown, and black, these fasteners are fiberglass-reinforced plastic with a stainless-steel insert added for strength. At $1.09 per sq. ft., they are the most expensive edge-mount option. Despite the name, the Ipe Clip Extreme can be used to fasten most hardwoods and synthetic decking that don't have a high rate of expansion and contraction. www.ipeclip.com

Undermounts: Truly Invisible

If you want to keep fasteners hidden and have an elevated deck that's easily accessible from below, an undermount strategy is worth considering. Systems based on steel strips are screwed to the top edges of deck joists before any decking goes down; they're great for flattening cupped or bowed planks. With small brackets like those from Invisi-Fast and Fasten-Master®, you can install fasteners one at a time. In all cases, it's necessary to have pressure bearing on the board from above during installation to ensure that each plank rests solidly on joists. Unlike edge-mount fasteners, undermounts offer the advantage of reversibility: If you can access the underside of the deck, you can remove the screws that hold a damaged deck board in place.

Shadoe® Track

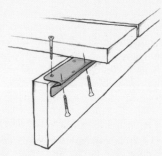

Offered in galvanized steel, stainless steel, and powder-coated steel, Shadoe Track is compatible with all types of decking. Sold in 4-ft. and 8-ft. lengths, the track can be cut to length using tin snips. The manufacturer offers a 30-year transferable warranty. Cost per sq. ft.: $1.05 to $1.33. **www.shadoetrack.com**

Deckmaster®

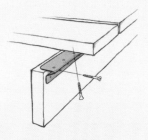

Available in powder-coated and stainless steel ($1.20 and $2.06 per sq. ft., respectively), Deckmaster is the most expensive of all undermount options. **www.deckmaster.com**

Even if you choose a synthetic material for the deck surface, the underlying pressure-treated framing lumber still poses a serious corrosion threat.

The use of hot-dipped galvanized fasteners is the minimum requirement according to building codes, but this protective coating can be difficult to apply to deck screws without clogging the recessed heads and congesting the threads along the shaft of the screw. Fortunately, many building inspectors now accept mechanical galvanization, which is a flash-coating of copper followed by a layer of zinc. The copper and zinc combine to make a thinner coating. But reports have shown mechanical galvanization to be a potential problem on sharp threads or on auger points where coatings get thinner.

The inherent corrosion resistance of stainless steel is the best defense against lumber preservatives and the harsh elements, but it's an expensive option compared to the hardened steel found in common nails and screws.

Invisi-Fast

These Lexan® equivalent material fasteners are clear (though they can be painted) and are compatible with nearly all deck planks. Fastener kits can be purchased with ACQ-compatible screws or stainless-steel screws. Cost per sq. ft.: 73¢; $1.10 with stainless-steel screws. **www.invisifast.com**

FastenMaster IQ

The IQ Hidden Fastening System's clear plastic fastener has an ingenious interlocking design that enables you to complete most of the decking installation from above. Fasteners can be screwed to a board before it's flipped over and slid into place. A toe screw and one face screw go with each fastener. Cost per sq. ft.: $2. **www.fastenmaster.com**

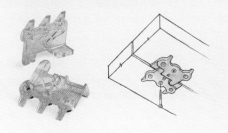

To combat the price of stainless steel and the problems that are associated with hot-dipped galvanization, several manufacturers now offer steel fasteners that have proprietary epoxy or powder coatings to help reduce costs without sacrificing durability. Because the benefit of these proprietary coatings is most obvious in small and intricate fasteners, they more commonly are found on screws—DeckMate and GuardDog are a couple of examples. Similar coatings are also available in some undermount brackets, such as Deckmaster

and Shadoe Track. Although it might not be a major concern, if this coating were to chip or crack, the underlying steel core would be exposed and would become susceptible to corrosion.

In the end, it's important to consider the life span of the deck itself. Stainless-steel fasteners are likely to outlive any deck material they secure, but the extra cost may not be sensible if the fasteners are used to install pressure-treated pine.

Some Hidden Fasteners Are More Visible Than Others

If you choose to fasten deck planks with nails, keep in mind that the heads will be hard to conceal and might pop up above the surface as the deck planks weather, shrink, and expand.

When choosing screws, remember that small-headed trim screws are less visible because the deck plank expands around the top of the fastener; this is especially true with softwoods and some synthetics.

Color-matched screws like DeckMate, Scrudini, TrapEase, and Headcote are a good compromise between cost and ease of installation. But remember to match the deck fasteners to the color that the deck planks will be after you've applied a stain or they've spent a few years in the sun; otherwise, the screw heads will become more obvious over time.

The ideal edge-mount system should have all of its components extruded from black metal, coated in a matte black finish, or color-matched to the deck planks to help them disappear in the shadowlines of the finished deck.

If you go with a steel strip-type undermount, try to match the hardware's coating color to the tone of your deck planks.

Justin Fink is senior editor at Fine Homebuilding.

Putting the Fast in Fastener

■ BY MIKE GUERTIN

Two qualities come to mind when I look at the evolution of decking fasteners over the past couple of years: speed and ease. Whether you're face-screwing deck boards or prefer the seamless look of a hidden-fastener system, manufacturers have begun focusing on tools and fasteners that help to get your deck finished faster than ever.

Plowing Pilotless Through Hardwoods

Years ago, fastening deck planks with screws was a time-consuming, two-step process: Drill a pilot hole in the face of the board, then drive the screw. A few years ago, screw makers engineered special screws that didn't require pilot holes for softwoods and many synthetic decking brands. The screws have tips that cut cleanly through decking and heads that neatly part the wood or composite surface for a neat, countersunk set. Only recently, though, have these pilotless screws been made compatible on hardwood decking like meranti, garapa, and ipé.

Manufacturers offering autofeed screw guns are on top of this category with the Ejector screw from Muro (www.muro.com), the #IPESS10212 from PAM Fastening Technology (www.pamfast.com), and the DHPD Hardwood Deck Screw from Simpson Strong-Tie (www.strongtie.com). If you're

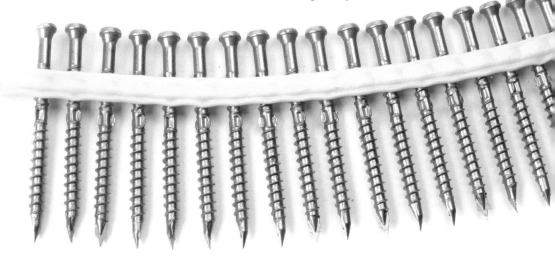

Headcote Razorback If you're using a standard screw gun, these screws will help minimize the chance of splitting.

DHPD Hardwood Deck Screws These screws are designed to fasten hardwood decking, like ipé.

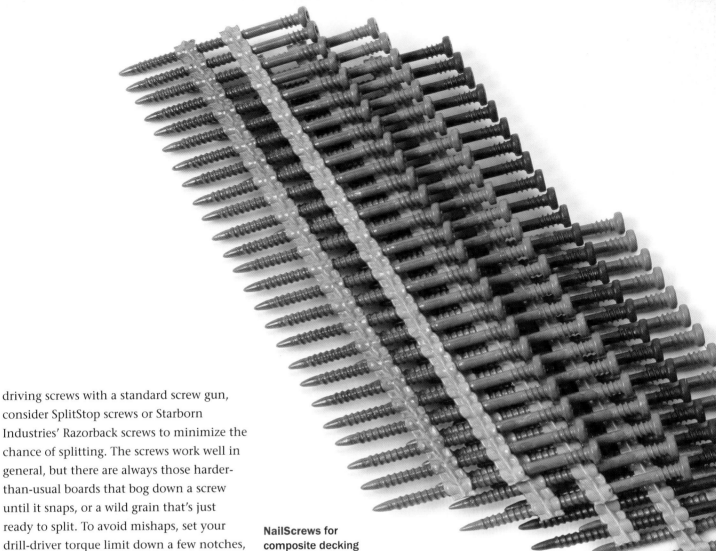

driving screws with a standard screw gun, consider SplitStop screws or Starborn Industries' Razorback screws to minimize the chance of splitting. The screws work well in general, but there are always those harder-than-usual boards that bog down a screw until it snaps, or a wild grain that's just ready to split. To avoid mishaps, set your drill-driver torque limit down a few notches, keep your eye out for wild grain, and take the time to drill pilot holes in butt joints between boards, just in case.

Screws That Nail?

If you think collated deck screws beat the pants off hand-driving loose screws, then you're really going to like pneumatically driven screws. Imagine tripling or quadrupling your deck-fastening efficiency using the framing nailer you already have. NailScrews® from Universal Fastener Outsourcing (UFO; www.911-nails.com) and Scrail® fasteners from Fasco® America (www.fascoamerica.com) are screws with ballistic points like those found on powder-actuated concrete nails. Just load the collated screws into a framing nailer, and blast down decking just like in the old days. Screw head too proud? Use a drill-driver and bit to spin it in further. Have to remove a board? Unscrew it. What's not to like?

NailScrews for composite decking

The pneumatically driven screw threads are unique; think of a cross between a ring-shank nail and spiral-shank nail. Like one-way barbs, the spiral threads drive into wood like a nail but won't pull out, only unscrew.

Here are a few pointers for a decent-looking job using pneumatically driven screws. Use a no-mar nose protector on your nailer, and switch to sequential (as opposed to bump-fire) mode for precise positioning of each fastener. Adjust the depth of drive so that the head of the screw is flush with the face of the board, not sunk below it. Avoid nailing butt joints; drill pilot holes and sink traditional screws in these spots.

Chances are that with the array of head styles, lengths, and color coatings available from UFO and Fasco, you may never return to spinning in screws again.

Decking Is Outdoor Flooring, Right?

Why not install decking with a flooring nailer? You can now with the HIDfast tool (www.hid-fast.com), a decking nailer that looks and works like a pneumatic flooring nailer. Compared to ordinary hidden deck-fastening systems, this one is lightning fast. The key to the concept is in the design of the fastener. The primary shank drives diagonally through the board and into the deck joist. At the head, there's a pin that sticks straight out, ready to engage the next plank that is installed.

A retractable stop registers the joist side so that the nailer drives the fasteners dead center on each joist. After driving fasteners through the decking into each joist, a mallet and block are used to tap the next deck board onto the pins. You also can use a deck-board-straightening tool to push the boards onto the pins. If you're using pregrooved deck boards, a baseplate attachment microadjusts the height of the fastener pin to match any groove level.

The HIDfast system works great with most square-edged synthetic and softwood decking. Hardwood decking and dense composite decking require a groove or bump slot in the edge of the oncoming plank to engage the fastener pins.

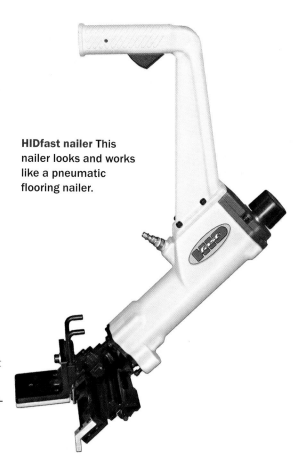

HIDfast nailer This nailer looks and works like a pneumatic flooring nailer.

The tool is pricey, but some lumberyards are renting or loaning them out with a minimum fastener purchase. This is a good option if you build decks only occasionally or just want to try out the HIDfast system before dipping too deep into your pocket.

Pneumatic Screws to the Rescue—Again

What if you take a metal-connector nailer, load it with pneumatically driven screws, and shoot the hidden-fastener clips in place? Tiger Claw and Sure Drive USA have done just that with the Tiger Claw Installation Gun (www.deckfastener.com) and the Eliminator tool (www.suredrive.com).

Tiger Claw's tool has a specially designed nosepiece that accepts the Tiger Claw TC-G and TimberTech Concealoc® hidden fasteners. Just slide a fastener onto the nose, orient the nailer and fastener to the slot in the deck plank, and pull the trigger. The pneumatically driven screw hits the mark

What's on Deck

The inventors aren't done yet. Be on the lookout for collated hidden decking fasteners that will be delivered to the nose of a nailer and attached with a pneumatically driven screw—kind of like a cap nailer for decking. Prototypes I've seen are sure to be the next step in the evolution of hidden fasteners for decking.

every time. The Eliminator works with SureDrive's Mantis hidden fastening clip. Slip a Mantis clip into the decking groove, fit the screw tip protruding from the nailer's nose—painted white for easy visibility—to the hole in the clip, and pull the trigger.

Some of you may be thinking that installing hidden decking fasteners pneumatically isn't anything new. You're right. Some EB-TY (www.ebty.com) users have been shooting down clips for years using a pneumatic stapler. I checked with EB-TY about this practice and was assured that the recommended stainless-steel staple has comparable holding power to a screw and can be used with all plastic EB-TY hidden fasteners.

Positive placement NailScrew and Mantis clip

Mike Guertin is a remodeling contractor in East Greenwich, Rhode Island, and editorial adviser to Fine Homebuilding. *His Web site is www. mikeguertin.com.*

Matchmaking: Decking and Fasteners

Decking is expensive, and synthetic-decking prices run close to and sometimes greater than those for premium wood decking. Be sure that the hidden-fastening system you use is compatible with the decking you plan to install. Many deck-plank manufacturers make the choice simple by offering proprietary fasteners, which are typically modified versions of common hidden-fastening systems. The benefit of these modified systems is the assurance that the fasteners match the slot width, depth, and height, and automatically gauge the proper joint spacing.

If your preferred brand of synthetic decking doesn't offer a hidden fastener, check to see if the manufacturer recommends a specific brand for its boards. You also can ask hidden-fastener companies with which brands their fasteners are most compatible.

EQUATOR®
Latitudes® Decking & Railing
(Universal Forest Products)
www.ufpi.com/product/latitudes/
accessories/equator.htm

SABRE™
CrossTimbers® (GAF)
www.gaf.com/decking/decking-
accessories.asp

CONCEALOC
TimberTech
www.timbertech.com/products/
finishing-touches/concealoc-
fasteners

FASTENATOR®
Correct Deck (GAF)
www.correctdeck.com/products/
decking/channeled.htm

TREX HIDEAWAY
Trex
www.trex.com/hideaway

CROWN CLIPS
Monarch®
www.monarchdeck.com/
decking_crownclips.php

FIBERON HIDDEN FASTENERS
Fiberon
www.fiberondecking.com/
products/hardware

EG 1-2-3
EverGrain® (Tamko)
www.evergrain.com/create/
decking/installation.jsp

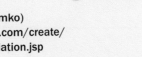

An Explosion of Decking Choices

For homeowners, the day a new deck is finished is a day of celebration, with anticipation of cookouts, family time, and quiet afternoons spent with a book on their pristine outdoor structure. The last thing they're thinking about is maintenance—or the fact that before the last deck board went down, nature was already hard at work trying to destroy their new prize.

Traditionally, decking has been wood in one of three sizes: 2×4, 5/4×6, or 2×6. That might be redwood, western red cedar, or pressure-treated southern pine, depending on what part of the country you live in.

Over the past 15 years, the tradition has changed. Other types of wood decking have become easier to find: Alaska yellow cedar, rainforest hardwoods such as ipé, and red meranti from Malaysia. Also, a whole new category of synthetic decking has flooded the marketplace. While purists will never accept a plank made of plastics, the latest generation of synthetic decking includes some pretty convincing facsimiles, and many are manufactured with recycled materials.

When building a deck, you choose materials by balancing your budget against durability, maintenance requirements, ease of installation, and aesthetics. It's not an easy balancing act; the up-front costs don't always give the whole picture. After considering the time and cost of annual washings and applications of preservative and the life expectancy of the product, a seemingly economical deck might end up costing as much as if you had gone with seemingly unobtainable planks.

This survey of popular decking choices arms you with the knowledge you need to weigh the relative pros and cons of materials. But remember, no matter which type you choose, it will perform as advertised only if the deck is designed and built to resist Mother Nature.

Fake Wood Never Looked so Good Of the four samples below, two are wood, and two are not. On the far left is a sample of Trex's Brasilia decking in cayenne. The piece of wood to its right is ipé. On the far right, it's Trex again, this time in burnished amber; to its left is a piece of Cambara mahogany.

Which one is ipé?

Which one is mahogany?

*Primary reporting by **Chris Green** and **Scott Gibson**, with help from **Daniel S. Morrison** and **Rob Yagid.***

Synthetic Decking: It Won't Crack, Rot, or Splinter

More than 60 manufacturers nationwide now produce synthetic decking products. We don't have space to feature every product, so we're focusing on those that are widely available, and those with unique features. Choosing won't be easy. Synthetics look better than ever, with convincing colors, textures, handrail systems, and trim profiles available. That said, distribution is spotty. Product availability will have a big influence on what you buy. Shop prices carefully; they vary, sometimes wildly within the same region.

Polyethylene-based composites

More wood-plastic composite decking is sold than all other synthetic decking combined, and polyethylene-wood blends lead the way. They are durable, strong enough to be used as decking, and easy to work with. They are, however, softer than the other plastics, which limits joist spacing and makes them wear a little more easily.

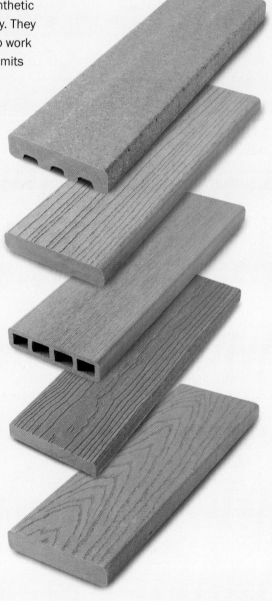

MOISTURESHIELD
A.E.R.T. Inc.
866-729-2378
www.moistureshield.com

TIMBERTECH
TimberTech
800-307-7780
www.timbertech.com

GEODECK
Green Bay Decking LLC;
877-804-0137
www.geodeck.com

EVERGRAIN
Tamko Building
Products Inc.
417-624-6644
www.evergrain.com

TREX
Trex Co. Inc.
800-289-8739
www.trex.com

Polypropylene-based composites

Polypropylene and wood-fiber composites are currently a smaller part of the market. They use a stiff, dense plastic capable of spanning longer distances. Using screws to fasten the decking without drilling pilot holes isn't recommended. The examples shown here have grooved edges to accept hidden fasteners.

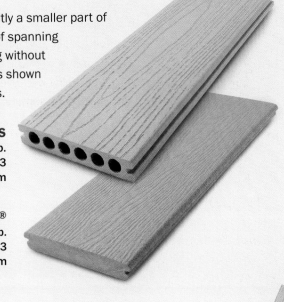

CROSSTIMBERS
GAF Materials Corp.
877-423-7663
www.gaf.com

CORRECTDECK®
GAF Materials Corp.
877-423-7663
www.gaf.com

Wood-free plastics

The popularity of plastic decking is growing fast and many major decking manufacturers are adding cellular PVC planks to their offerings. Some are all plastic. Others are mostly plastic with some nonwood fiber added. The benefit is that problems with mold and seasonal movement caused by the moisture in wood are eliminated.

Deck Lok

Bear Board

BEAR BOARD™
Engineered Plastic Systems
847-289-8383
www.epsplasticlumber.com

DECK LOK™
Royal Outdoor Products
800-488-5245
www.royalbuildingproducts.com

Eon

Azek Deck

EON®
CPI Plastics Group Ltd.
866-342-5366
www.eonoutdoor.com

AZEK DECK
Azek Building Products
877-275-2935
www.azek.com

Wood Decking: Redwood, Cedar, and Tropical Hardwoods Resist Insects and Decay

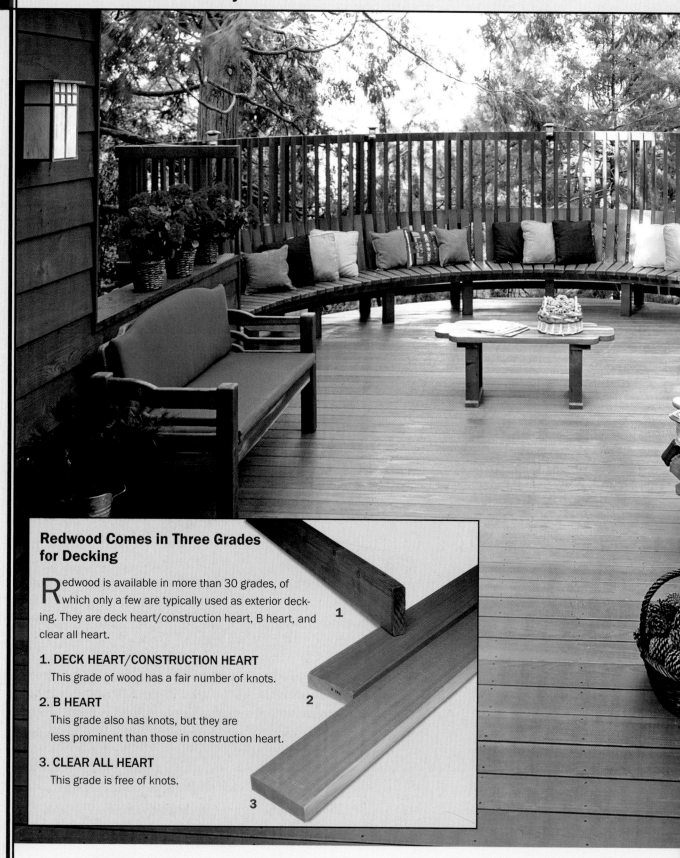

Redwood Comes in Three Grades for Decking

Redwood is available in more than 30 grades, of which only a few are typically used as exterior decking. They are deck heart/construction heart, B heart, and clear all heart.

1. DECK HEART/CONSTRUCTION HEART

This grade of wood has a fair number of knots.

2. B HEART

This grade also has knots, but they are less prominent than those in construction heart.

3. CLEAR ALL HEART

This grade is free of knots.

Resistance to decay and insects comes naturally to some wood species and can be improved chemically in others. But even the hardiest of wood decking requires attention from time to time, especially if you want to maintain the rich colors of a new deck. Wood decking is available in a number of different grades. Clear grades (without knots) are most expensive; the price drops as the number of defects rises. More important, look for planks cut from heartwood, which resists decay. Sapwood, the tree's soft outer layers, has virtually no natural protection against rot.

Redwood

You can't blame John Muir for idolizing these giant forest dwellers, some of them 300 ft. or more high. Top grades of redwood decking are equally prized for their performance. Although lighter and not as tough as some decking material, redwood is stable, with little in-service movement and not much pitch. Its heartwood, which has a pleasing reddish-brown color, is highly resistant to insects and decay. Redwood is easy to work, and it holds finishes well.

What more could you want? Well, a lower public profile might be a start. Past battles over logging the remaining old-growth forests were bitter and well publicized, and have probably scared some people away from considering redwood for decking. According to the California Redwood Association (www.calredwood.org), however, nearly all of the redwood on the market is second- and even third-growth wood cut from private land. California forestry laws are stringent, and what little old-growth wood being cut is not as a rule going into decking. The association estimates that 500 million to 700 million board feet of the fast-growing redwood is cut annually. FSC-certified (Forest Stewardship Council) redwood is available.

Although the heartwood in redwood is exceptionally resistant to both rot and insects, sapwood is not. This factor is a key difference in some redwood grades: Construction common contains sapwood, for instance, while deck heart/construction heart does not. Although grades of B heart and deck heart/construction heart both have knots, those in B heart are less prominent.

The California Redwood Association suggests applying a protective finish on a redwood deck every few years. Use one that contains mildewcides, water repellents, and ultraviolet protection.

Cedar

Western red cedar and Alaska yellow cedar are a lovely pair of Pacific Northwest woods. The heartwood of both species is highly resistant to decay, and they are both straight-grained, easy to work, and dimensionally stable. Both are readily available as decking, particularly on the West Coast. Despite sharing these attributes, the woods are different.

The heartwood of western red cedar has a red-to-brown color. It is lighter in weight than Alaska yellow cedar or even redwood, and is the softest of the three. Western red cedar has little shock resistance, but it also shows little shrinkage after it has been seasoned. It can be brittle and splintery. Alaska yellow cedar is stronger and heavier with greater shock resistance and bending strength. It has a clear, bright color and is not as brittle. Alaska yellow cedar, which also might be marketed as Alaska cypress, weathers to a silver-gray.

Grades developed by the Western Red Cedar Lumber Association (www.wrcla.org; 866-778-9096) range from architect clear to custom knotty. But as is the case with other species, suppliers can develop their own trade names, a practice that even the Western Wood Products Association admits is "difficult and confusing."

According to Bear Creek Lumber (www.bearcreeklumber.com; 800-597-7191), Alaska yellow cedar shrinks more than western red as it dries. As a result, it is often kiln-dried to minimize problems after installation. Because the wood is harder than red cedar, it is somewhat more difficult to stain. Even though the heartwood of cedar naturally resists rot, regular application of a water-repellent preservative is a good idea. It helps to protect the wood surface from mildew and weathering.

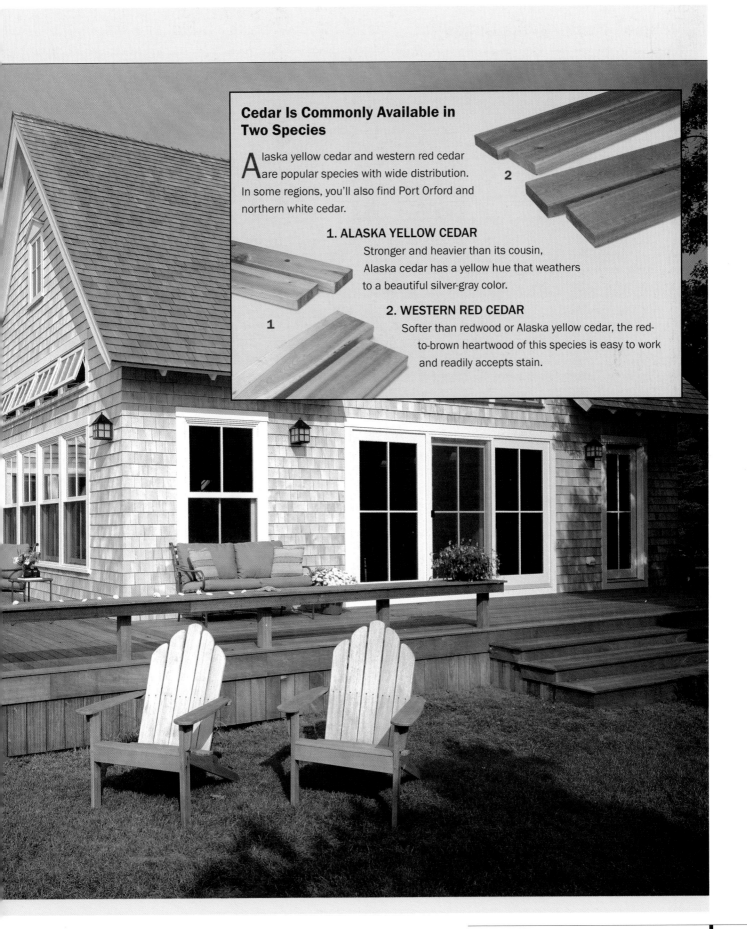

Cedar Is Commonly Available in Two Species

Alaska yellow cedar and western red cedar are popular species with wide distribution. In some regions, you'll also find Port Orford and northern white cedar.

1. ALASKA YELLOW CEDAR

Stronger and heavier than its cousin, Alaska cedar has a yellow hue that weathers to a beautiful silver-gray color.

2. WESTERN RED CEDAR

Softer than redwood or Alaska yellow cedar, the red-to-brown heartwood of this species is easy to work and readily accepts stain.

Tropical Hardwoods

Lumber grades and designations for tropical woods can be even more confusing than those for more-familiar North American species. You can search in vain for standardized grading rules or span tables. Also, trade names can be confusing, if not downright misleading. Ironwood and Pau Lope, for instance, are not species of trees; they're trade names like Kleenex or Xerox®.

All that aside, tropical hardwoods can make great decking. Ipé, a related group of South American hardwoods, stands up exceedingly well to very demanding use. Although it is too hard to treat chemically, it is highly resistant to rot and insect damage without treatment. Although ipé is not easy to work, the wood should make an extremely durable decking surface. When newly milled, ipé has a beautiful red-to-brown color. Decking in 1× dimensions spans 16-in. on-center framing; 5/4 stock spans 24 in.

A number of companies in the United States have what's called "chain of custody" certification for ipé under Forest Stewardship Council guidelines. But according to Jon Jickling of SmartWood, these lumber brokers have nonexclusive contracts, meaning they technically can sell both certified and noncertified wood. You just have to ask for the one you want. Any company selling FSC-certified wood should be able to provide you with a chain-of-custody code to prove it.

Like many products in the green marketplace, demand for certified lumber is growing, even though it costs a little more. Plenty of online dealers like Naturally Durable (www.naturallydurable.com) specialize in certified lumber. The cost for certified wood is roughly 5 percent to 10 percent higher than noncertified decking. Just seven years ago, the premium for certified wood was 20 percent.

Other tropical hardwoods that can be used as decking include cambara and meranti. Cambara is lighter in color and not as hard as ipé. Cambara is stiffer and heavier than any decking produced in North America, and is reported to be resistant to insects and decay. It gained popularity a few years ago when it cost 25 percent to 50 percent less than ipé. The price has risen, however, and it can be hard to find. Dealers recommend that cambara be treated periodically with a water repellent and preservative.

Meranti is a name for a number of species from Malaysia, the Philippines, and other parts of Southeast Asia. Widely available from lumber dealers, it might be called Philippine mahogany or lauan. The Forest Products Laboratory rates this wood as moderately decay-resistant, a step below redwood, cedar, and ipé. Treatment with a water repellent is recommended. Strength properties are comparable to red oak.

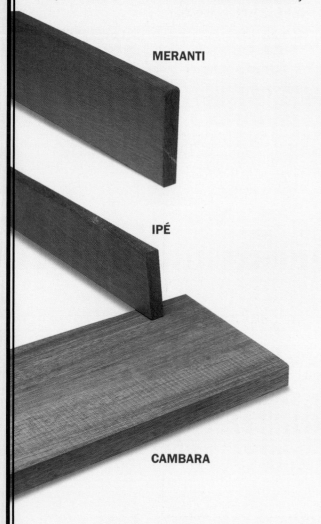

MERANTI

IPÉ

CAMBARA

Is Third-Generation Pressure-Treated Wood Already at Your Lumberyard?

Preservative treatments for rot-resistant lumber are something of a moving target. Manufacturers claim the treatments are much less corrosive than ACQ and CA and that it's OK to use standard joist hangers and aluminum flashings. They also boast that the preservatives are more environmentally benign than CCA. The most widely available, MicroPro®, uses copper as its preservative, but in fine particles that make treated wood no more corrosive than the old CCA.

Wolmanized L³ Outdoor Wood uses a combination of fungicides, insecticides, and water repellents as its preservative, so corrosion isn't a concern. However, one of the insecticides has been banned in France because it's suspected of contributing to die-offs in the bee population; the U.S. Agriculture Department is researching the supposed link. PureWood® protects wood via a heating and steaming process that changes the composition of the wood's sugars into a substance inedible by mold, fungus, and insects.

Micropro

SOURCE Osmose® www.osmose.com

TREATMENT Copper cobiocides

USES Above ground, ground contact, freshwater immersion, saltwater splash

PRICE/AVAILABILITY Comparable to ACQ, CA; available east of the Rocky Mountains

Wolmanized L³

SOURCE Arch Wood Protection www.archchemicals .com

TREATMENT Fungicides, insecticides, and water repellents

USES Above ground

PRICE/AVAILABILITY Comparable to ACQ, CA; limited availability

Purewood

SOURCE Bay Tree Technologies www.purewoodproducts .com

TREATMENT Heat and steam

USES Above ground, ground contact, freshwater immersion, saltwater immersion

PRICE/AVAILABILITY To be determined; limited availability

Pressure-Treated Decking: Readily Available and Safer Than Ever

Alkaline copper quaternary and copper azole are the two copper-based wood treatments that have been the industry standard for residential use since chromated copper arsenate was phased out in 2003. Readily available, ACQ- and CA-treated lumber products have established a reliable track record against moisture, mold, and insect damage over the past 20 years. However, the transition from CCA to ACQ and CA has not been seamless.

Eliminating arsenic and chromium reduced treated lumber's toxicity but significantly increased the wood's corrosive effect on steel fasteners and hardware, as well as on some types of flashing. The high copper content means that treated wood is particularly corrosive to aluminum. When building anything with pressure-treated lumber, you need to choose every fastener and flashing that contacts ACQ and CA wood carefully (see "Deck-Fastener Options," pp. 54–61).

By the way, there's no need to panic about existing CCA-treated structures. The EPA says that they're fine. But if you're nervous about the chances of leaching chromium and arsenic, you can make your deck or swing set safer by coating it with an oil-based penetrating stain every couple of years.

The absence of chromium in ACQ and CA lumber allows more copper to leach out into the environment. That's a problem for aquatic organisms and could lead to government restrictions in the future. As a result, the industry sees ACQ and CA as a step on the way to third-generation treatments (see the sidebar on p. 75).

Most water repellents can be applied immediately to ACQ and CA pressure-treated wood. But you should wait for the lumber to dry before applying an oil-based semitransparent stain. How long you should wait before applying the stain varies depending on where you live. In New Mexico, you probably should wait six weeks; in New Orleans, six months would be more preferable.

Pay Attention to the Labels

Brand name

End-use application

American Wood Preservers Association standard

Retention level 0.1 lb. per cu. ft.

Preservative type Copper azole, type B

Name of wood treater

Third-party inspector

FOR ABOVE GROUND USE

AWPA UC3B C2, C9 STDS

CA-B

0.10

AUDITED BY:

TP

NORTHEAST TREATERS, INC
BELCHERTOWN, MA   ATHENS, NY

Lifetime Limited Warranty

Natural Select

WOLMANIZED

ACQ and CA treatments use more copper than CCA did, so their cost is higher than the old treatment method (5/4×6 planks are about 80¢ per lin. ft.). To control costs, companies vary the retention level of the chemicals in the wood to suit its end use. The American Wood Preservers Association (AWPA) sets standards for retention levels, the building code approves the standards, and a third-party inspector verifies compliance by wood treaters. You'll find this information on a tag stapled to the lumber.

GROUND CONTACT

4× and 6× stock used for deck posts and freshwater docks gets a higher level of treatment.

ABOVE GROUND

2× stock for framing, rails, and balusters is approved for outdoor use.

DECKING

The lowest retention level is used for 5/4 deck boards.

PWF

Lumber for permanent wood foundations might have a higher retention level or higher lumber standards, depending on the brand.

The Care and Feeding of Wooden Decks

■ BY JON TOBEY

The Eskimos have five dozen words for snow. Here in the waterlogged Pacific Northwest, weather forecasters have an equally diverse vocabulary, whether they're calling for light rain, showers, isolated storms, sprinkles, drizzle, mist, driving rain, or mizzle. If you live here, you can expect to get wet nearly every day from September through June. I can't imagine a less hospitable place to build a wooden deck. But to the average Seattle homeowner, a house with less than half the yard covered by cascading decks is unfinished.

I'd be happier if everyone built stone patios. But homeowners depend on me to make sure their decks aren't reduced to a heap of compost. Fortunately, I can assure them that with modern technology and periodic maintenance, a deck can enjoy a long, productive life.

Penetrating Finishes Are Better Than Paints

Materials for wooden decks vary from region to region, but none of them is maintenance-free. I use the same procedures for all wooden decks. When homeowners ask me beforehand how to finish a new deck, I caution against paint or solid stain. Any horizontal surface, especially one subjected to foot traffic, is extremely difficult to keep paint on. Even solid alkyd stains, which for years have been recommended for decks, are too brittle and merely sit on top of the wood (like paint), awaiting the opportunity to peel off.

I prefer penetrating finishes. Properly applied penetrating finishes such as semitransparent alkyd stains and clear wood preservatives are absorbed into the wood fibers to protect better against mold, mildew, rot, and UV-degradation. Penetrating finishes are also easier to recoat because over time, they fade rather than flake.

The best penetrating finish I've found is CWF-UV® from The Flood Co., which enhances the wood's natural beauty but can also be tinted like a stain. CWF is an emulsified oil, so it cleans up like a latex but offers the protection of a petroleum product. I have found it far superior to the more popular paraffin-based coatings (such as Thompson's Water Seal®) that require biannual re-treatment to be effective. Even

For maximum cleaning with minimal abrasion, the author holds the 15-degree spray tip 6 in. to 9 in. above the deck and gradually sweeps across the boards in a flattened pendulum motion.

Applied using a garden sprayer, a specially formulated deck cleaner dissolves dirt and oxidation and kills mold and mildew on contact.

To protect vulnerable end grain, the author covers the tops of 4×4 posts with ready-made copper caps.

with the best finishes, however, the surface of the deck needs to be recoated every three years to provide maximum protection for the wood.

Cleaning and Pressure-Washing Come First

Unless they've been painted, I treat older decks basically the same as new ones. Every deck gets a thorough broom cleaning; while I'm sweeping an older deck, I check for damaged spots and mark any boards that need to be replaced. After all the leaves and dog hair have been swept away, I spray on a specially formulated deck cleaner, such as Cuprinol® Revive or Simple Wash from Bio-Wash®. Applied full strength with a garden sprayer (see the photos above), the

deck cleaner kills mold and mildew and cuts through dirt and oxidation. It also removes mill glazing from new decks, which means you don't have to let new lumber "silver" for a year before applying a finish. The deck cleaner works almost immediately, so as soon as I'm finished spraying it on, I return to the starting point and begin a light pressure-washing.

A lot of people are afraid of using a pressure washer on a deck, and with good reason. Used improperly, a pressure washer can do more harm than good. In the right hands, however, a pressure washer prepares a deck for refinishing quickly and effectively. For cleaning decks, I use a 9-hp, 2500-psi machine with a 15-degree spray tip (15 degrees is the angle formed by the fan of water as it shoots from the tip).

After the cleaning process has left these old deck boards looking their age, an oxalic-acid based wood brightener quickly restores their youthful sparkle. The brightener is allowed to stand for 20 minutes, then is rinsed off with the pressure washer.

To avoid wasted motion, I spray a 6-ft. wide swath, then overlap the next swath by 12 in. to 18 in. to make sure that the edges blend together. For maximum cleaning power with minimal abrasion, I hold the spray tip 6 in. to 9 in. above the surface of the deck and sweep the wand over the boards in a flattened pendulum motion, lifting the wand away from the deck at the end of one pass and lowering it gradually back at the beginning of the next (see the top right photo on the facing page).

When I'm able to wiggle underneath the deck, I give the underside a quick pressure wash as well. I usually don't find much mold or mildew, which would require an intensive wash; mostly I'm just concerned with cleaning out spider webs, splashed mud, and other debris. It's a dirty job, but somebody really ought to do it. After I wash the underside, the top gets another quick rinse.

Preparing the Railings

While I'm spraying the deck, I also pressure-wash both sides of the railings. For the most effective cleaning, I keep the fan of water as perpendicular to the vertical surfaces as I can. At the same time, I also direct the spray deep into the crevices to drive out all the bugs and gunk that have taken up residence.

After washing the deck, I give the railing assembly the once-over, checking for signs of rot. I pay attention to the top of the handrail, especially if it has exposed fasteners, and to the end grain at the top of uncapped support posts. If I find any rotten spots, I use liquid borates to kill the rot organism; then, after it has been allowed to dry, I use epoxy to repair the damage.

With so much end grain exposed to the elements, uncapped support posts are always

a problem. If the design permits, I simply cut back the posts to solid wood, then install inexpensive but good-looking copper caps, which are available at any hardware store (see the bottom right photo on p. 80).

Brightening Follows Cleaning

Preparing a deck for finish actually involves two chemical treatments. A side effect of the cleaning stage is that it leaves even brand new decks looking tired and gray. But that's just temporary. As soon as I finish pressure-washing, I fill up the garden sprayer with an oxalic-acid based wood brightener and spray a liberal coating over all the bare wood. Oxalic-acid brighteners quickly restore wood darkened by age or chemicals to a like-new appearance. I usually let the brightener soak into the wood for 20 minutes or so, then rinse the deck lightly with the pressure washer.

Penetrating finish won't soak in unless the wood is dry, so after I'm done swabbing the decks, I allow them to dry for a minimum of three warm, rain-free days before I apply the finish. During the interim, I usually move on to another job, but before I leave, I replace the boards that I previously determined were too rotten

to save. To make the new boards blend in, I pick a semitransparent stain from my collection that closely matches the color of the weathered deck boards. By the time the stain wears away, the new board will be almost unnoticeable.

Sprayed Finish Gets Nooks and Crannies

There's no reason you can't finish a deck using brushes and rollers, but it's much faster to use spray equipment. You can also get better coverage using a sprayer because it enables you to force the coating into tight spots that would be difficult or impossible to reach with a brush. Spray equipment is expensive to buy, but compared with the cost of labor, it's cheap to rent. Sprayers and pressure washers are offered for rent at many paint-supply houses as well as at most rental centers.

With a brush, I'd start outside the deck on the tops of the railings and work my way down to the deck, then in toward the house. Spraying is tougher because I have to use masking to control overspray.

Which Comes First, Deck or Railings?

When all the surfaces are getting the same finish, I generally spray both sides of the railings and leave the deck boards for last. If the railings are getting a different finish than the deck surface (as was the case on this job), I have to spray the deck first.

On this job, the railings were originally painted to match the trim of the house.

Dealing with Paint

Stripper is applied with bucket and brush.

Pressure-washing removes paint and neutralizes stripper.

Painting a deck is a bad idea to begin with; so whenever a painted deck needs to be refinished, I prefer to remove the paint and start over with bare wood. Unlike most paint removal, stripping paint from the surface of a deck is incredibly easy, thanks to a product called Stripex®.

After donning heavy rubber gloves and oversize rubber boots, I use an acid brush to swab the stripper over the surface of the deck (top left). When that's done, all it takes is a gentle rinse with a pressure washer, and the paint is history (bottom left). Unlike some paint strippers that must be rinsed with a neutralizer, Stripex is water-neutralized, so no additional step is required after the product is washed off. One advantage to this process is that instead of being covered with plastic, nearby plants can be merely wet down with water for protection during application. Don't let the ease of its use fool you, however. Stripex is a powerful base that can inflict serious burns on unprotected skin. I have the scars to prove it.

Although it's easy to strip the surface of a deck, it's much harder to strip painted railings completely, so I concentrate on problem areas such as the top of the handrail and anyplace else where the paint is flaking off. If the handrail is peeling badly, I use a mechanical paint scraper to get down to bare wood quickly. I use hand scrapers to remove loose paint elsewhere on the railing; then all the surfaces get a light going-over with a palm sander loaded with 80-grit sandpaper. I also make sure to recaulk all the joints.

Although I prefer to use a penetrating finish on a deck, whenever I've had to cover a solid finish (paint or stain), I've gotten good results using Sherwin-Williams® Woodscapes® Solid Latex Stain. This stain can be tinted to match any house color; in the past, I have used it over bare wood, solid stain, and paint without any failures.

Stripping all the paint would have cost a fortune, so I'd previously scraped and sanded the loose spots (see the sidebar above). When the deck finish was dry, the railings would get a fresh coat of stain.

Using an airless paint sprayer with a #617 spray tip, I apply the CWF coating, moving lengthwise along the deck boards from one end of the deck to the other (see the top left photo on the facing page). I hold the spray gun 12 in. to 18 in. from the surface and move just fast enough to put down an even, wet coat. After every couple of passes, I put down the spray gun and roll the finish using a ½-in. nap, 9-in. wide paint roller (see the top right photo on the facing page). After rolling, the deck boards should have an even, glossy sheen. If the penetrating finish soaks in completely, as it often does on thirsty, weathered boards, I spray another light coat before moving on to the next section. When I'm spraying alongside the house or the railings, I use a 4-ft. wide painting shield to control the overspray (see the top left photo on the facing page).

TIP

Cover the deck with tarps, wrap the first floor of the house with plastic sheeting, and mask the outside of the railing. After coating the inside of the railing, remove the paper and spray the outside.

After the top of the deck has been coated, I crawl underneath, if it's accessible, and soak the bottom of the boards, the joists, the beams, whatever I can get. In my experience, treating the underside of a deck even once can double its life span.

Mask Carefully before Spraying the Railings

The downside to spraying the deck first is that I have to let it dry for 24 hours to 72 hours (depending on humidity) before I can finish the railings. When the deck is dry enough to walk on without leaving footprints, I start masking off the surfaces I don't want painted. To protect the house from overspray, I wrap the first floor with a 9-ft. wide strip of plastic sheeting. I spread clean painter's tarps and masking paper over the deck surface and then run a strip of 3-ft. wide kraft paper around the outside of the balusters.

These railings were painted, so after removing the loose paint, I applied a coat of Sherwin-Williams Woodscapes Solid Latex Stain (for more about recoating painted finishes, see the sidebar on p. 83). To spray the railings, I switch to a narrower (#213) spray tip, which puts out a more compact, directional spray fan than the tip I use for the deck boards. I start on one of the inside corners and work counterclockwise, spraying the handrail in long, horizontal strokes, and the balusters in vertical strokes. Keeping the spray tip about 12 in. away from the railing, I cover the balusters on three sides and also try to coat as much of the underside of the railing as possible. At the end of each pass with the spray gun, I brush the finish using a disposable painting pad (if I'd been applying a penetrating finish, I would have used a lamb's wool mitt).

Once the railing's interior surface is dry to the touch (on a warm day, usually an hour or less), I remove the kraft paper and spray the outer surfaces of the balusters, as well as any other spots I wasn't able to reach

from the inside. I don't need to rehang the paper on the inside because all the vulnerable surfaces are already covered. As soon as I finish this application, the rest of the masking is pulled, a few small touch-ups are made with the disposable pad, and I am done. Unless homeowners really like having me around, I urge them to sweep the deck frequently and to wash it lightly once a year.

Jon Tobey is a painting contractor in Monroe, Washington.

Avoiding Deck Problems

Unfortunately, cleaning and refinishing a deck are not cure-alls. A lot of the problems I see with decks stem from the original construction and landscaping. By far the worst problem is improper flashing where the deck's rim joist is attached to the house. This critical detail must be carefully designed, or the house as well as the deck will suffer.

Another common problem is placing the deck too close to the ground (see the bottom right photo). The proximity of the moist earth encourages rot to thrive as evaporation pulls moisture directly into the bottom of the deck. I like to see at least 1 ft. of airspace between the bottom of the joists and the ground. If a deck must be built closer to the ground, I recommend providing special drainage beneath the deck and then dipping all of the lumber in preservative before installation.

Fasteners can also be a problem. Deeply countersunk screws or air nails create hundreds of tiny petri dishes for rot to thrive in. Builders should try to set their fasteners flush with the deck surface (or you can try one of the concealed-fastening systems that are now available). In my experience, however, even deep pockets aren't a problem as long as the deck is regularly cleaned and recoated.

Railings are always a problem, especially when the handrails are made of wide, flat boards. Wide, flat surfaces are great places to set potted plants or to rest drinks, but they're also great places for water to collect, which eventually causes cupping, checking, and rot. To reduce cupping, the handrail needs to be relatively thick for its width; a 2×6 is far preferable to a 1×6. If the homeowners will stand for it, the top of the handrail should be beveled to shed water. To prevent cupping further, the handrail should be installed so that the annular rings curve down.

Plants and decks don't mix

Deck boards need air circulation to keep them healthy.

1. Don't place immovable potted plants on the deck.

2. Maintain airspace between decks and shrubbery.

3. Don't allow debris to accumulate between deck boards.

4. Place a barrier between mulch and ground-level framing.

Start Your Railing Right

■ BY MIKE GUERTIN

I must be getting old. I'm starting to take safety a lot more seriously than I did years ago, especially when it comes to building. When I'm building a deck, I focus on two points of potential failure: the ledger and the railings. Here, I'll take up the more troublesome part of the railing system: the posts.

There are a lot of ways to build a deck railing, but most have a common element in the posts, which transfer loads applied to the top rail into the framing.

Often-used methods of screwing or bolting posts to deck joists or rim joists just aren't strong enough to meet the building code's structural requirement, and here's why: Posts can act as levers. An outward force applied along the railing (someone leaning on the rail, for instance) is multiplied at the point where the post

is attached to the rim joist. The force can overload the fasteners or pull away the joist connected to the posts.

One of the most secure installation methods is to mount guardrail posts to the deck frame with metal hardware that transfers the load to the deck joists. There are several pieces of hardware that are available and a fastening arrangement for just about every place where you might locate posts. I'll show you the best way to install posts, then discuss options for the hardware placement that completes the post installation.

Mike Guertin is a remodeling contractor in East Greenwich, Rhode Island, and editorial adviser to Fine Homebuilding. *His Web site is www. mikeguertin.com.*

Posts That Pass Inspection

The 2009 International Residential Code (IRC) offers performance criteria only for railing systems (table R301.5) and leaves it up to deck builders to devise a solution for mounting guardrail posts to the deck frame. Local building officials may approve or reject that solution, but most accept an engineer's stamped design or other supporting documents. One example that addresses the methods I've described here is the American Wood Council's Prescriptive

Residential Deck Construction Guide (DCA #6). The current version, published in fall 2009, is based on the 2009 IRC. Code officials generally recognize the prescriptive details presented in American Forest & Paper Association (AFPA) documents. Inspectors also often accept hardware manufacturers' product-installation guides, which in some cases are backed up by ICC-ES (International Code Council Evaluation Services) reports.

Securely Mount Guardrail Posts to the Deck Frame with Metal Hardware

1. Holes must be straight and square. After cutting the posts to length, use a ¼-in. plywood template to locate the bolt holes. With a nail set and a hammer, mark the locations for the drill-bit point, then mark the line that represents the top of the deck joist. A drill press is the best tool to drill the ⁹⁄₁₆-in. pilot holes on the posts. Another method is to mark the bolt holes on both sides of the post and, with a handheld drill, bore from both sides toward the center.

2. Clamps make post installations a one-person job. Attach a clamp just above the register mark to set the height of the post automatically. Next, use a second clamp to attach the post to the joist. A third clamp holds a 2-ft. level to the side of the post to free hands for drilling.

3. Use the post as a drilling guide. After locating and plumbing the post, follow the pilot holes, and drill through the joist. The best types of bolts to use are ½-in.-dia. hot-dipped galvanized hex-head bolts with washers that have a broad bearing surface. Don't overtighten the nut, because crushing the wood fibers reduces the holding power of the connection.

Details Depend on Post Location

When you lean on a post, the bottom of the post acts as the fulcrum of a lever, and the top bolt receives the greatest force. Therefore, this is the logical location for dedicated hardware that ties the post back into the joists. The specific details of hardware placement depend on the post location. Note: These illustrations show only general recommendations. Follow manufacturers' instructions for specific hardware installations.

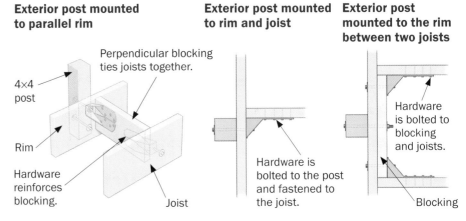

Exterior post mounted to parallel rim

4×4 post

Perpendicular blocking ties joists together.

Rim

Hardware reinforces blocking.

Joist

Exterior post mounted to rim and joist

Hardware is bolted to the post and fastened to the joist.

Exterior post mounted to the rim between two joists

Hardware is bolted to blocking and joists.

Blocking

4. Hardware completes the installation. To strengthen the post's attachment to the deck, install galvanized brackets that tie the rim joist and post to an adjacent joist. The DeckLok bracket (see the bottom photo at far right) is bolted to the frame and has been tested for a number of common post-to-rim-joist connections. In addition, two newer pieces of dedicated hardware (see the photos at far right) became available in the fall of 2009. They mount with structural screws that are faster to install than bolts and are more cost-effective in terms of materials and labor.

SIMPSON STRONG-TIE'S DTT2Z

UNITED STEEL PRODUCTS' DTBTZ

DECKLOK BRACKET

5. Use a strap to reduce wobble. If you bolt on posts at the framing stage, you'll notice that the posts on parallel rim joists will have a lot more deflection than those along perpendicular joists. Once the decking is installed, the deflection diminishes. Go one step further to help stiffen these posts by nailing a 16-ga. metal strap across the top of the rim joist and the next three or four inboard joists.

Exterior posts at outside corner

4×4 blocking

Each post shares two brackets, one high (blue) and one low (purple).

Interior post mounted at intersection of rim and joist with a single bracket

Interior post mounted to rim between two joists

Post is braced with one bracket high: 2× blocking is braced with a low bracket.

Interior post mounted to parallel rim

Post is braced with one bracket high: 2× blocking is braced with a low bracket.

Interior post at outside corner

2× blocking is added as reinforcement.

Deck Railings Grow Up

■ BY SCOTT GIBSON

Trex started a stampede of new building materials in the 1990s with the
introduction of an alternative decking made
from wood flour and recycled plastic. Many
other manufacturers since have introduced
their own composites, and low-maintenance
decking options have grown to include a
variety of plastics and metal. Yet the development of matching railings lagged behind.
Now that's changing, too.

Wood still accounts for as much as
80 percent of all residential deck railings.

But a number of other choices offer the
same advantages that are behind the steady
rise of composite decking: resistance to
insects and decay, weather hardiness, and
the need for very little maintenance.

Of these low-maintenance options,
wood/plastic composite railings make up
a fast-growing category, but there's also
aluminum-reinforced vinyl, stainless-
steel cable, cellular polyvinyl chloride
(PVC), molded polyurethane, and powder-
coated metal. Even at the low end, these

What the Code Says about Railings

The International Residential Code (IRC) is straightforward about railings on
residential decks. However, some areas are more restrictive than others in
their interpretation. For example, although not prohibited by the IRC, some local
inspectors won't allow horizontal installations; critics claim that the railing pres-
ents a ladder structure that's not childproof. It's a good idea to check with your
code-enforcement officer before you build. In a nutshell:
- No part of the railing can allow passage of a 4-in.-dia. sphere.
- Any deck more than 30 in. off the ground needs a guardrail.
- Residential railings must be at least 36 in. high (commercial railings,
  42 in. high).
- Guardrails must withstand a concentrated 200 lb. force in any direction
  plus a safety factor for tested assemblies.
- Railing infill (balusters, cables, etc.) must withstand a 50 lb. force ap-
  plied to a 1 sq. ft. area plus a safety factor.

alternatives are more expensive than wood. PVC railings are often the most affordable, and they can be three or four times as expensive as a pressure-treated rail. At the other end of the scale, molded urethane can top $150 per running foot for the heaviest, most elaborate styles.

Newer rail systems, however, are often easier and faster to install. At their most basic, lumberlike composite railings assemble the same way as the wood they are displacing. But producers have devised special clips, brackets, and templates to speed up the job. Some rail comes packaged in 6-ft. or 8-ft. ready-to-assemble kits that manufacturers say can be installed in minutes per foot.

"The more consumers are getting educated to new railings . . . the more they want them," says Steve Scholl, a busy deck builder in the Detroit metro area. None of this will ever satisfy anyone who wants real wood, but to a generation with an increasing aversion to maintenance, it's very appealing.

Scott Gibson, a contributing writer to Fine Homebuilding, *lives in East Waterboro, Maine.*

Shop Notes

As *Fine Hombuilding*'s shop manager, I assembled the sample railings the manufacturers sent to us for the photos in this chapter. Below are some of my observations.

The **manufacturer's instructions** are often poorly written and/or misleading. I'm experienced in building railings, so I was able to muddle through. Less experienced builders might have a harder time, though. It's a good idea to check the manufacturer's Web site for a preview of installation guides before buying the product.

If **irregular baluster spacing** drives you crazy, then think long and hard about the type of railing you buy and the post spacing on your deck. Any railing system that has predetermined baluster spacing (Trex, Genova, Eon, etc.) must be installed with post locations that correspond to the length of the railings (6 ft. on center, for example), or the baluster spacing on each side of the post will be difficult to match.

In high winds, **noisy railing systems** can be a problem. Balusters that drop into precut holes in the rails can rattle when disturbed.

Many of the **post sleeves** are made slightly oversize to fit easily over potentially twisted wood posts. Because the sleeve material is often thin, it deforms when the railing sections are attached if it's not shimmed. —John White

Cable Rail: Less Is More

Cable rail is one railing alternative that doesn't look like wood. It's made from the same kind of wire and hardware used for sailboat rigging, and it won't block a million-dollar view.

Stainless-steel cable is typically ⅛ in. dia. for residential railings and heavier for commercial applications. The most common (and one of the strongest) is known as 1×19, made up of 19 individual strands of wire.

Cable railing is moderately expensive, starting at $65 to $75 per running foot for an all-metal horizontal installation but about half that cost when cable and fittings are combined with wood posts and top rails. Both surface-mounted and through-post cable terminations (see the bottom left photos on the facing page) are available; turnbuckles allow the cable to be tightened as needed. Keeping railing turns to a minimum will reduce hardware and installation costs.

PROS	CONS
• Unobtrusive. Won't block scenic views. • Flexible. Can be built with a variety of wood or metal post and rail components as well as tensioning hardware. • Cables can run horizontally or vertically.	• More expensive than some other options. • Horizontal railings barred in some areas because they pose a "climbing hazard." • Not compatible with all architectural styles.

A

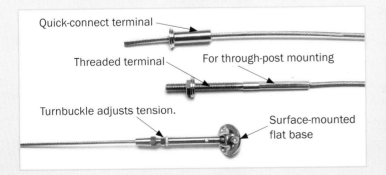

A. This style is strong and transparent. Custom steel posts and stainless-steel cable open the views to this lakeside deck. The posts were fabricated and designed by Keuka Studios in Honeoye Falls, N.Y. Cable assembly by Feeney.

B. Cable rail can be surface-mounted. If you use wood, corner posts have to be sturdy. Producers usually recommend a 4×4 at minimum because the 11 cables typical for a 36-in.-high rail exert a great deal of lateral force. Railing by Atlantis.

C. There's an upcharge for a different look. Vertical installations require beefy top and bottom rails as well as more cable terminations and labor. Railing by Atlantis.

Quick-connect terminal

Threaded terminal

For through-post mounting

Turnbuckle adjusts tension.

Surface-mounted flat base

Metal: Old-World Look with a Friendly Price

There is no mistaking powder-coated aluminum and steel railings for something else. These railings are not trying to look like any material other than metal.

Given the strength of metal parts, baluster and post styles tend to be thinner and less massive than other alternatives. Metal also is a versatile material that can be fabricated into many styles, from plain to ornately detailed filigree, as in the example from Anderson Welding (see the photo below).

Producers point to speedy installation as another advantage. Rail sections arrive already assembled so that the installer only has to mount the posts, cut rails to length, and attach them. Post-to-post spans of 10 ft. are possible without any intermediate supports.

Aluminum, iron, and steel railings might look the same, but it could be best to stay away from ferrous metals in saltwater areas. Although powder-coating offers good protection from the elements, even a pinhole can allow moisture below the paint film, where it leads to rust.

Basic aluminum railings are typically more expensive than vinyl but not as costly as many composites. Expect to pay about $35 to $40 per running foot.

PROS
- Quick installation.
- High strength and long unsupported spans.
- Material highly adaptable to custom shapes.
- Very low maintenance.

CONS
- Appearance might not be appropriate with some architectural styles.
- Railings made from ferrous metals can rust if finish is damaged.

Don't let corrosion start.
When bolting metal posts to the deck, use nylon washers to prevent cracking the powder coating on the mounting flange. Railing above by L&L Ornamental Railings.

Vinyl: A Very Long-Lasting Paint Job

Polyvinyl chloride is a widely used plastic that has become standard in everything from siding to window and door frames as well as deck railings. Vinyl is supposed to look like freshly painted wood, but as producers like CertainTeed® (see the photo at left) are fond of saying, it doesn't have any of the maintenance problems that go along with wood. Vinyl doesn't rot or warp, never needs paint, and is unaffected by insects.

Now in very wide use even on upscale houses, vinyl has done a lot to shed its image as a cheap building material. Alcoa®, for example, guarantees its vinyl railing for as long as you own the house. Yet some homeowners complain that vinyl railings can be squeaky when flexed.

Vinyl railing tends to be one of the least expensive wood alternatives and should be available for about $20 to $25 per running foot.

Posts are still wood. Many railing systems come with a post sleeve that fits over the 4×4, as in this Alcoa railing; the railings are attached through the sleeve into the post. Vinyl sleeves tend to be thinner-walled than composite sleeves.

The mechanicals are hidden. Rail/post connections typically are made with the help of metal brackets that are screwed through the post sleeve into the wood beneath. Some models' brackets are hidden by a trim cover, as in this Genova railing.

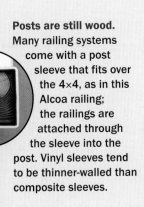

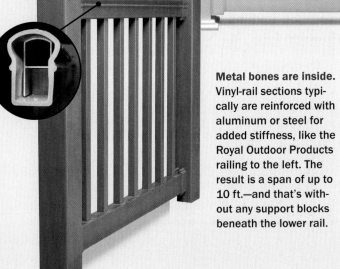

PROS
- Durable; very low maintenance.
- Longer unsupported rail spans than wood-plastic composites.
- Has the appearance of painted wood.
- Railing comes in kits that can be assembled quickly.

CONS
- It's still plastic, which won't appeal to all homeowners.
- Limited color selection.
- Some consider the manufacturing process environmentally hazardous.

Metal bones are inside. Vinyl-rail sections typically are reinforced with aluminum or steel for added stiffness, like the Royal Outdoor Products railing to the left. The result is a span of up to 10 ft.—and that's without any support blocks beneath the lower rail.

Composites: A New Life for Wood Chips and Plastic Bags

Composites are a recycling success story, keeping millions of pounds of plastics per year out of landfills. Although they still make up a small slice of the deck and railing business, composite producers are elbowing their way into the market in increasing numbers.

Composites are fairly flexible—polyethylene products like Trex more so than polypropylene composites—so bottom rails must be supported by squash blocks as frequently as every 18 in. so that they don't droop.

A newer type of composite (see the photo on the facing page) is capped with a layer of PVC in a process that is called co-extrusion. This process gives the railing the look of a painted finish that, like solid-PVC railings, is nonporous and is not as susceptible to fading.

Composites are available as dimensional lumber that can be used to make railings conventionally or as kits that are designed to go together more quickly. Costs start at about $45 per running foot.

PROS

- Appears more wood-like than other low-maintenance options, so railings blend nicely with wood-composite decking.
- Feels more like wood than plastic railings.
- Wider color selection than vinyl.
- Unlike wood, won't split, crack, or warp.
- Trex railings can be ordered in curved sections.

CONS

- Relatively expensive.
- Because wood composites contain organic material, they can support the growth of mold.
- With the exception of the PVC-coated variety, dark colors can fade in sunlight. Effect varies by brand.
- Requires support blocks under bottom rail to prevent sagging.

A

B

Site-built rails offer more assembly options. Composite railings like the Alcoa Oasis shown on the facing page are made from solid, lumberlike stock.

A. They are built the same way as wood railings. Railing kits such as Trex's co-extruded Artisan are made of preregistered and precut parts.

B. They may be faster to assemble, but their design isn't as flexible in terms of baluster spacing, railing height, and other design options.

The Other Plastics: Variations on a Theme

Elegance comes at a price

Molded-urethane railings are made by Fypon®, which produces a line of well-known trim under the same trade name; it is the most expensive railing option I found. Prices go above $150 per running foot for large-scale railings and oversize balusters with the proportions of carved stone. But the look is unlike just about anything else (see the photo at left). Styles can be very ornate, better-suited to period homes than the more limited offerings in vinyl or wood composite. Rail widths range from 5 in. to 12 in.

Urethane railing components, which are reinforced with PVC pipe (see the photo at right), are available in straight and curved sections. Newel posts also are reinforced with PVC pipe. Railings can span up to 12 ft. between posts (10 ft. for the 5-in. system) with squash blocks required below the bottom rail every 4 ft. to 5 ft. Fypon arrives primed and can be painted. It won't absorb water, crack, or rot.

Fiberglass rivals aluminum in strength

Fiberglass railings made by Armor-Rail® (see the photo at far right) are similar in composition to a fiberglass ladder and, the manufacturer says, are about as strong as aluminum. They are made with "pultruded" fiberglass, a process in which continuous glass strands are pulled through a die.

Posts are hollow in section with walls about ¼ in. thick. They can be installed over a 4×4 or mounted over a proprietary support (see the photo at right) that's bolted to the deck framing.

Rail sections come completely assembled. The maximum distance between posts is 12 ft., with one squash block below the bottom rail. There are several rail and baluster styles and four colors to choose from. These railings cost more than vinyl but not as much as some composites.

Foam and wood are another composite recipe

Cellular PVC is a type of plastic foam that is molded into different profiles for railing parts. It's made by several companies and typically is reinforced with another material to meet code requirements for strength. Novaline's® Wood Collection railings use a composite higher than most in wood-fiber content plus cellular PVC. Novaline's hollow posts can be installed on 4×4s or over the company's steel-tube stanchion (see the photo below). The railing is in about the same price range as wood composites.

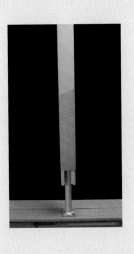

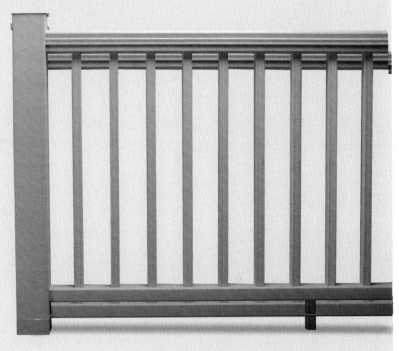

Sources

CABLE RAIL

Atlantis Rail Systems
www.atlantisrail.com

CableRail by Feeney®
www.cablerail.com

Secosouth
www.secosouth.com

Ultra-Tec®
www.ultra-tec.com

METAL

Anderson Welding Inc.
www.steelandironwork.com

Fortress Iron Railing
www.fortressiron.com

L & L Ornamental Railings
www.llrailings.com

VINYL

Alcoa Oasis
www.alcoa.com/alcoahomes

CertainTeed
www.certainteed.com

Genova
www.genovaproducts.com

Royal Outdoor Products
www.royalcrownltd.com

COMPOSITE

Alcoa Oasis
www.alcoa.com/alcoahomes

CertainTeed
www.certainteed.com

CorrectDeck
www.correctdeck.com

Latitudes
www.latitudesdeck.com

Timber Tech
www.timbertech.com

Trex
www.trex.com

OTHER PLASTICS

Armor-Rail
www.armor-rail.com

Eon
www.eonoutdoor.com

Fypon
www.fypon.com

Gossen
www.gossenmouldings.com

Harmony Select Railings
www.royalcrownltd.com

Novaline
www.rdirail.com

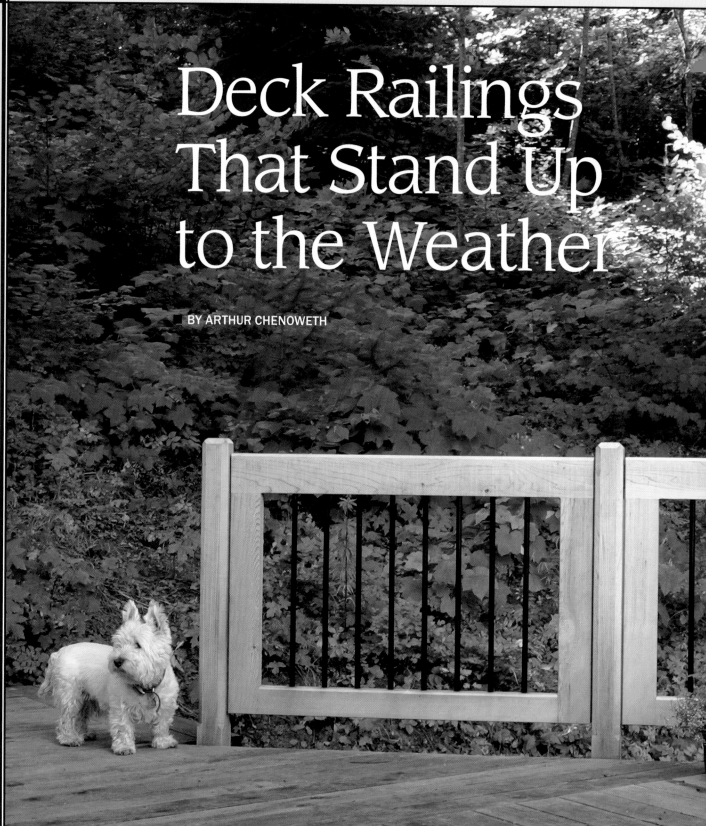

Deck Railings That Stand Up to the Weather

BY ARTHUR CHENOWETH

In Oregon's Hood River valley, the average rainy season is nine months long. All that rain makes for the sweetest cherries on the planet, but it's murder on decks. The deck on our house had long since succumbed to Mother Nature, and I ended up replacing many of the Douglas-fir joists as well as all the old decking. The real challenge was replacing the railing with one that would stand up to the climate. In my experience, stains and rot begin with exposed fasteners. Consequently, I tried to find ways to keep fasteners to a minimum in this project. My solution was to construct rail sections with a mortise-and-tenon frame and electrical conduit as balusters. Hidden splines hold the rail sections in place.

Foundation Bolts Secure the Newel Posts

The new 4×4 newel posts are clear cedar. I chamfered the top 36 in. of each post on all four edges. A simple router jig made quick work of the chamfers (see the top photo on p. 103). I put a 1-in. straight bit into a router with two 45-degree guide blocks screwed to the base. A carriage held the post at a 45-degree angle, and I ran the router from the top end to a measured point. I finished the chamfers with a chisel, leaving the last 14 in. of each post with square edges.

Putting in newel posts and getting them plumb is a tedious process, so I borrowed a method that I use to brace strongbacks (temporary supports) to concrete-wall forms using J-bolts. The location of the joists determined the placement of the newel posts at less than 8 ft. apart.

For this railing, I drilled two bolt holes through each post and the rim joist. Then I drilled corresponding holes through the joist at a right angle to the first holes (see the middle photo and drawing on the facing page). The hook end of the J-bolt goes into the hole in the joist, and the threaded end runs through the rim joist and the post. (The hole through the joist can be drilled oversize or elongated vertically to ease installation of the hook end.) Tightening the nuts on the bolts pulls the newel post tight to the rim joist, making it easy to plumb the posts in both directions (see "Start Your Railing Right" on p. 86 for another post securing method).

This system worked fine, except where the deck had a 45-degree turn. Here, I used regular bolts through a doubled rim joist.

Railing Sections Are Built in the Shop

The new deck boards that I had installed were tight-knot cedar; that type of cedar wasn't suitable for the railing, however. I doubted the wood's strength and knew the difficulty of working with knots in the joinery, so I opted instead for clear western red cedar for the frames. It cost about four times more than the decking but lacked the disadvantages. That fact combined with the clear cedar's appearance made it worth the price.

The 2× stock wasn't uniform, and some pieces were slightly warped. I ran all the stock across the jointer, ripped it to width, and planed it to the right thickness. Then I cut all the stiles (vertical frame members) and rails (horizontal frame members) to length.

I joined the stiles and rails for each section with mortise-and-tenon joints. With about 60 mortises looming, I bought a freestanding hollow-chisel mortiser with a ⅝-in. bit. Two days' work with the mortiser let me finish a job that would have taken forever with the usual method of boring and chiseling.

On my tablesaw, I beveled the top edges of both the bottom and top rails 45 degrees so that they shed water. I configured the mortises and tenons of the railing frames to keep the end grain of the stiles out of the rain. Each end of the top rail has a mortise cut into it that's about 3¼ in. deep. The bottom rail has ⅝-in.-wide tenons cut into each end. Correspondingly, each stile has a tenon at the top and a mortise on the bottom (see the bottom photo on p. 104). Tenoning the bottom rail into the stiles adds strength for those inevitable occasions when someone decides to stand on the bottom rail.

Cutting the stile tenons on the tablesaw was easy, but the bottom rails were too long to cut that way because of the 10-ft.-high ceiling in my shop. I cut those tenons with a sliding compound-miter saw, making multiple kerf cuts and finishing the cuts with a sharp chisel.

Spindles Are Made of Conduit

Before assembling the frames, I cut ½-in. electrical metal tubing (EMT) for the deck balusters. On the top rail, each baluster slides into a 2-in. deep, ¾-in.-dia. hole, wide enough for the outside diameter of the EMT. I bored the holes on a drill press, spacing them 4 in. on center.

If I had simply drilled holes in the bottom rail for the balusters, those holes would have filled with rain. Instead, the balusters fit over ⅝-in. wooden dowels that I drilled and glued into the bottom rail. They project up 1 in. (see the bottom photo on p. 105).

The inside diameter of ½-in. EMT is just less than ⅝-in. To pare down the diameter of the dowels to fit the EMT, I ran a ¾-in. hole saw over the stub of each dowel. I also cleaned the tubing and then sprayed it with many coats of gray primer and flat black paint.

Newels Take Shape

A simple jig for chamfering. To get the chamfers on the edges of the newel posts, 45-degree angle blocks guide a router equipped with a 1-in. straight bit.

PLAN VIEW

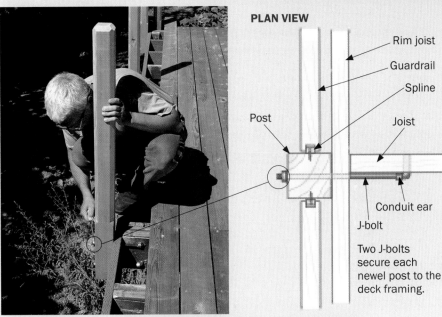

Rim joist

Guardrail

Spline

Post

Joist

Conduit ear

J-bolt

Two J-bolts secure each newel post to the deck framing.

These fasteners aren't standard. Adopted from concrete formwork, the only fasteners in this railing are the J-bolts that hold the posts to the rim joist. Conduit ears hold the bolts in place during installation.

Alignment splines. Wood splines glued and screwed to the sides of each newel post fit into grooves on the sides of the railing sections. The top of the spline marks the lower edge of the top rail.

Rail Sections Are Assembled in the Shop

Holes on the top, dowels on the bottom. Before the frames are assembled, provisions are made for pipe balusters, which fit into holes in the top rail. On the bottom rail, the balusters slide over dowels (far left). A hole saw reduces the dowels' diameter to that of the pipe.

Waterproof glue binds the joinery. To assemble each frame, I glue the mortise-and-tenon joints and clamp the sections until the glue sets.

Frames Don't Have to Fit Exactly

To assemble the frames, I used a waterproof Titebond® glue (www.titebond.com) on the mortise-and-tenon joints. I then clamped the whole assembly until the glue set. For added strength, I pinned each corner with two ¼-in. dowels. After sanding, I applied WoodLife® Classic Clear Wood Preservative (www.wolman.com) to prevent moss from growing on the railing.

The next step was slipping the rail sections into place (see the top photo on the facing page). When cutting the frame pieces, I had cut ⅝-in.-wide by ½-in.-deep slots into the outside edges of the stiles. These slots fit over clear Douglas-fir mounting strips that I glued and screwed to the newel posts (see the bottom photo on p. 103).

As part of the system, I undersized each section by ½ in., resulting in ¼-in. gaps on each end at the newel post. The narrow gap looks nice and helps to hide discrepancies in the frames or the posts (see the top left photo on the facing page).

I spread glue on the mounting strips to add a little lubrication during installation and to seal the joint after the frame was in place. The final step was putting in the balusters. They insert into the holes in the top rail and then slide down over the dowels in the bottom rail (see the bottom photo on the facing page). The 45-degree bevel on the bottom rail facilitated this process.

I probably won't glue the balusters to the dowels. We don't have children around, and if the balusters aren't pulled up and out, they won't move.

Arthur Chenoweth is a carpenter in Oregon.

Frames Slide Down, Balusters Slide Up

Railings are glued to the posts. Slots cut in the stiles of the frames slide over mounting strips on the newel posts (right). Making frame sections smaller than the opening results in a ¼-in. reveal that helps to disguise any small variations in the frames or the posts (below).

Painted balusters slide up and then down. Large nails partially driven into an old beam hold the conduit spindles as they're painted (inset). As the final step, I push the balusters up into the holes in the top rail and then down over a protruding dowel.

Deck Railings

■ BY ANDREW WORMER

One of the first decks I ever built didn't have a railing. Technically, it didn't need one because it wasn't high off the ground and didn't have stairs, but something about it always felt wrong to me.

Not long ago, I drove by the house with this old deck; the house had been bought and sold a couple of times since I worked on it. The first thing I noticed on the deck was a new railing. Although unremarkable, the railing added a sense of completion. The deck now was more a part of the house than an afterthought.

Although there are lots of options when it comes to building deck railings, not all of them are good. One railing design I've seen far too often is a rickety 2×4 post-and-rail assembly with a balustrade of lumberyard-variety pressure-treated lattice. Although it looks substantial, the flimsy, stapled-together lattice can splinter easily, and a toddler with a good head of steam can break through. In addition to that, the lattice blocks the view.

Although my New England roots make me partial to wood railings with full balustrades, other railing designs use different materials, such as steel and even glass. Use of such materials can make a railing that's not only safe and secure but also unique in design.

Safety First

In most areas, local building codes establish only minimum guidelines for rail safety (see the sidebar on p. 108). Often, common sense is a more reliable guide. For example, it's a good idea to install some type of rail whenever a person can fall more than the actual thickness of the deck framing. Also, it's safer to have a 42-in.-high railing (36 in. generally is the code minimum) for decks that are high off the ground.

Common sense also has it that deck railings endure weather. Naturally rot-resistant redwood, cedar, cypress, and even steel are good alternatives to pressure-treated lumber.

On any wood deck railing, beveling or rounding over edges helps minimize splintering, which is especially important on a top rail that meets a lot of rumps and forearms. Making connections from underneath also helps a wood railing because it protects fastener holes from rain and snow. And maintaining the railing with an appropriate finish will help keep out water and make the wood less prone to checking.

Andrew Wormer is a builder and writer in Vermont.

Code Requirements for Deck-Rail Safety

Most local building codes follow guidelines spelled out in national codes, such as the International Residential Code (IRC). The IRC requires a guardrail when a deck is more than 30 in. above the ground and a handrail whenever there are more than two risers on a stairway. Guardrail height is a minimum of 36 in. off the finished deck surface and 34 in. off the nose of stair risers. Handrail height along stairways must be between 34 in. and 38 in. off the nose of the treads. Spacing between the components of a rail system should be less than 4 in., which means that a ball 4 in. in diameter shouldn't be able to pass through the rail.

There are two exceptions to the 4 in. limit—the triangular spaces between the tread, riser, and bottom rail of a guard rail system where the space must be less than 6 in., and the space between rail components alongside stairs where the space must be less than 4⅜ in. Although that may seem to be a pretty small opening, children have been known to get into (and through) some pretty small spaces.

The grip size of a stairway handrail should have a circular cross section with a diameter between 1¼ in. and 2 in. Other handrail profiles are possible, but the largest cross-sectional dimension should not exceed 2¼ in., and the perimeter dimension should fall between 4 in. and 6¼ in. The main concern for the handrail is that it be graspable: A rail design that is appropriate on the guardrail of the deck may be inappropriate on the handrail of the stairway.

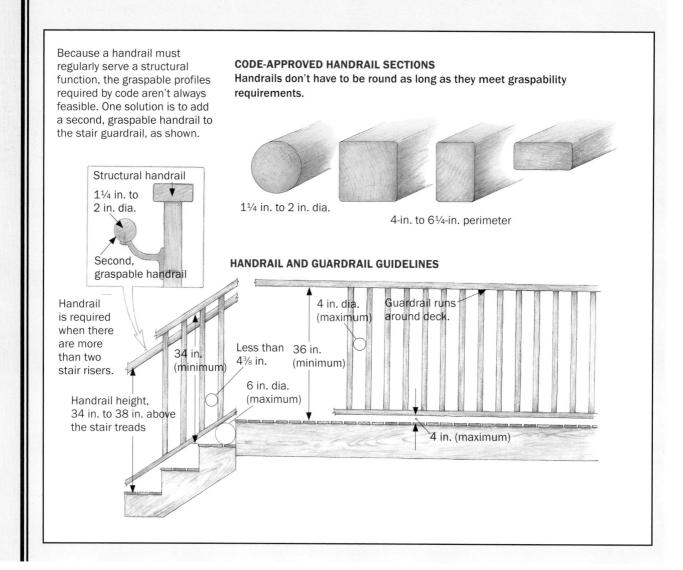

Because a handrail must regularly serve a structural function, the graspable profiles required by code aren't always feasible. One solution is to add a second, graspable handrail to the stair guardrail, as shown.

CODE-APPROVED HANDRAIL SECTIONS
Handrails don't have to be round as long as they meet graspability requirements.

1¼ in. to 2 in. dia.

4-in. to 6¼-in. perimeter

Structural handrail
1¼ in. to 2 in. dia.

Second, graspable handrail

HANDRAIL AND GUARDRAIL GUIDELINES

Handrail is required when there are more than two stair risers.

Handrail height, 34 in. to 38 in. above the stair treads

34 in. (minimum)

Less than 4⅜ in.

6 in. dia. (maximum)

4 in. dia. (maximum)

36 in. (minimum)

Guardrail runs around deck.

4 in. (maximum)

Cable Railings Are Strong, but Check Your Local Codes

STEEL-AND-REDWOOD DECK RAILING

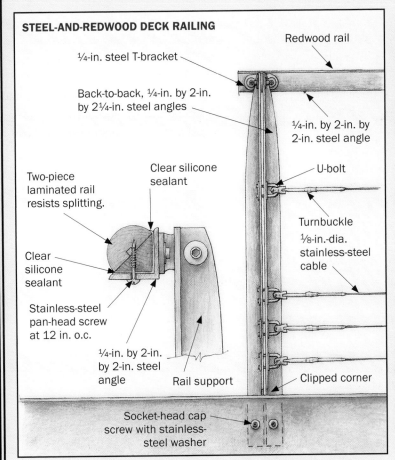

- ¼-in. steel T-bracket
- Redwood rail
- Back-to-back, ¼-in. by 2-in. by 2¼-in. steel angles
- ¼-in. by 2-in. by 2-in. steel angle
- Two-piece laminated rail resists splitting.
- Clear silicone sealant
- U-bolt
- Clear silicone sealant
- Turnbuckle
- ⅛-in.-dia. stainless-steel cable
- Stainless-steel pan-head screw at 12 in. o.c.
- ¼-in. by 2-in. by 2-in. steel angle
- Rail support
- Clipped corner
- Socket-head cap screw with stainless-steel washer

Cedar and stainless steel stand up to weather. This gray-stained cedar railing designed by Clay Benjamin Smook uses stainless-steel fittings and plastic-coated stainless-steel marine cable in its balustrade. Plastic sleeves line drilled holes in the center post.

A maritime feel in central Wyoming. The gray-painted steel frame, stainless-steel marine cable and fittings, and redwood decking and handrail evoke the feel of the sea on this deck, which was designed by Eric Logan.

Any sailor can tell you that stainless-steel marine hardware will hold up well to the weather, a prime consideration when choosing potential deck-railing material. Long used for railings and lifelines on boats, stainless-steel cable and fasteners are strong and versatile, and they don't obscure the view.

Plastic-coated stainless-steel cable can be used in conjunction with a conventionally framed post and top-rail system. In the deck railing shown in the top right photo, the cable is attached to cedar posts with stainless-steel I-bolts and threaded through holes in the center post that are lined with plastic sleeves.

A turnbuckle puts tension on the continuous cable.

Although located far inland in central Wyoming, the redwood and steel deck designed by Eric Logan and built by Greg Pope certainly evokes images of the sea (see the bottom right photo). Custom-fabricated gray-painted steel posts are bolted directly to the steel framing, and stainless-steel fasteners connect the cable to the posts (see the drawing above). The handrail is milled from two pieces of redwood and screwed to the ¼-in. steel angle. All of the decking, the handrails, and the post caps are sealed with three coats of Sikkens® polyurethane.

Although this deck and rail were designed to meet the specifications of a childless couple, it should be pointed out that most local codes would frown on this balustrade detail because of the spacing between cables. However, the balustrade could easily be brought into compliance with minimal visual impact by adding more horizontal cables and reducing the spacing between them to 4 in.

Battens Simplify Baluster Assembly

Slip tenons reinforce this redwood railing. The bottom rail on this redwood railing drops onto slip tenons mortised into the posts. The balusters are premounted onto ¼-in.-thick by 1½-in.-wide battens to make a balustrade, which is then attached to the top and bottom rails.

BY STEVE ORTON

I wanted to build an elegant deck railing for my small bungalow in Pasadena, Calif., that would be simple enough for on-site construction and not involve specially milled lumber.

Because I think that the weakest part of this rail system is the joint where the bottom rail meets the post, I wanted this joint to remain tight and strong. Before installing the posts, I mortised them for slip tenons. Then the bottom rails were mortised on both ends and were dropped over the slip

tenons and screwed to the posts (see the drawing on the facing page).

The heart of the rail system is the baluster assembly, which is simply two lengths per section of ¼-in.-thick by 1½-in.-wide battens cut to the length of the section. The battens were nailed to the top and bottom of the 2×2 balusters spaced 5½ in. on center. This assembly created a balustrade, which was then dropped into place on top of the bottom rail.

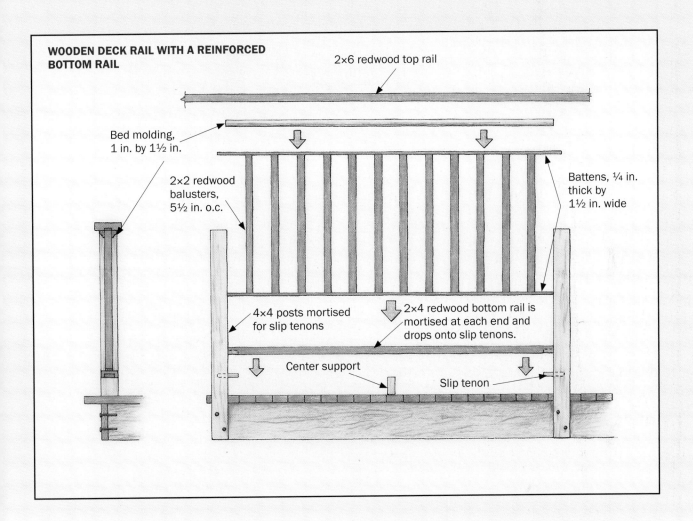

WOODEN DECK RAIL WITH A REINFORCED BOTTOM RAIL

2×6 redwood top rail

Bed molding, 1 in. by 1½ in.

2×2 redwood balusters, 5½ in. o.c.

Battens, ¼ in. thick by 1½ in. wide

4×4 posts mortised for slip tenons

2×4 redwood bottom rail is mortised at each end and drops onto slip tenons.

Center support

Slip tenon

With a router and an adjustable fence, I cut a 1½-in.-wide groove into the center of the underside of the top rail to receive the top batten of the balustrade. To finish, I installed 1-in. by 1½-in. bed molding against the balusters on both sides and under the top rail and put supports under the center of each bottom rail.

The hard part was priming and painting the railing, which took longer to do by hand than it had taken to build it. But this was before I bought high-volume low-pressure (HVLP) spray equipment, which makes finishing almost fun.

Steve Orton is a retired builder and is now a furniture maker in Seattle, Washington.

A Railing You Can See Through

Tempered glass panels don't obscure the view. Salvaged tempered-glass panels from failed thermopane sliders make a strong and unobtrusive deck railing.

BY KEN SIMMONS

On a recent project, my clients asked for a railing that wouldn't intrude on their exceptional views of the mountains that surround their vacation home. Because the deck was 18 ft. off the ground and had to withstand visits from their grandchildren, it had to be safe as well.

My solution was to use cast-off tempered safety glass salvaged from failed double-pane glass doors. Many glass companies keep these discarded panels, separate the glass, and sell the individual tempered plates for around $20 each. Measuring 76 in. by 33 in. and nearly impossible to break, this glass is ideal for railings.

The first step was to lay out the posts, remembering that tempered panels can't be cut. Although a glass company can sup-

ply smaller sizes of tempered glass, the cost per square foot goes up considerably (around $6 per sq. ft. in my area), so I laid out the posts carefully—I used 4×4 posts 90 in. on center—and used full-size glass panels wherever possible.

For the bottom rail, I used a 2×4 with a support block in the middle to keep the rail rigid. The top rail was a 2×6, and the side stiles were 2×2s. I routed out 3/16-in. wide by 1/4-in. deep grooves down the centers of the stiles and rails to accept the glass (see the bottom drawing on the facing page), and I've also ripped 3/4-in. by 3/4-in. stops, nailed them to the stiles and rails with 4d galvanized finish nails, and set the glass that way (see the top drawing on the facing page). Routing the stiles and rails requires

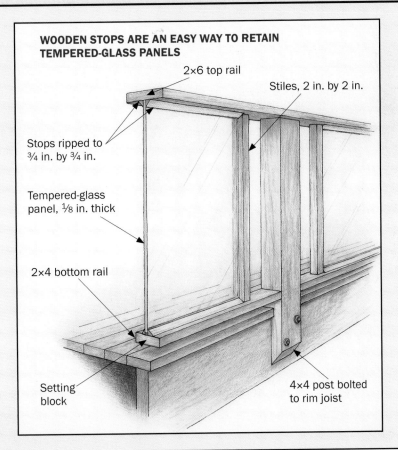

WOODEN STOPS ARE AN EASY WAY TO RETAIN TEMPERED-GLASS PANELS

2×6 top rail

Stiles, 2 in. by 2 in.

Stops ripped to ¾ in. by ¾ in.

Tempered-glass panel, ⅛ in. thick

2×4 bottom rail

Setting block

4×4 post bolted to rim joist

a bit more care but results in a cleaner look. In both cases, I use beads of clear silicone around the perimeter of the glass to seal the joint against seepage and to prevent the glass from rattling in the wind.

I left about ⅛-in. extra space in the frame for expansion, and set the glass on setting blocks (you can get them from a glass company), which keep the glass from resting directly on the framing. Check with your local building code to make sure that this detail is code-compliant.

Ken Simmons is a builder in Rumney, New Hampshire.

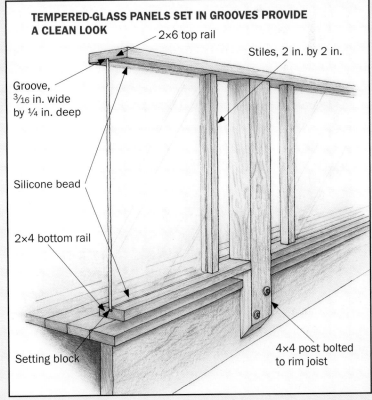

TEMPERED-GLASS PANELS SET IN GROOVES PROVIDE A CLEAN LOOK

2×6 top rail

Stiles, 2 in. by 2 in.

Groove, ³⁄₁₆ in. wide by ¼ in. deep

Silicone bead

2×4 bottom rail

Setting block

4×4 post bolted to rim joist

Lighted Railing Is Pretty and Safe at Night

Pittsburgh-area deck designer and builder Robert Viviano's technique for illuminating an outdoor newel-post and handrail system is an interesting blend of low- and high-tech (see the photo below). The central component is commercially available acrylic rod that reflects light along its length from a light source mounted in the newel post.

These rods are mounted in a groove routed in the handrail and usually are either ½ in. by ½ in. square or ½ in. dia. The tubes extend into the newel post right to the light source, which typically is a 7w fluorescent bulb that is mounted in a porcelain fixture, and function like oversize fiber optics (see the drawings on the facing page). Another groove routed in the two-piece handrail carries electrical cable from newel post to newel post.

Acrylic rods help light the way. Inset into the handrails, solid acrylic rods reflect light from fluorescent fixtures concealed in the newel posts.

LIGHTED NEWEL POST AND RAIL

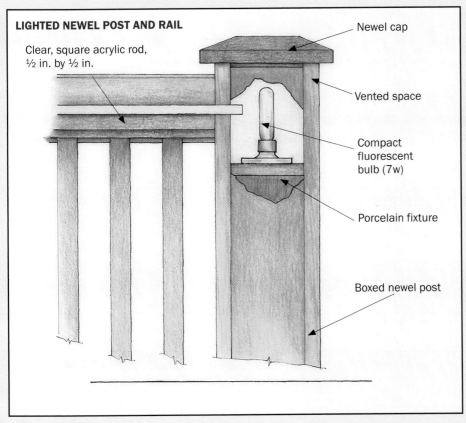

Clear, square acrylic rod,
½ in. by ½ in.

Newel cap

Vented space

Compact
fluorescent
bulb (7w)

Porcelain fixture

Boxed newel post

CROSS SECTION OF LIGHTED RAIL

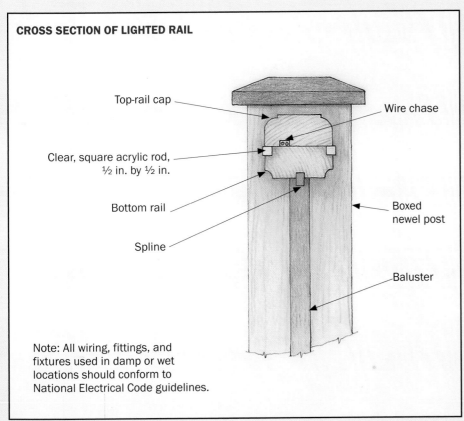

Top-rail cap

Wire chase

Clear, square acrylic rod,
½ in. by ½ in.

Bottom rail

Boxed
newel post

Spline

Baluster

Note: All wiring, fittings, and
fixtures used in damp or wet
locations should conform to
National Electrical Code guidelines.

Railing Against the Elements

■ BY SCOTT MCBRIDE

The original railing around the deck over the garage rotted out prematurely, so the owner of the house commissioned a new railing of a slightly different design. Carefully detailed of cypress and cedar, the new railing should last a long time.

The moist climate of New York's Hudson Valley isn't exactly ideal for carpenters like myself. We have muggy summers, slushy winters, and three months of rain in between. As we struggle through weeks of unremitting precipitation with fogged-up levels and wet chalklines, there is but one consolation: come April, a billion fungal spores will bloom, reaching into every water-logged mudsill, fascia, and doorstep. That means a guaranteed crop of rot-repair jobs in the coming season.

Of all the woodwork exposed to the elements, none is so vulnerable as the white pine porch railing. With the right combination of faulty detailing and wind-driven rain, a railing can be reduced to shredded wheat in about eight years. I typically rebuild several of these railings each year. In this chapter I'll describe one such project.

Getting Organized

A railing around the flat roof of a garage had rotted out and the owner asked me to build a new one. This wasn't a deck that was used, so the railing was decorative rather than functional, and one of my worries was installing the new railing without making the roof leak (more about that later). On a house across town, my customer had spotted a railing that he liked and asked if I could reproduce it. I said I could and took down the address.

Before leaving the job site, I made a list of the rail sections I would be replacing, their lengths, and the number of posts I would need. Later that afternoon I found the house with the railing my customer liked, strolled up the walk, and began jotting down measurements. The family dog objected strenuously to my presence, but no one called the police.

Back at the shop, I drew a full-scale section of the railing and a partial elevation

Spacing Balusters

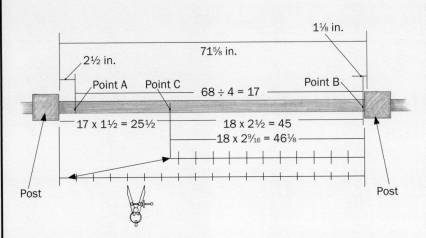

- 2½ in.
- 71⅝ in.
- 1⅛ in.
- Point A
- Point C
- 68 ÷ 4 = 17
- Point B
- 17 x 1½ = 25½
- 18 x 2½ = 45
- 18 x 2⁹⁄₁₆ = 46⅛
- Post
- Post

S pacing balusters correctly is a simple trick, but it's surprising how many carpenters are stumped by it. The object is to have equal spaces between each baluster and between balusters and posts.

Suppose your railing is 71⅝ in. long, your balusters are 1½ in. sq., and you want a spacing of 4 in. on center—that is, 1½ in. of wood, 2½ in. of air, 1½ in. of wood, and so on.

Begin the layout from the post on the left by tentatively laying off a 2½-in. space ending at point A in the drawing. From there you stretch a tape and see how close you come to the post on the right with a multiple of 4 in. In this case, 68 in. (a multiple of 4) brings us to point B, which is 1⅛ in. from the right-hand post. Forget about this remainder for the moment.

Dividing 68 by 4 tells you that you will have 17 intervals containing one baluster and one space, plus the extra space you laid out at the start. That makes 17 balusters and 18 spaces. Now you're going to lay out the combined dimensions of all 17 balusters (17 x 1½ in. = 25½ in.) from the left-hand post. That brings you to point C. From there you're going to lay off the combined dimensions of all the spaces, bringing you to point B— close, but not close enough. To land directly at the post, divide the remaining 1⅛-in. by 18 (the number of spaces) and add the quotient to each space. How fortunate 1⅛ ÷ 18 = ¹⁄₁₆. That gives you a nice, neat adjusted dimension for the space of 2⁹⁄₁₆ in.

If the numbers don't divide evenly, I'll use a pair of spring dividers to find the exact space dimension by trial and error, stepping off the distance from point C to the post. When I find the right setting, I lay off the first space. Then I add this dimension to the baluster width, reset the spring dividers to the sum distance, and step off the actual spacing. This method avoids the accumulated error that happens when using a ruler and pencil, not to mention all that excruciating arithmetic.

showing the repeating elements. The next bit of work was to make layout sticks (or rods) showing the baluster spacing for the different rail sections. This would tell me the exact number of partial-and full-length balusters that I would need.

The Right Wood

I'm fortunate to have a good supplier who specializes in boat lumber. He carries premium grades of redwood, cedar, cypress, and Honduras mahogany, all of which resist decay well. I used cypress for the rails and balusters because it's less expensive and because the rough stock is a little thicker than the others. Cypress is mostly flatsawn from small trees, though, and the grain tends to lift if the wood isn't painted immediately.

Much of the western red cedar at this yard is vertical grain—the annual rings run perpendicular to the face—and hence inherently stable. I typically use it for wider pieces where cupping could be a problem. Square caps on posts fit this description because they are so short in length. They should always be made from vertical-grain material or they'll curl in the sun like potato chips.

For this job, I bought 2-in.-thick cypress for the rails and balusters, 5/4 red cedar for the rail caps and post caps, and 1-in. cedar boards for the box newel posts.

Bevels and Birds' Mouths

After cutting the lumber into rough lengths with a circular saw, I jointed, ripped, and thickness-planed the pieces to finish dimensions. Using a tablesaw, I beveled the top, middle, and bottom rail caps at 15 degrees. Besides looking nice, the bevels keep water from sitting on what would otherwise be level surfaces.

I had to cut a bird's mouth on the bottom of each baluster so that the baluster would fit over the beveled cap on the bottom rail. I devised a shortcut to making these, as explained in the sidebar below. I also cut birds' mouths in the full-length balusters with the same setup, but cut them one at a time because they were wider. These uprights also have decorative stopped chamfers routed into them. The chamfers bounce light smack into your eye in a most appealing way.

Next, I set up the dado cutterhead on my tablesaw. I plowed a shallow groove for

When fungi sprout from railings, it's a rotten sign. Here is a close-up of the railing the author was hired to replace.

the partial balusters in the underside of the middle rail and another to receive the full-length balusters in the underside of the top rail. Although these grooves are a mere ⅛ in. deep, they made assembling the railing much easier and ensured positive alignment of the vertical members. The tops of the partial balusters are housed completely in the groove, but the tops of the full-length balusters also have stub tenons, cut on the radial-arm saw.

Of all the woodwork exposed to the elements, none is so vulnerable as the white pine porch railing.

Shortcut for Cutting Birds' Mouths

Rather than make each bird's mouth individually for the balusters, I first crosscut my 2×6 baluster stock to finished length and jointed one edge. I then ripped just enough off the opposite edge to make it parallel to the jointed edge. With the blade on my radial-arm saw raised off the table and tilted 15 degrees, I made an angled crosscut halfway through the thickness of the baluster stock. Flipping the piece, I made the same cut from the opposite face. Individual balusters were then ripped from the 2×6, with each bird's mouth already formed.

Box Newel Posts

Each box newel post is a two-part affair. I cut rough posts from pressure-treated 4×4 yellow pine and outfitted them with soldered copper base flashing (see the drawing on p. 120). This flashing would later be heat-welded to the new roof surface (more on that in a minute). A finished cedar box newel post would slip over the rough post and receive the railings.

Because the sides of the box newels were to be butt-joined, two sides were left their full 5½-in. width, and the other two were ripped down to 3¾ in. so that the finished post would be square in cross section. I saved the rippings to make the quarter-round molding that's under the bottom rail cap.

The box newels were glued up with a generous helping of resorcinol to keep out moisture. Glue also does a better job of keeping the corner joints from opening up than nails do. To align the sides of the box newels during glue-up, I used three biscuit joints along the length of each side.

The last parts to be fabricated were the post caps. The square lower part of the cap is a shallow truncated pyramid, produced by making four consecutive bevel cuts on a tablesaw. I made the round upper part on a shaper. The two parts were glued together with the grain of each parallel to the other, so they would expand and contract in unison.

Railing Anatomy

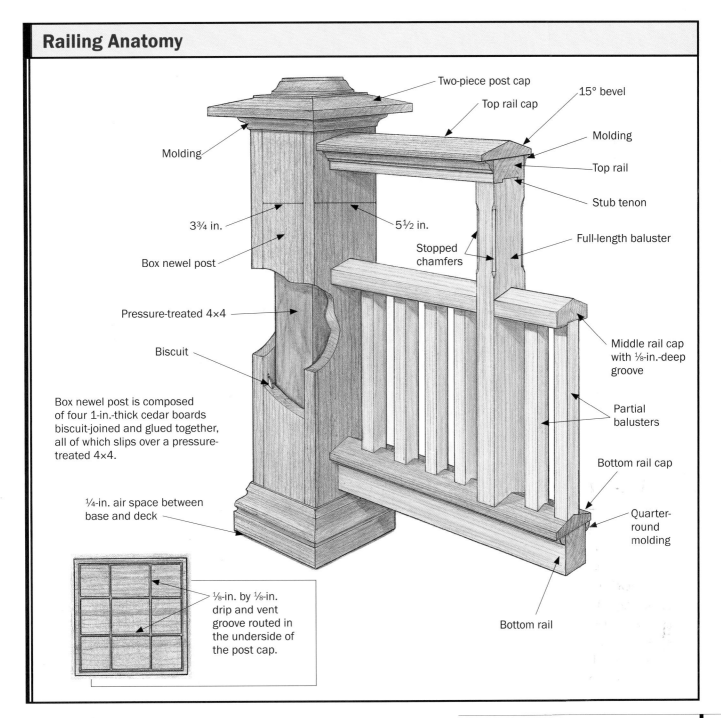

Two-piece post cap
Top rail cap
15° bevel
Molding
Top rail
Stub tenon
Molding
Full-length baluster
3¾ in.
5½ in.
Stopped chamfers
Box newel post
Middle rail cap with ⅛-in.-deep groove
Pressure-treated 4×4
Biscuit
Partial balusters
Box newel post is composed of four 1-in.-thick cedar boards biscuit-joined and glued together, all of which slips over a pressure-treated 4×4.
Bottom rail cap
Quarter-round molding
¼-in. air space between base and deck
⅛-in. by ⅛-in. drip and vent groove routed in the underside of the post cap.
Bottom rail

Flashing a Post Base

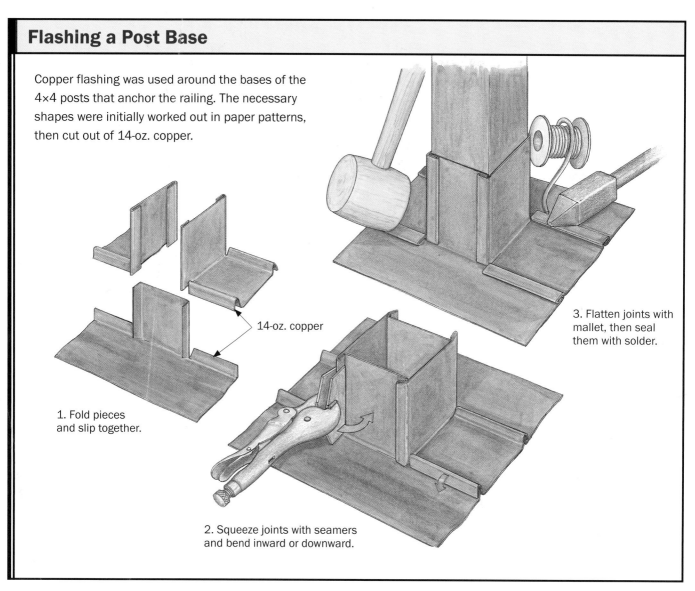

Copper flashing was used around the bases of the 4×4 posts that anchor the railing. The necessary shapes were initially worked out in paper patterns, then cut out of 14-oz. copper.

14-oz. copper

1. Fold pieces and slip together.

2. Squeeze joints with seamers and bend inward or downward.

3. Flatten joints with mallet, then seal them with solder.

Where a roof deck is subject to heavy use, the posts should be securely anchored to the framing.

To reduce the amount of water running down the face of the post, I cut a drip groove around the underside of the cap with a ⅛-in. veiner bit mounted in a router table. Using the same bit, I also routed a series of ventilation grooves into the underside of the cap in a tic-tac-toe pattern (see the detail drawing on p. 119). They allow air taken in at the bottom between the rough post and the box newels to escape at the top without letting in rain.

Assembling the Rail Sections

I assembled the rail sections in the shop where I could count on dry weather and warm temperatures. The first step was to face-nail the bottom rail cap to the bottom rail. I placed the nails so that they would be covered subsequently by the ends of the balusters.

I toenailed the balusters in place with 4d galvanized finish nails. This was easy to do because the bevel and bird's-mouth joinery prevented the balusters from skidding around as I drove the nails.

The middle rail was cut into segments to fit between the full-length balusters. I took the lengths of the segments, along with the spacing for the partial balusters, directly from the layout on the bottom rail cap. Every other segment of the middle rail could be attached with 3-in. galvanized screws through the uprights. The intervening segments were toenailed with 8d galvanized finish nails. Then I face-nailed through the middle rail down onto the tops of the partial balusters. The top rail was screwed down onto the full-length balusters. I left the top-rail cap loose so that it could be trimmed on site for a tight fit between the newels.

Still in the shop, I caulked all the components with a paintable silicone caulk, primed the wood, and then painted it with a good-quality latex house paint. With a truckload of completed rail sections and posts, I headed for the job site with my crew.

Installation

My roofing contractor had replaced the existing 90-lb. rolled roof over the garage with a single-ply modified-bitumen roof. One advantage of modified bitumen is that repairs and alterations can be heat-welded into the membrane long after the initial installation. This meant I didn't have to coordinate my schedule with that of the roofer to fuse the copper base flashings to the new roof. Flashing strips of the bitumen were melted on top of the copper flange, providing two layers of protection (including the copper) around the base of the post and a "through-flashed" layer of roofing beneath the post.

The railing is U-shaped in plan, and I anchored the two ends into the house. However, I didn't want to penetrate the roof membrane with framing or fasteners, so the newel posts are attached to the deck only by way of their flashings. Although this method of attaching the posts provides superb weather protection, the intermediate posts are a bit wobbly. This was okay for this particular deck because the railing is strictly decorative. Where a roof deck is subject to heavy use, the posts should be securely anchored to the framing.

With the rough posts in place, installation of the railing was straightforward. Box newels were slipped over the 4×4s and roughly plumbed. We stretched a line between corner newels and shimmed the intermediate newels up to the line. All box

One of the advantages of a single-ply modified-bitumen roof is that repairs and alterations can be heat-welded to the membrane long after the initial installation. Here, flashing strips of bitumen, which cover the copper base flashings around the 4×4 posts, are being fused to the roof membrane.

newels were held up off the deck at least ¼ in. to allow ventilation. The difference between the rough post dimension (3½ in. by 3½ in.) and the internal dimension of the box newels (3¾ in. by 3¾ in.) allowed for some adjustment. When the newels were just where we wanted them, we simply nailed through the shims and into the rough posts.

In some cases, rail sections had to be trimmed. When the fit was good, top, middle, and bottom rails were snugged up to the posts with galvanized screws. All that remained was to glue cypress plugs into the counterbored holes and shave them flush.

Scott McBride is the owner of Mustard Seed Builders (www.mustardseedbuilders.com) in Sperryville, Virginia.

Deck-Stair Basics

■ BY SCOTT SCHUTTNER

Lay Out and Cut the Stringers

Determine total rise. Use a level and a measuring tape to find the total rise. Remember to factor in a concrete pad if one will be installed later. Use the calculations explained on the facing page to figure out the number of steps and the total run.

Stair buttons ensure an accurate layout. Small clamps known as stair buttons screw onto a framing square to mark the unit rise and the unit run on a stringer. Working from bottom to top, slide the square up the stringer, marking each notch the same way. The bottom of the stringer is marked parallel to the tread cuts, but the first riser must be shortened (see the drawing on the facing page) by the thickness of the tread.

Start the cuts with a circular saw. Cut the notches on the waste side of the line. Stop the blade just shy of the intersecting line, and finish the cut square and plumb with a jigsaw, a handsaw, or a reciprocating saw.

Building even a simple set of stairs can seem pretty intimidating if you've never done it before. But once you understand how to lay out the stringers, you'll see it's largely a matter of measuring the overall height, or rise, of the stairs and determining a comfortable, safe depth for the treads, known as the run. The hardest work is done by the time you get out your saw. If your project calls for a basic stair or if you just need to understand the fundamentals so that you can confidently tackle a custom project, the notched-stringer stairs shown here will get you started.

*This chapter was adapted from **Scott Schuttner's** book,* Building a Deck *(The Taunton Press, 2002).*

How many steps?

Divide the total rise by a comfortable riser height (7 in. is standard); the result is the number of risers, plus a fraction. Divide the whole-number portion back into the total rise to get the exact rise per step. The number of treads will be equal to or one less than the number of risers, depending on how the stairs are attached to the deck. Multiply the number of treads by their depth for the total run.

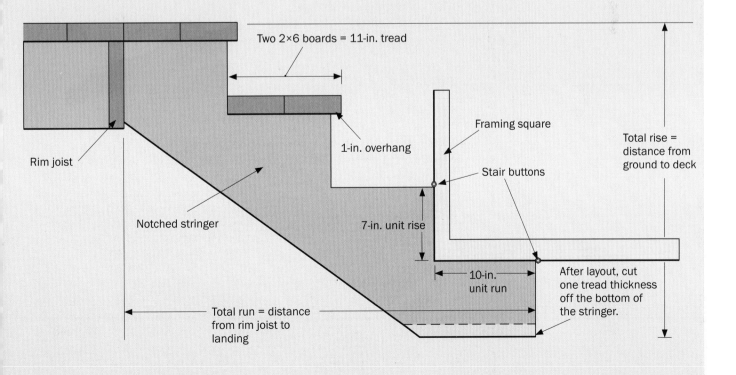

Two 2×6 boards = 11-in. tread

Rim joist

Notched stringer

1-in. overhang

7-in. unit rise

Framing square

Stair buttons

10-in. unit run

After layout, cut one tread thickness off the bottom of the stringer.

Total rise = distance from ground to deck

Total run = distance from rim joist to landing

Durable Deck Stairs

■ BY SCOTT GRICE

Deck stairs for a small yard had better be beautiful to look at because there's no way to hide them. Although this might sound like a risky situation, it is also an opportunity. Deck stairs done well can add a sense of balance and unity to a small yard and can become a feature to be celebrated rather than a utilitarian eyesore.

I recently took on a job where I had just such an opportunity. The homeowner's backyard was small, and the landscaping had been mostly destroyed during a remodeling project that was nearing completion. The homeowner had a fresh slate for landscaping, and the deck stairs that I built would be the first feature there. I knew that in the future the stairs would be a prominent part of a fastidiously landscaped backyard haven.

The Finished Look Affects the Framing

For both durability and aesthetics, ipé was the decking choice. Ipé is highly resistant to rot, it is incredibly dense, and when sealed with tung oil, it develops a dark-brown patina over time. Also, ipé is heavy and hard to cut, and it has been known to pull itself loose from framing because of the extreme

force it exerts with seasonal movement. The ipé risers for these stairs are made from ¾-in.-thick decking, but the treads are 2×12s. I frame stairs as strong as possible, but because this deck called for ipé, the framing was particularly important.

I did a few things to ensure the framing was strong enough. First, I minimized the distance the stringers had to span by eliminating one step. This increased the stair rise to 8 in., which is tall but still within acceptable range. To ensure the stringers wouldn't flex under load, I used pressure-treated 2×12s (the largest dimension available at the lumberyard). Also, I nailed 2×4 strongbacks to both sides of the middle stringer and to the inside of each outside stringer. Strongbacks dramatically increase the rigidity of stringers, so I never build exterior stairs without them.

The transitions at the top and bottom of the stairs also affected the framing. At the top, the last riser needed to continue seamlessly as the deck's fascia. The fascia was spaced off a 4×8 supporting beam by the thickness of the newel posts, which complicated the stringer attachment. I solved the problem by using the stringer strongbacks and the top newel posts to help support the stairs (see the drawing on p. 127).

Stronger Stairs, Top to Bottom

At the top of the stairs, newel posts are incorporated into the framing to create a seamless transition from stairs to deck. At the bottom of the stairs, a rigid box is incorporated into the landing step using epoxy, ½-in.-dia. bolts, and ¼-in.-dia. all-thread. This ensures sturdy newel posts and a solid connection to the concrete slab. The stringers that connect the deck and the slab are strengthened with 2×4 strongbacks.

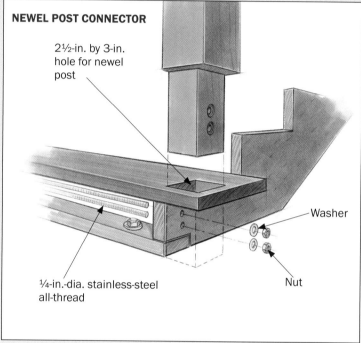

NEWEL POST CONNECTOR

2½-in. by 3-in. hole for newel post

Washer

Nut

¼-in.-dia. stainless-steel all-thread

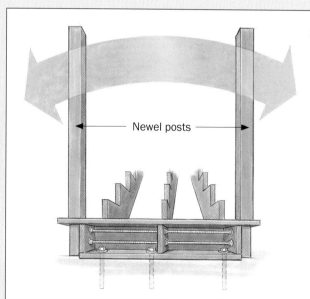

STABILIZING THE LANDING

Two ¼-in.-dia. rods of all-thread stabilize the landing newel posts to prevent them from racking with lateral pressure. The top, bottom, and sides of the landing-step box add extra stability by tying all three stringers together.

Newel posts

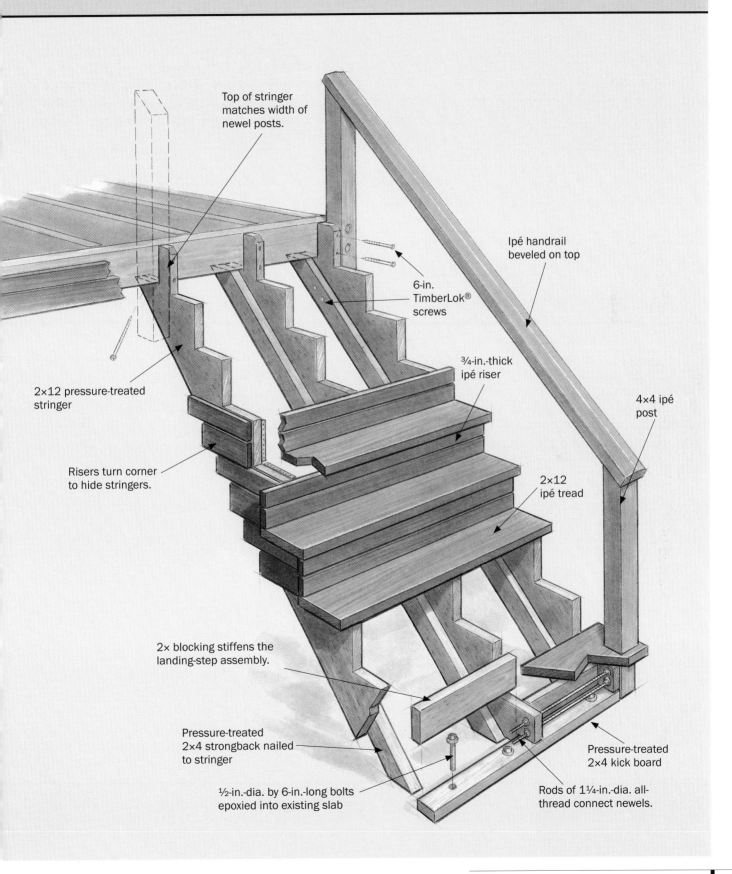

Top of stringer matches width of newel posts.

Ipé handrail beveled on top

6-in. TimberLok® screws

¾-in.-thick ipé riser

4×4 ipé post

2×12 pressure-treated stringer

2×12 ipé tread

Risers turn corner to hide stringers.

2× blocking stiffens the landing-step assembly.

Pressure-treated 2×4 strongback nailed to stringer

Pressure-treated 2×4 kick board

½-in.-dia. by 6-in.-long bolts epoxied into existing slab

Rods of 1¼-in.-dia. all-thread connect newels.

Supporting Stairs Without a Slab

When I don't have the luxury of an existing slab, I build a big footing and hide it under the stair framing. A stair footing is simply a block of reinforced concrete that carries the weight of the stairs and prevents the bottom of the stairs from kicking out. I usually make the footing big enough to support the stair framing fully but small enough to be hidden when the stairs are finished. The back side of the footing is under the stairs, so I run it thicker than necessary to give myself a little wiggle room.

With the footing laid out, I excavate to below frost level, compact 2 in. of gravel at the bottom, and build a form. I keep the top of the form no more than 1 in. above grade, but high enough to keep the bottom of the stringers out of the dirt, if possible. The form is typically small enough that I can mix the concrete I need by hand. Depending on the depth of the form, I add one or two pieces of rebar across the width to reinforce the concrete. Once the concrete has cured and the stair stringers are connected to the kick board, I drill holes with a rotary hammer and use epoxy to secure ½-in.-dia. by 6-in.-long bolts through the kick board and into the footing.

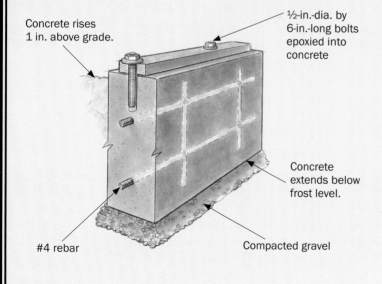

Concrete rises
1 in. above grade.

½-in.-dia. by
6-in.-long bolts
epoxied into
concrete

Concrete
extends below
frost level.

#4 rebar

Compacted gravel

The bottom transition incorporated an existing concrete slab to support and secure the stairs. To ensure solid newel posts and to protect the entire stair assembly from racking or twisting, I beefed up the landing step. With extra blocking and all-thread rods, I created a rigid box at the bottom of the stairs that includes the newel posts. I bolted this assembly to the concrete slab.

Meticulous Stringer Assembly Pays Off

Beefy stringers don't do much good if they are not cut or crowned properly. Stringers are the backbone of the staircase, and I've found that less-than-perfect stringers compound problems down the road. Perfect stringers begin at the lumberyard. Pressure-treated lumber is not high quality in the first place, so I take the time to select stringer boards that are free of big knots. I choose boards with a slight crown (I orient the crown up to help fight gravity), but without cups, twists, bows, or checks. Also, I buy lumber that is long enough to catch the framing square when I'm laying out the cuts for the top and bottom connections.

I use stair gauges on a framing square to lay out stringers. To increase accuracy, I use a Speed Square to mark the transition from one step to the next (see the top left photo on the facing page). When I draw and number the steps, I leave a little room at the top and bottom of the board. At the top step, I draw the way the stringer will attach to the deck. Once that is done, I make adjustments for tread thickness. If I had cut these stringers and installed them without accounting for tread thickness, the first step up from the concrete would have been taller than the other steps.

Accounting for tread thickness is easy. From the height of the first riser, I subtract the thickness of the tread. I mark a new cutline on the stringer and label it. Typically, I account for the thickness of the decking

Be Organized and Accurate When Making Stringers

The first step in constructing deck stairs is to figure out where and how the stringers will connect the deck to the ground. Once I establish the exact number and size of treads and risers, I draw all the elements on the stringer before I begin cutting. I take the time to be as accurate as possible and double-check my measurements. Also, even for a small set of stairs, I ensure that the stringers are strong enough to carry the load and are protected against rot.

Take time to be accurate. When laying out the stair's rise and run on a pressure-treated stringer, I use a Speed Square placed against the stair gauges to mark the exact location of the next rise. When marking the next rise and run, I align the framing square to that line. This reduces the margin of error introduced when marking each step.

Use the stringer as a story pole. Before making any cuts, I draw all the cutlines as well as any other important elements, such as the height of the decking, the thickness of the treads, and the top of the concrete.

Make stringers that last. To protect stringers against rot, I coat each cut surface with wood preservative. To prevent a stress failure, I attach one strongback (a 2×4 cleat nailed flush to the back edge of the stringer) to each side of the center stringer and one strongback to the inside of each outside stringer.

Use Newel Posts to Strengthen Stringer Connections

Top and bottom stringer connections are potential weak points for any set of stairs. At the top, a combination of TimberLok screws secures the stairs to the deck. At the bottom, I created a box assembly with enough rigidity to anchor the landing newel posts firmly. I secured this box assembly to the existing slab to prevent the stair stringers from moving away from the deck over time.

TimberLok screws secure the top. I secure the top of the stringer to the deck's beam by driving 6-in. screws through the vertical face; however, this mainly prevents lateral movement. To carry the load, I drive fasteners up through the strong-backs into the deck beam. Additionally, the newel posts (installed later) at each side of the top of the stairs help to carry the load by being fastened to both the beam and the stringers. Check with your building official for local stair stringer mounting requirements.

The newel post slips through the tread. I cut down the bottom of the newel post to allow it to pass through a hole in the tread. Because the tread helps to stabilize the newel post, I keep the tolerances between the hole and the post as tight as possible.

Connect the newels through the base. I pass ¼-in. all-thread through holes I've drilled in the base of the newels and matching holes drilled in the ends of the stringers. Countersunk into 1-in. holes, nuts tightened over washers secure the newels and can be used for plumb adjustment. To increase adjustability, I place washers and nuts on the all-thread rods at both sides of the center stringer.

at the top of the stairs by including it in the overall height calculation. But just to make sure, I draw and label the decking on the stringer along with all the other framing elements that affect stringer framing or stair height.

Before I start cutting, I double-check measurements and layout marks for accuracy. I use a circular saw to make cuts. At inside corners, however, I finish the cuts with a handsaw instead of overcutting and weakening the stringer. After the first stringer is cut, I use it as a template by clamping it to an uncut stringer board and tracing the outline. After I've cut all the stringers and fastened the strongbacks, I coat all the fresh-cut surfaces with wood preservative.

Finishing Details Affect the Experience

You don't typically hear someone say, "I had a great experience with my deck stairs today," but any casual observation of a backyard party assures us that deck stairs are used for more than simply climbing up and down. People set plates on them. They sit and lounge on them. They stop to talk midspan. During quieter times, deck stairs collect flowerpots and garden art and even substitute as a potting bench. Consequently, I like to make the deck stairs as inviting as possible.

Wide is better than narrow. I like the stairs to be at least 3½ ft. wide at the inside of the newel posts, and wider if possible. I make the treads at least 11 in. from front to back to allow enough room for people and pots. I chamfer all sharp edges and sand rough spots. Finally, I hide all the fasteners by screwing from underneath or countersinking the screws and plugging the holes. As I mentioned, hiding the fasteners improves the look of the stairs and reduces the chance of water damage, but it also

makes the stairs nicer to the touch and eliminates the fastener location as a source of slivers.

Obviously, all deck stairs should conform to local code requirements. I installed the cable-rail system according to the manufacturer's specifications. I beveled the top of the handrail to shed water and to make it more comfortable to grab. In some code jurisdictions, I also would have to install an additional handrail that is easier to hold.

Scott Grice *is a builder in Portland, Oregon.*

Add Durability by Adding Detail

A little attention to detail will raise the craftsmanship of stairs from pure utility to an ornamental feature in the yard. The easiest way I've found to improve the look of deck stairs is to hide the fasteners and framing lumber. This not only creates a better look but also can help the stairs to last longer.

Screw the treads from underneath. I use the Deckmaster hidden-fastener system (www.grabberman .com) because I found the galvanized J-channel system is strong enough for ipé, a dense wood that exerts a lot of force with seasonal movement. Also, securing the treads from below does not create a place for water to penetrate the framing and potentially cause rot.

Hide the stringers. I continue the riser detail around to the sides of the stringers, spacing the boards ⅛ in. to allow for water drainage (see the photo below). The gaps also add to the visual interest of the stairs.

Streamline the post connection. The top riser is continuous with the deck's fascia for a clean transition. The outside course of decking is full width and is notched around each newel post.

Plug all locations screwed from above. It's not possible to hide all the fasteners by screwing from below. There are always some locations, like handrails, where it is much easier to drive a fastener from above. I don't worry about it, but I take the time to plug every location screwed from above to maintain a stream-lined appearance and to prevent water penetration.

Curved Deck Stairs

■ BY MIKE GUERTIN

When I designed a multilevel curved deck for clients, I didn't consider adding curved stairs. I'd never built a set of freestanding curved stairs and wasn't ready to offer that option. But while I was away on vacation, the design plans changed, and my brother Bruce framed the deck. When I returned home from my trip, I learned that Bruce had volunteered curved stairs and that I was responsible for building them. I guess it was payback for having taken two weeks off.

I'd previously built curved interior stairs that relied on the surrounding walls to support the treads and risers; but exterior deck stairs would have to rely on open stringers. Curved stringers require a form, and I didn't know where to start to calculate the geometry. After a day of swearing at my brother under my breath, an idea popped into my head that seemed too simple to work. And it wouldn't require any more math than a simple rise-run calculation for common stringers.

My plan was to lay out and frame temporary curved walls like those on an enclosed set of curved stairs. Using the walls as both a form and a layout instrument, I could build and cut precise, curved laminated plywood stringers in place.

The framing and support system for a set of curved stairs isn't conventional, so check with your local building department during the design phase to ensure code compliance.

Mike Guertin is a remodeling contractor in East Greenwich, Rhode Island, and editorial advisor to Fine Homebuilding. His web site is www.mikeguertin.com

Curved Stud Walls Create the Form

A plywood floor defines the stairs. My first step in this process was to establish the stair radius. I covered the ground directly below the stair location with a monolithic sheet of plywood made from two layers cross-lapped at the seams; one edge was butted against and secured to the deck posts. Next, I determined the axis by driving a stake into the ground, parallel to the deck face. Now I could hook a measuring tape onto the stake and draw arcs for the inner and outer edges of the stairs. The tread widths were marked next. I knew the approximate stair run and calculated 7-in. rise, so starting beneath the deck edge, I stepped off 14 15-in. marks on the outer arc, then snapped chalklines between the axis point and the marks. After making a mirror image of the template, I transferred the tread marks to it, raised it in place, and built the stud wall.

Establish radius and treads. Driven into the ground at a point in line with the upper landing, a stake becomes a pivot, anchoring the tape and chalkline used to draw the stair's shape and treads.

Create a mirror image for the upper template. After marking and cutting a second identical plywood template, the author doubled the plywood, then transferred the tread marks from the lower to the upper, and snapped connecting lines.

Raising the template walls. Hoisted atop temporary staging, the upper template is fastened to the deck's rim joist for stability. Studs are screwed to the tread-position marks on both templates. With the walls in place, the studs are braced plumb.

STAIRCASE LAYOUT

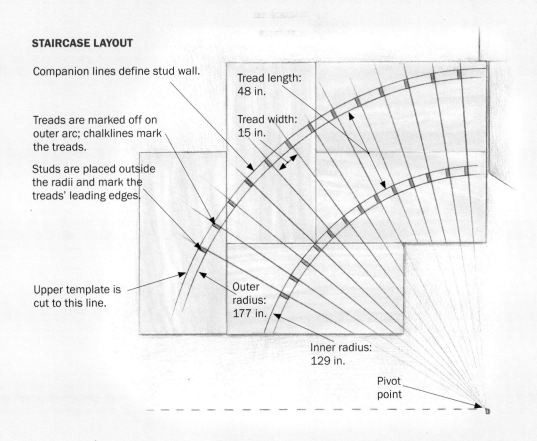

Companion lines define stud wall.

Treads are marked off on outer arc; chalklines mark the treads.

Studs are placed outside the radii and mark the treads' leading edges.

Upper template is cut to this line.

Tread length: 48 in.

Tread width: 15 in.

Outer radius: 177 in.

Inner radius: 129 in.

Pivot point

Layers of Plywood Make the Rough Stair Frame

Locate the stringers

After establishing a level reference line across both walls, I found the stringer location by first subtracting the riser height plus the rough-tread thickness from the top of the deck and marking the first pair of studs, then repeating for each subsequent tread position. The marks then describe the top of the stringer.

Prebend the stringers. After ½-in. pressure-treated plywood was ripped to 16 in., the stringer laminations were screwed inside the walls to prebend them (above). Heel and plumb cuts were made on a template from a short piece of stringer stock. Four laminations were screwed together on each wall.

Add glue. After unscrewing all but the first layer, the author rolled on a coat of two-part epoxy (top), then fastened successive layers with more epoxy, exterior-grade screws, and clamps where needed (above). Polyurethane construction adhesive can be used instead of epoxy.

Use the studs to mark notches

The point where the stringer and stud's back edge meet is the intersection of the tread and riser. I drew the tread line by carrying a level line from the intersecting point back to the next stud (below left). The riser cut is drawn plumb from the same point (below right).

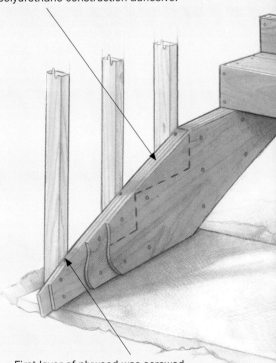

2× pressure-treated rough tread

Laminated riser of pressure-treated ½-in. plywood

Fortifying the assembly
A doubled ½-in. pressure-treated plywood riser serves as backing and tread ledger. It is secured with galvanized screws and polyurethane construction adhesive.

Stringers are laminated from four layers of ½-in. pressure-treated plywood, glued with two-part epoxy fortified with microfibers or polyurethane construction adhesive.

First layer of plywood was screwed into the studs for easy removal later. Subsequent layers were attached with exterior-grade screws. Care was taken not to place screws in areas to be cut.

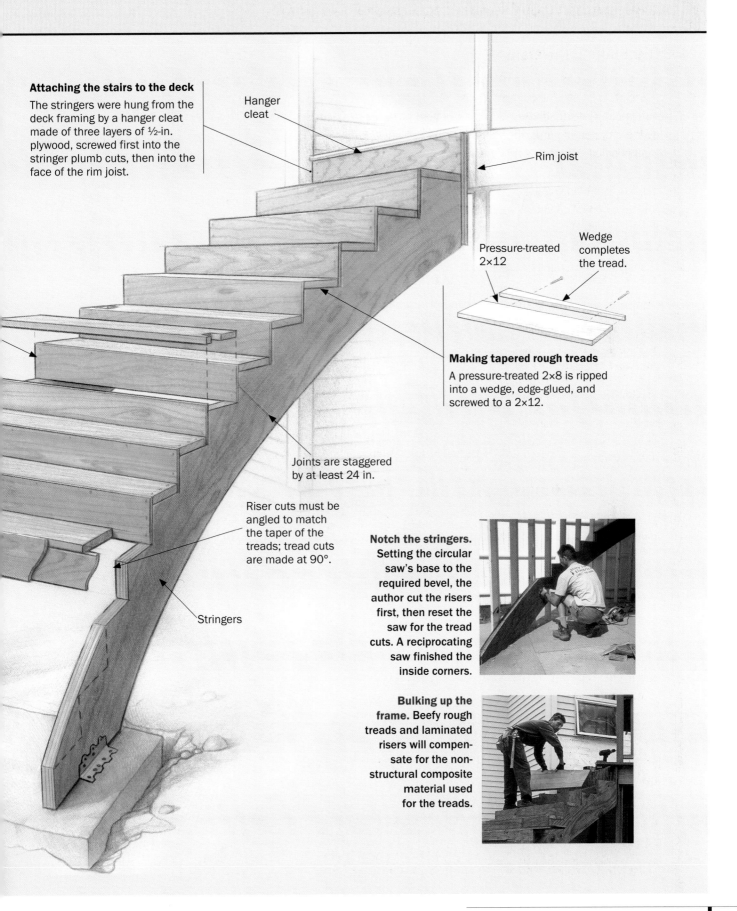

Attaching the stairs to the deck

The stringers were hung from the deck framing by a hanger cleat made of three layers of ½-in. plywood, screwed first into the stringer plumb cuts, then into the face of the rim joist.

Hanger cleat

Rim joist

Pressure-treated 2×12

Wedge completes the tread.

Making tapered rough treads

A pressure-treated 2×8 is ripped into a wedge, edge-glued, and screwed to a 2×12.

Joints are staggered by at least 24 in.

Riser cuts must be angled to match the taper of the treads; tread cuts are made at 90°.

Stringers

Notch the stringers. Setting the circular saw's base to the required bevel, the author cut the risers first, then reset the saw for the tread cuts. A reciprocating saw finished the inside corners.

Bulking up the frame. Beefy rough treads and laminated risers will compensate for the non-structural composite material used for the treads.

Cedar Trim Details Finish the Stairs

Dressing Up the Frame

Bruce Guertin finished the stairs. First, in the mid- and upper-post locations, he cut holes in the rough treads, then marked, notched, and attached the posts. The bottom posts were notched over the first step and screwed in place. Next, he bent and nailed the cedar skirtboards along the sweep of the stringer, then installed the cedar risers and composite decking treads. He built the railings in sections by tracing the stair's radius onto cedar 2×8s in place on a stringer and cutting the profiles on a router table. This method of cutting rails doesn't produce the helical twist a continuous rail would require, but the intermittent posts conceal the inaccuracy. The balusters were captured between two 1×2s ripped to the same radius; lengths of rail then were screwed to the balusters, and the completed section was installed between two posts.

Curved rails from straight stock
Cut to fit between posts, 2×8 cedar is laid on top of the skirt.

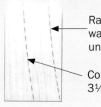

Radius of skirt was traced onto underside.

Companion line is drawn 3½ in. to outside.

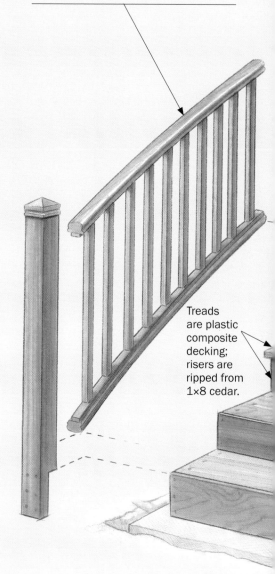

Treads are plastic composite decking; risers are ripped from 1×8 cedar.

Bending the skirts with gentle persuasion. Each cedar skirtboard was attached at the stringer top and worked into shape with clamps, polyurethane construction adhesive, and stainless trim screws (left). After the skirts were done, the cedar risers were nailed in place (right).

One section at a time. To ensure the correct radius and baluster spacing, each segment of railing was cut and assembled for a specific pair of posts.

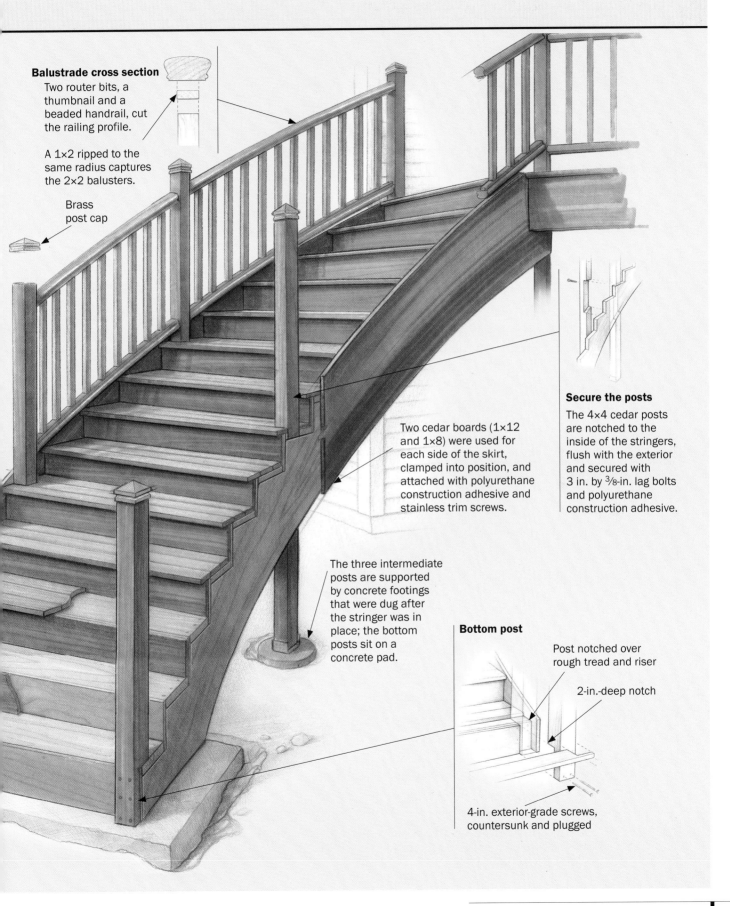

Balustrade cross section
Two router bits, a thumbnail and a beaded handrail, cut the railing profile.

A 1×2 ripped to the same radius captures the 2×2 balusters.

Brass post cap

Two cedar boards (1×12 and 1×8) were used for each side of the skirt, clamped into position, and attached with polyurethane construction adhesive and stainless trim screws.

The three intermediate posts are supported by concrete footings that were dug after the stringer was in place; the bottom posts sit on a concrete pad.

Secure the posts
The 4×4 cedar posts are notched to the inside of the stringers, flush with the exterior and secured with 3 in. by $\frac{3}{8}$-in. lag bolts and polyurethane construction adhesive.

Bottom post

Post notched over rough tread and riser

2-in.-deep notch

4-in. exterior-grade screws, countersunk and plugged

Fantail Deck Stairs

■ BY JOSÉ L. FLORESCA

started working with curves about 10 years ago. I learned from a master carpenter, Tom Pratt, who taught me how to build curved forms for concrete pools. What made this different from rectilinear construction was that we used plywood for the top and bottom plates. To follow the different radii for the curved surfaces of the pool, we cut the plates with a jigsaw or a bandsaw. A similar technique worked when I built a circular soffit in my kitchen. But my appetite for challenging curved projects hadn't been really nourished since Pratt moved out of town in 1987.

A new challenge presented itself when my partner, Steve Cassella, and I saw the plans for a remodel/deck addition designed by Dwayne Kohler that included a set of exterior stairs that fanned out in a quadrant, or quarter circle. Questions arose about the stair's construction: How many stringers are necessary to support the treads? How should the stringers be supported? What kind of calculations would be necessary to build the stairway?

After we got the job, and before we could build the quadrant stairs, we first enlarged the home's existing upper deck and built a new lower deck. That was the easy part of the job.

Calculations and Cogitations

The plans called for a straight set of stringers to run from the upper deck down to a landing. From the landing a second set of stringers would fan out in a quadrant. The total rise of the stairway—from upper deck to lower—is 93 in. We divided the height into 12 risers. More risers would have meant more treads, resulting in longer stringers. And longer stringers would have taken up more space on the lower deck. The rise (93 in.) divided by the number of risers (12) gave us an individual riser height of 7¾ in. We cut 10-in. treads because 10 in. is a good tread width for three 2×4s with ⅛-in. drainage space between the boards and a ¾-in. nosing.

After we determined the length of our stringers, we framed the landing and installed the straight-run stringers to the upper deck. We could now concentrate on the quadrant stairs.

The calculations for cutting the stringers of the quadrant stairs are the same as those for the straight run above. The big question was how many stringers did we need to support the treads? We decided that the span between the stringers at their widest point

Quadrant Stringers

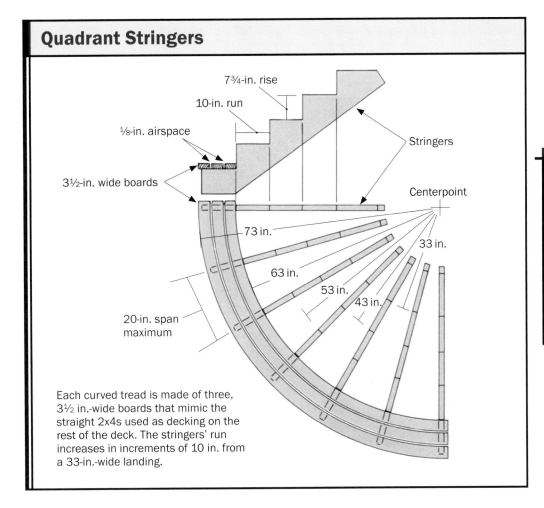

7¾-in. rise

10-in. run

⅛-in. airspace

3½-in. wide boards

Stringers

Centerpoint

73 in.

63 in.

53 in.

43 in.

33 in.

20-in. span maximum

Each curved tread is made of three, 3½ in.-wide boards that mimic the straight 2x4s used as decking on the rest of the deck. The stringers' run increases in increments of 10 in. from a 33-in.-wide landing.

Rather than support each stringer individually, I visualized a single, curved brace that each stringer would bear against.

(the outside edge of the bottom riser) should not exceed 20 in. because the grain of the treads is not consistently perpendicular to all of the stringers they rest on.

The landing is 33 in. wide. We used this dimension as the radius for the top risers of the quadrant stair stringers. Because our treads are 10 in. wide, the radii for the other risers are larger in 10-in. increments (the width of each tread); i.e., 43 in., 53 in., 63 in., and 73 in.

To calculate the number of stringers for the bottom step, we first had to calculate the circumference of the circle formed by the radius of the bottom step. Knowing that 2πr = circumference (r is the radius), we plugged in the numbers: $2 \times 3.1416 \times 73 = 458.6736$ in. The stairs occupy a quarter circle, so we divided the circumference by four. This figure was divided by the desired stringer span, 20 in., which gave us the number of

All the stringers are supported by a single, curved brace, which was notched to accommodate each stringer. A 2×10 leg runs between the deck joist and the brace.

Accuracy was essential, so we laid out the curved treads on the level floor of our cabinet shop.

20-in. spaces in the quarter circle. Rounding our quotient to the nearest whole number gave us six spaces, so we'd need seven stringers.

A Curved Brace for the Stringers

Installing the stringers posed yet another challenge. How should we support the tops of the stringers? Rather than support each stringer individually, I visualized a single, curved brace that each stringer would bear against.

I cut the brace from a 2×12. The curve of the brace is a segment of a circle. Its radius was determined by finding a centerpoint that was perpendicular to the center stringer and equidistant to the backs of all the other stringers, roughly 3 in. from their tops. We added 1 in. to the circle's radius to allow the brace to be notched around each stringer for lateral support. The brace was attached to the framing in such a way that its face is perpendicular to the back of the center stringer (see the photo on p. 143). A 2×10 leg supports the curved brace and was nailed to the top of one of the deck's joists. The top of the leg was cut at a compound angle and

nailed to the curved brace (see the photo on p. 143). With both pieces nailed in place, we then notched the curved brace with a jigsaw to accommodate the stringers.

The bottoms of the stringers sit on the lower deck and are toenailed in place. To provide nailing for the landing's deck boards, we added blocking between the stringers about 3 in. behind the top risers.

Determining Tread Length

To calculate the length of the treads along their circumference, we multiplied the radius of the lowest riser by two to get its diameter. We then multiplied this diameter by π (3.1416) to obtain the circumference. Because the arc of the stairway is a quarter circle, we divided the circumference by four.

For each of the four treads, it was necessary to cut three rows of boards (to simulate 2×4s): the inner board, which butts up against the riser above; the middle board; and the outer board whose nose hangs over the riser below. Each board of each tread has both an inside and an outside radius. The inside radius of the inner board is the same as the radius of the riser above—33 in.,

Three 3½-in.-wide curved boards make up each tread. The curves were laid out using a marking device made out of a 1×2, an adhesive-backed tape measure, and a set of trammel points. After layout, the authors cut the boards on a bandsaw.

43 in., 53 in., etc. The outside radius of each board is always 3½ in. (the width of a 2×4) greater than the inside radius. The inside radius of the next concentric tread board is greater by ⅛ in. (airspace) than the outside radius of the previous tread.

To calculate the lumber necessary for the treads, we used the same formula as that used to determine tread length. We calculated for each of the 12 tread boards plus one for the quarter-circle edge on the landing. To our total lengths we added an additional 10 percent as a safety factor. We added it up and purchased tight-knot cedar 2×10s in this linear quantity. Although this figure was derived as a length along a curve, it allotted for additional material needed so that we could stagger joints on the stringers.

Marking and Cutting the Treads

Accuracy was essential, so we laid out the curved treads on the level floor of our cabinet shop. Steve made a marking device out of a 1×2, an adhesive-backed tape measure, and a set of trammel points. One point was set at zero. The other was adjusted to the lengths of the curves determined

when we calculated the tread lengths (see the drawing on p. 143). When marking the curves on the 2×10s, we avoided using checked ends, and we placed knots so as not to create holes or cracks.

We first cut the curves with a jigsaw, which was inadequate because the cuts were not consistently square. The bandsaw cut the curves, but it became a two-man job because of the long lengths involved. We left the ends of the boards long and cut them to length during installation. We routed a ¼-in. radius on all visible edges.

Installing the treads was fairly straightforward. We predrilled the nail holes where necessary so that we wouldn't split the ends, and we staggered the joints.

Curved work has a natural character to it. It adds life to the otherwise rectangular dimensions of most carpentry. Enter some geometry, a bandsaw, and—voilà—quadrant stairs.

José L. Floresca is a carpenter in Seattle, Washington. Steve Cassella co-authored this chapter.

Custom Details Make a Better Deck

■ BY MICHAEL AYERS

Decks often are referred to as outdoor rooms, and this added living space can receive as much furnishing attention as any room in the house. These outdoor rooms are subject to outdoor weather, though, which affects durability and usability. Most home-owners accept the fact that they won't be able to use an outdoor room in December, but they expect to be able to use the deck full-time in August. Even in cold climates like Montana's, the August sun gets hot. Shady seating can be provided with store-bought chairs, benches, and umbrellas, but a more elegant option is to build in the seating and the shading. A pergola is an attractive way to create shade, and as long as you're building one, why not add some benches to sit on underneath?

had been wicking in through an old porch. Rather than devising a complicated strategy for attaching and flashing the new deck ledger—the board that typically connects a deck to a house—we thought, "Why not make the deck freestanding?"

By simply adding a couple of beams and their associated posts and piers, we could eliminate the need for flashing a ledger altogether. This design has the added benefit of eliminating joist hangers because the deck joists sit atop site-built beams that are bolted through 6×6 posts. And because we had called in an excavator to dig the deep holes needed for piers in Montana, where the frost line is about 3½ ft. below the surface, adding a few more holes didn't add much more to the cost.

Freestanding Decks Don't Cause Rot

One of the most difficult aspects of a deck is how to attach it to a house without allowing water to infiltrate house framing. When my crew and I started work at the house featured here, we found considerable rot in the rim joist and sill plate where moisture

Posts Must Be Aligned Perfectly

Taking time to ensure a good layout is the key to making the job easier as you move from framing the deck to building the pergola and the benches. Some deck posts in this design run continuously through the deck and support the bench and the pergola above, one runs through the deck to support the bench framing, and the others support only floor framing.

Because of this design, the posts must be placed thoughtfully, and they must be aligned perfectly. Thoughtful post placement means that they won't interfere with windows, doors, or travel paths. Equally important, they need to be spaced to support the floor beams adequately. Post placement starts with excavation, but you have opportunities to refine their position: when setting the concrete tubes in the holes and with adjustable bases used to anchor the posts.

Beams Are Built in Place

In Montana's high mountain desert, using pressure-treated lumber for durable decks is unnecessary except in ground-contact situations. If the deck is close to the ground, we use pressure-treated lumber for the floor framing, but not for the visible wood. On this deck, the posts, the benches, and the pergola are fir. The framing is pressure-treated, and the decking is composite (www. trex.com). The post bases elevate the posts enough to keep moisture from wicking into them.

Because the posts are finish work, they need to look good. I chamfered the post tops before installation. To calculate post length, you can use a rotary laser or a transit to establish the high point of the ground, which is used as the benchmark, to figure out how much you need to add to each post to keep the tops level. It's not imperative that the tops be perfectly level because they'll be integrated into a pergola frame, but they should be within ¼ in.

The more important aspect of establishing level is beam placement. For a grade-level deck such as this one, the elevations can be tricky. The decking should be about 1 in. below the door threshold, and the beams should be above the ground. To squeeze a

The Design Revolves

Anchored to concrete piers, the tallest posts extend through the deck, bench, and pergola; beams are bolted to the posts to support deck joists, bench framing, and pergola rafters. This freestanding design eliminates the need for a ledger. Because the posts are central to the design, aligned and plumb installation is critical.

Begin with a benchmark. The post in the foreground sits on the highest base and is marked "zero" as the benchmark. All the other posts are marked relative to the benchmark to ensure level beam installation.

Bore for carriage bolts. Deck joists will be supported by pairs of 2×10s secured to 6×6 posts. Tack each 2×10 to its post with a framing nail, making sure to keep the top edges level. Then drill through the post-and-beam assembly and install bolts. Check with your building official that bolting the beam to the post without additional support complies with the local building code.

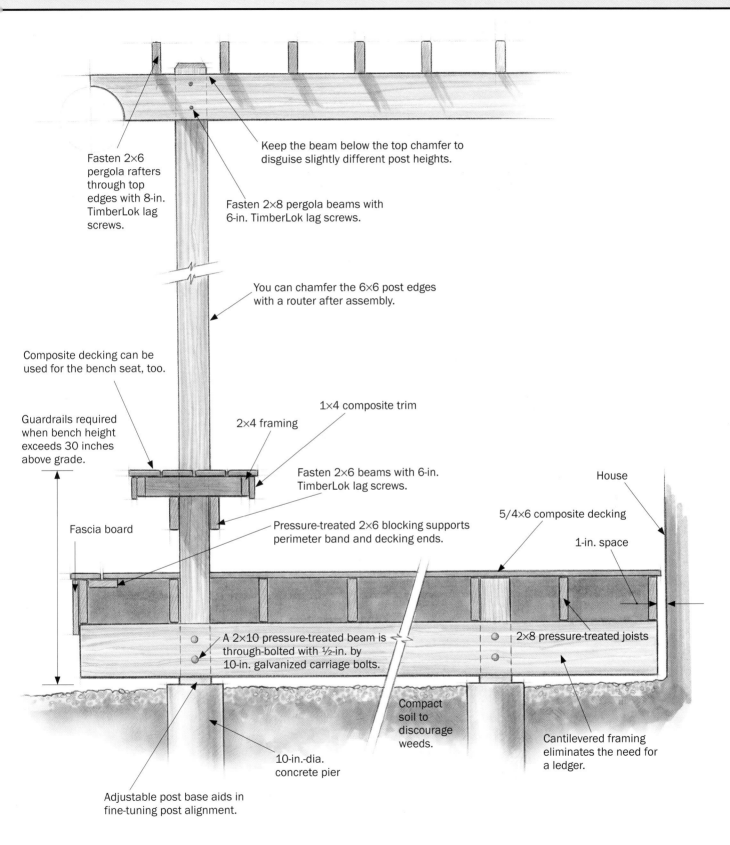

Fasten 2×6 pergola rafters through top edges with 8-in. TimberLok lag screws.

Keep the beam below the top chamfer to disguise slightly different post heights.

Fasten 2×8 pergola beams with 6-in. TimberLok lag screws.

You can chamfer the 6×6 post edges with a router after assembly.

Composite decking can be used for the bench seat, too.

1×4 composite trim

Guardrails required when bench height exceeds 30 inches above grade.

2×4 framing

Fasten 2×6 beams with 6-in. TimberLok lag screws.

House

5/4×6 composite decking

1-in. space

Fascia board

Pressure-treated 2×6 blocking supports perimeter band and decking ends.

A 2×10 pressure-treated beam is through-bolted with ½-in. by 10-in. galvanized carriage bolts.

2×8 pressure-treated joists

Compact soil to discourage weeds.

10-in.-dia. concrete pier

Cantilevered framing eliminates the need for a ledger.

Adjustable post base aids in fine-tuning post alignment.

Frame the Floor and Then Slide It over to the House

Face-nailing is faster than installing joist hangers. Because the rim joist isn't attached to the house and the joists lay over a beam, you can eliminate the need for 20 joist hangers, which will save a lot of time. Frame the floor far enough away from the house to provide nail-gun clearance. Then, with some assistance, slide the deck into place.

Toenail joists to beams. Straight joists mean straight lines of screws in the decking. After toenailing the joists on the layout, add blocks around the posts to catch the ends of decking boards (below).

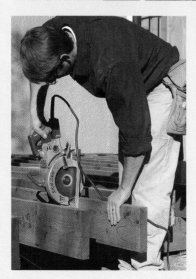

Cut the joists with deck boards in mind. During installation, let the outboard ends of the joists run long. Then calculate the depth the deck needs to be to finish with a full-width deck board. This saves time and improves the deck's finished appearance. After snapping a line to establish uniform joist length, you can cut the joists in place.

beam and floor joists into the space between the threshold and the ground, we used 2×10s for the beam and 2×8s for the floor joists. Along with 1-in. decking, this puts the beam 1 in. to 2 in. above the ground. Post placement and joist spacing need to be part of the equation when choosing lumber dimensions, so consult applicable span tables in code books or ask your local building official.

With a felt-tip pen, I mark the highest post zero; this is the benchmark. The other posts are marked with the fraction of an inch that they differ from the benchmark (+⅛, +¼). When nailing the posts into the bases, it's the last chance to align them accurately. It's also a good idea to plumb them at this point; temporary braces can help to hold them in place.

To find the top of the beam, hook a tape measure to the bottom of the post, and add the fraction written on the post to the beam height (9¼ in. in this case). I tack the beams to the posts with a framing nail, making sure the two-piece beams are level to each other. Then I drill through each post and beam with a ⅝-in.-dia. auger bit and use carriage bolts to tie everything together. It's a good idea to double-check that the posts are plumb and spaced properly before you really tighten the carriage bolts and move on to the floor framing.

I spread the joists on layout atop the beams, then attach the rim closest to the house first. With that end of the floor framed, I slide the frame in place, leaving it about 1 in. from the house, and toenail the joists to the beams.

Next, I cut the joists to length, but not just any length. Instead, I calculate the number of deck boards needed to cover the distance, including trim board, gaps, and overhang. This way, I won't have to rip the last deck board where it meets the house. It takes about the same amount of time to calculate this number as it does to rip the final board, and it looks a lot better. After cutting the joists, I attach the opposing rim

Use Spacers to Keep the Expansion Gaps Consistent

Ends and edges need gaps. Composite decking shrinks and swells with temperature variations, so spacing joints is necessary. Cut the spacers a little wider and narrower than the specified gaps to keep the decking parallel to the house.

Template for speedy screw placement. If you don't want to place screws by eye, mark a Speed Square with a felt-tip pen. Slide the square along, or mark the boards individually.

and any blocking needed to support the deck boards around the posts (see the photos on p. 150) and along their ends where they butt into the perimeter band.

Space the Decking Consistently

With the deck framed, I square up the outside corner, apply a fascia board to the deck's rim, and lay deck boards along the perimeter, mitering the corners. I overhang this "picture frame" past the trim by about 1 in.

Because the joists' lengths are calculated precisely to accommodate a particular number of deck boards, it's important to gap the deck boards consistently as you work back toward the house. As with other composite-decking materials, Trex requires specific spacing between boards and at butt joints because the material shrinks and swells with temperature variations. The gap size depends on the temperature during installation; the specs are printed on the end tags. You can cut a few shims on a tablesaw to keep the gaps consistent (see the photos at left).

To space the ends of the decking consistently away from the house, I use a scrap of ½-in. oriented strand board (OSB) as a spacer. I also check the decking as I proceed toward the house; staying parallel to the house is important. After notching around the posts, I snap a chalkline as a guide, and when I get about halfway across the deck, I start measuring from the house to the deck boards.

This also confirms that I can finish with a full-width deck board. If the numbers are a little off here, I can make a correction using a larger or smaller spacer at one end or the other. Then I can phase in the correction over many boards so that it won't be as visible.

Detail the Ends of the Pergola Beams and Rafters

Multiple cuts warrant a template

The ends of the beams and rafters are detailed with a simple curve. Because the beams are wider than the rafters, they need a slightly different radius to maintain the same proportions. Scraps of OSB make good templates. Trace the outline, and rough-cut it with a jigsaw (photo 1). Cut a line with a razor knife (photo 2) to avoid tearout caused by a pattern-cutting router bit (photo 3). Clean up the finished cut with a sander.

Frame the Benches and the Pergola

The beams carrying the pergola are 2×8s lag-screwed to the posts with TimberLok screws (www.fastenmaster.com); the pergola rafters are 2×6s. Both framing members have decorative cuts on their ends. Square or angular cuts can be made with a circular saw or a sliding compound-miter saw. Rounded or notched details can be cut with a jigsaw and a router. When cutting 2× stock with a jigsaw, the final cut probably won't be square. You either need to clean it up with a belt sander or make a router template of ½-in. OSB. The template guides a pattern-cutting bit. At the end overhanging the house roof, I cut an angle to match the slope of the roof, leaving at least an inch of clearance off the roof shingles.

The benches are framed the same way as the deck, only on a smaller scale: a frame atop a beam bolted to posts (see the drawing on p. 149). In this case, the beams are 2×6s attached to the posts with small lag screws. The 2×4 bench frame is built on top of the beam. The width of the frame again is set by the number of full-width deck boards that

The Benches Are Like Long, Skinny Mini-Decks

Deck boards dictate the bench width. The 2×4 bench framing should be sized to accommodate full-width deck boards, an overhang, and a 1×4 trim board. The bench's perimeter, like the deck's, is picture-framed with mitered corners.

will be placed on top, which eliminates the need to rip any deck boards to fit. I wrap the bench frame with 1×4 finish trim and then I run the decking on the benches. As with the deck boards, I picture-frame the benches, screwing the outer frame in place first, then decking the interior. This gives a finished look to the ends of the benches, capping the end cuts.

The pergola rafters are set north and south, which casts a wide afternoon shadow over the deck on hot summer days but allows sunlight into the house during cold winter months. If more shade is needed, a perpendicular layer of 1×2 material can be added to the top of the rafters.

With a couple of light fixtures mounted in the corners and a gas grill outside the kitchen door, the pergola and built-in benches lend a cozy feel to this inviting 300-sq.-ft. outdoor room.

Michael Ayers is a finish carpenter and remodeling contractor in Missoula, Montana.

A Comfortable Outdoor Bench

■ BY DAVID BRIGHT

A good carpenter always takes pride in a well-done job, but some projects are especially gratifying. Such was the reward that Mark Schouten and Doug TeVelde got from building a red-cedar bench on a deck overlooking the placid waters of Lake Whatcom near Bellingham, Washington. The bench was designed by David Hall.

The bench had to meet three criteria: It had to be truly comfortable; it had to survive in a damp, rainy climate; it had to complement its spectacular setting and yet blend with it.

Many wood benches are uncomfortable. They make you slouch forward, or they make you wish you could. Some benches cut you behind the knees or across the back. But this bench is made for comfort. The back leans out 10 degrees from vertical, and the seat dips in a curve about ¾ in. below horizontal—just enough to allow your back to rest naturally against the rails.

As well as making the bench comfortable, the slopes and the curves diminish the number of horizontal planes on the bench and allow few places for rainwater to collect.

Comfort that stands up to the weather. By slanting or curving most of the surfaces on this bench, the builders were able to create a seat that is truly comfortable. The slopes and the curves also eliminate horizontal planes on which standing water can collect.

To further the bench's weather resistance, the wood was spaced to allow air to circulate, and all fasteners were galvanized or made of stainless steel.

Back and Seat Supports

Before assembling the bench, all the pieces of clear red cedar used in the construction were run through a surface sander. The extra effort spent dressing the wood in the beginning saved considerable time at the end when it was time to apply the finish to the bench.

The bench frame consists of seat supports and back supports. The back supports are made of 2×4s. Before attaching them to the deck, we dadoed the supports to accept the 1×4 back rails. The back supports are canted 10 degrees from plumb and, as the drawing below shows, we cut the bottom ends of the back supports to fit against the deck frame, where two galvanized carriage bolts and a little construction adhesive hold them solid and tight. Two back supports sandwich each seat support.

The seat supports are made of 2×4s laminated with exterior urethane resin glue. To attach the seat supports to the deck, we angled 4-in. stainless-steel screws through the decking from underneath. Throughout the assembly process we tried to fasten either from underneath or on a vertical surface; our idea was to avoid areas where water could penetrate the wood through the holes made by the screws. We also wanted to avoid showing any fasteners.

We ran a horizontal 2×6 face piece around the inside perimeter of the seat. The face piece is flush with the top edge of the seat support and was beveled (on a tablesaw) to continue the curving top plane of the seat support. The face piece helps finish the

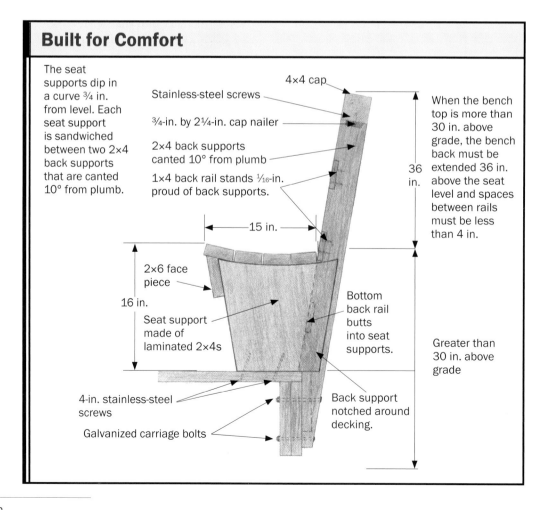

Built for Comfort

The seat supports dip in a curve ¾ in. from level. Each seat support is sandwiched between two 2×4 back supports that are canted 10° from plumb.

4×4 cap

Stainless-steel screws

¾-in. by 2¼-in. cap nailer

2×4 back supports canted 10° from plumb

1×4 back rail stands ¹⁄₁₆-in. proud of back supports.

15 in.

When the bench top is more than 30 in. above grade, the bench back must be extended 36 in. above the seat level and spaces between rails must be less than 4 in.

36 in.

2×6 face piece

16 in.

Seat support made of laminated 2×4s

Bottom back rail butts into seat supports.

Greater than 30 in. above grade

4-in. stainless-steel screws

Galvanized carriage bolts

Back support notched around decking.

The finished bench complements its spectacular setting.

design of the bench; it also supports the first row of 2×4s that make the seat.

Curves, Cants, and Compound Miters

The first row of 2×4s that make the bench's seat extends over the face piece about ½ in. The 2×4s were installed beginning at the inside edge—the edge that your knees rest against. Working toward the back rest gave us room to fasten screws into the miter joint at the bench's two inside corners. If we had started from the outside and worked inward toward the front, the previous row of mitered 2×4s would not have allowed us to fasten the next row. A good adhesive caulking seals the end grain of the miter and helps keep the joint tight.

If the seat had no curve, mitering its joints would have been a matter of cutting good, familiar 45s. But the curve demanded a compound miter, and a different one for each row—a fact that will no doubt be lost on the folks who will sit there. On the inside row, the miter must be undercut; on the second, not so much; the third is almost perpendicular; and the last miter is shorter

on the surface than on the bottom. The safest way to get the right compound cut was to use two scrap pieces of 2×4 to test the angles. You may draw like Frank Lloyd Wright and calculate like Einstein, but when it comes to making that critical cut, you'd better test first.

If you're off a bit, you can change the angle of your blade or remove some wood with a chisel or a block plane. Remember, red cedar is soft, and it's easy to overcorrect. (You know the story: Soon your board is too short, and your temper is shorter.)

The horizontal back rails are 1×4s, which were carefully let into the canted 2×4 back supports. The rails extend about ¹⁄₁₆-in. past the back supports. Because of the 10-degree angle of the back, the corner miters are compound angles, too. Construction adhesive and two nails from each direction hold the corners tight. To avoid splitting, we predrilled the corners before nailing. The mitered corners seem to hang in midair, but they are as strong as can be.

Before the rail cap was installed, a ¾-in. by 2¼ -in. cedar strip running the length of the back rest was notched flush into the top of each 2×4 back support. This strip provided a way to screw from underneath into the 4×4 cedar cap. The corners of the cap were also mitered at a compound angle very similar to the first miter of the seat.

After the cap was installed, we touched up the wood with 150-grit sandpaper. For comfort's sake, we made sure all the sharp edges of the bench were eased with sandpaper. Sanding also removes nicks and pencil lines that are unavoidable during construction. We didn't want these small imperfections to get sealed into the wood. After sanding, the bench was sealed with a semitransparent stain.

It's not often that people in our business get to build a project so perfectly suited to its location. We did our best, and the results rewarded us.

David Bright is a custom home builder in Lynden, Washington.

For comfort's sake, we made sure all the sharp edges of the bench were eased with sandpaper.

A Furniture-Grade Deck

■ BY SCOTT FLEMING

Hungry deer prowl the sunburned hills of Danville, California. When spring rolls around and flowerbeds full of tender sprouts make their annual push, the deer practically paw the ground in anticipation. But not at Steve and Celeste Butterfield's house.

On their steep hillside, the Butterfields had grown weary of feeding the deer a steady diet of pedigreed plants with Latin names. The only shrubs that the deer wouldn't eat were the ones they couldn't reach—like the ones in pots out on the decaying deck. Deer don't like stairs, or wooden floors for that matter.

Landscaping seemed like a losing proposition, so Steve and Celeste decided to put their outdoor-improvement money into replacing the old deck. They hired me to lavish attention on the new deck as though it were a piece of furniture and to make it last by avoiding the mistakes made in their original deck.

Why Decks Go Bad

The Butterfields' original deck didn't have much of a chance at longevity. Its deck boards were too close together, and the oak leaves that collected in the narrow crevices between the boards held moisture and

promoted rot. The deck's ledger was nailed directly to the plywood siding, and the lack of an airspace caused rot both in ledger and in plywood. At the butt joints between the deck boards, nails—too close to the board ends—caused splits and potentially dangerous slivers that angled upward toward oncoming feet.

At our earliest design sessions, we nailed down the important details to be included in the new deck. It would be made of the best-quality redwood that we could find, and it would be detailed to shed water and to promote ventilation. All exposed edges would be rounded to make them soft to the eye and to the touch, and all decking fasteners would be hidden from view. The railing would be unobtrusive and include a discreet lighting system. Finally, a pair of stairways to the hillside below would make for easy access to the area under the deck. With these marching orders, I set out to design and build the ultimate deck.

Following the Lay of the Land

As the defunct deck was being torn down and hauled off, Barry Pfaff and I began the layout for the new one. The old deck was 10 ft. wide, and we all agreed that a wider

With quality materials and finely detailed design elements, this multi-level deck was built to last.

A Wraparound Deck

Beginning with a basic L-shape, the author added two lower-level bump-outs to this deck to create separate sitting areas and stair landings. At 12 ft. wide, the deck is broad enough to set up dining tables and still allow comfortable circulation.

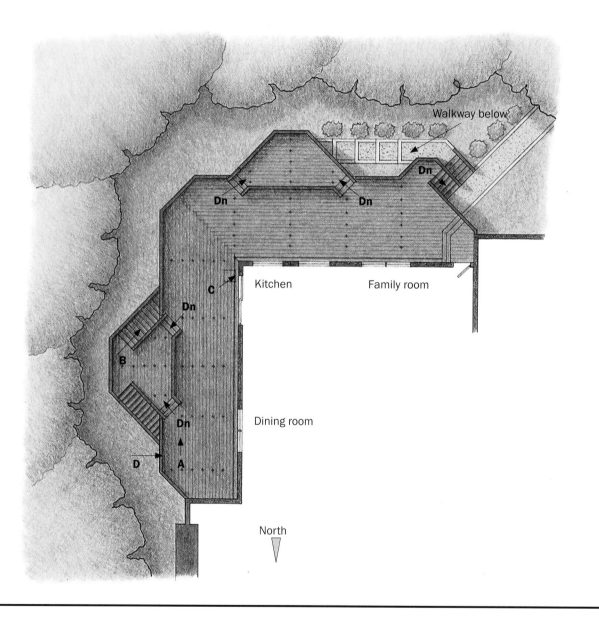

Walkway below

Dn

Dn

Dn

Kitchen

Family room

C

Dn

B

Dn

D   A

Dining room

North

deck would be a more useful deck. We settled on 12 ft., which leaves enough room to have a table and chairs on the deck with circulation space to the sides.

As shown in the drawing on the facing page, the deck wraps around two sides of the house, with a couple of triangular bays that are 20 in. below the main deck. The bays serve several functions. First, their triangular shapes are inherently strong, adding diagonal bracing to the horizontal plane of the deck. Second, we didn't want to cut any of the limbs of the splendid oaks that ring the house. By lowering the bays, we could project the deck into the treetops without pruning any limbs, which gives the bays a cozy, tree house feeling. Finally, the

bay on the east side of the house is also the landing for the two stairways that lead to grade. By code, the stairs can't have more than 18 risers in a single run. By lowering the landing, we could take the stairs down to grade in straight runs.

Don't Forget the Space under the Deck

Two conditions made it tough to get around under the original deck. A forest of posts and diagonal braces made an obstacle course out of the hillside next to the house. And the clay soil turned to grease during the rainy season. Steve and Celeste wanted an easy-to-use path under the deck. So before we got

The new deck would be made of the best-quality redwood that we could find, and it would be detailed to shed water and to promote ventilation.

Pathway as retaining wall. Stepped concrete grade beams under the deck create a terrace of steps that help stabilize the hillside. Photo taken at B on floor plan.

Hidden fasteners attach deck boards. Galvanized-steel angles affixed to the joists provide a flange for screws driven from below.

into carpentry, we did our time as concrete workers.

First we poured stepped concrete grade beams that roughly follow the perimeter of the deck. The grade beams are 4 ft. apart, and in several places they are affixed to the deck piers by tie beams. In combination with pressure-treated 2×12s, these tie beams double as risers for a path that steps down the hill in 4-ft.-sq. increments.

The walkway connects the three stair landings and the door to the utility room below the deck. We filled the path's 4-ft.-sq. cells with smooth, 2-in. blue pebbles and spread a layer of gravel on the soil underneath the deck.

Pressure-Treated Lumber Gets Special Care

We used the old concrete piers wherever possible to support the new deck. By using some 6×12s and several custom-made ⅜-in. steel brackets, we were able to pick up almost all of the loads from the new, expanded deck. Only four additional piers were required, mostly where the new deck had multiple levels.

All the new posts, beams, and joists are Douglas fir and have been treated with ACZA preservative. I guess the companies that apply the preservative to this lumber search out the lowest grades of structural material, reasoning that it will all end up out of sight someplace. Not here. We combed through the piles of treated lumber, searching with little success for straight sticks with no twist. To fix the pieces we ended up using, we had to break some new ground, prepwise. We ran pressure-treated posts and joists over a jointer. This unlikely scenario was especially important for the deck joists, which all had wicked crowns. On a job such as this, with fastidious clients who wanted straight, true lines of deck boards, there really wasn't any other way to go. We had to change knives six times before we were through jointing the stuff.

We chamfered all visible edges of the posts and recoated all the pressure-treated material with a copper-based wood preservative to even out the color. This color turned out to match the trunks of the indigenous live oak and tan oak quite nicely, so the substructure of the deck virtually disappears.

Hidden Fasteners Anchor the Decking

Back at the shop, we prepared the 6-in.-wide deck boards for installation. They are mostly 20-footers, which started out at a true, roughsawn 2-in. thickness. We surfaced them down to 1¾ in. thick and radiused their top edges with a ⅜-in. roundover bit. On site, the indefatigable Lalo Arjona cut the deck boards to length, radiused their ends, and then coated them, top and bottom, with Penofin® from Performance Coatings Inc. This preservative is specially formulated for redwood. It has some reddish pigment in it, but not enough to impart the chalky, orange color that some stains leave on redwood.

Railing Sections Include Circular Cutouts

The railing design includes a horizontal 2×6 that's halfway between the 3×6 railing cap and the deck. The 2×6 has round or oval cutouts flanking a diamond-shaped recess in the middle. Semicircular cutouts at each end create the prongs that connect to the posts. Above and below the 2×6s, a pair of 1-in. copper pipes on 4½-in. centers complete the railing.

The post-to-post distances were kept under 48 in. to minimize deflection. We cut the copper to length with a zero-hook blade on a chopsaw. Short sections of the pipe worked fine as dowels to join 2×6 railing sections with the posts.

The circular cutouts on the wooden railing sections begin on the drill press with a 2½-in. hole bored with a Forstner bit. The 1⅛-in. holes in the end grain were bored with a horizontal milling machine.

Next, a bandsaw removes the waste from the rail ends.

Short sections of copper pipe act as dowels to connect the rails with their posts.

Housing the garden hose. A wire basket topped with a trap door conceals the hose. Behind it, a band of ebonized redwood borders the deck. Photo taken at C on floor plan.

We spaced the deck boards a generous ¼ in. apart. Large gaps make it easier to keep the deck clean but can trap spike heels. (Of course, a redwood deck is not the place to wear high heels, as Steve and Celeste would be quick to point out.)

The decking is affixed to the joists from below by way of 22-in. Deckmaster deck clips. These sheet-metal clips are T-shaped in section. The top of the T is attached to the top of its joist, where it also serves as a flange for screwing the deck boards from below (see the photo on the facing page) with 1½-in. galvanized deck screws. The flanges elevate the deck boards slightly above the joists, promoting air circulation.

The deck wraps around the corner of the house in a series of herringbone steps. At this strategic corner, equidistant to both

Fabricating posts. With the post fixed at the correct angle, mortises for the 1-in. copper pipe rails were bored with a 1⅛-in. Forstner bit.

ends of the deck, we placed a basket covered by a trap door to house a length of garden hose (see the bottom photo on p. 163).

One deck board out from the house, a band of ebonized redwood borders the edge of the deck. The strong line established by the ebonized strip draws your attention away from the tapered deck board next to it, made necessary by the out-of-square corner of the house. Incidentally, ebonized wood has simply been coated with black stain.

Ebonized redwood diamonds add another decorative touch to the deck. They are ¾ in. thick, and they are held in place by a single plugged screw. The diamonds occur over joists, between deck boards to ensure good drainage. After the deck boards had been installed, we cut the recesses for the diamonds with a bearing-guided router following a pattern clamped to the deck.

Low-Voltage Wiring Is Concealed in the Railings

There are 108 posts in the railing of this deck, and each one has a minimum of six holes drilled in it for bolts and for the 1-in. copper pipes that serve as railings. To ensure accuracy and to speed things up as much as possible, all the holes were bored in the shop using a drill press fitted with a fixture to hold the posts in the right place (see the photo above).

At less than 4 ft., the 1-in. copper pipe is plenty sturdy to be a railing on a deck. It is also light, durable, splinter-free, and easy to install. And although gaudy in its initial brightness, the copper rails slowly oxidize to a soft reddish brown that is compatible with redwood. The copper rails barely affect the view on this deck, and they are maintenance free.

Curved posts meet straight stairs. Held together by dovetailed splines, curvy posts made of three sections of 4×4 anchor the balustrade at stair landings. The posts nest in shallow mortises in the underside of the cap rail. Photo taken at D on floor plan.

The copper pipe also serves as a conduit for a 12V lighting system. A 700W transformer in the utility room powers 40 lamps, 30 of which illuminate the deck and stairs. The remaining 10 are on the walkway below. We pulled the wires for the lighting as we assembled the railing section by section, drilling out the posts in the appropriate spots for the lamps.

The Railings End at Curvy Posts

On your basic California deck, a 2×6 cap rail covers 4×4 posts. Cap sections abut atop the posts, where they are nailed into the end grain of the posts. After a couple of seasons in the sun and rain, the cap rails split around the nails. It's ugly.

On the Butterfields' deck, the cap-rail sections meet in midair between posts that are 4 in. apart. They are held together by dovetailed splines made of Honduras mahogany that were soaked in Penofin until they were slippery enough to drive into their dovetailed slots. The rails end at the stairs, where built-up posts of 4×4s flair out, Deco style, to catch the ends of the cap rails.

By the way, a deck like this needs regular maintenance. The Butterfields give it an annual coat of Penofin for protection from the sun and rain. When we started, Penofin still contained VOC solvents, which have now been outlawed by California's air-quality laws. The new formulation, according to Steve and Celeste, seems to work just as well as the old one.

Scott Fleming is a builder/designer who lives in Honolulu, Hawaii, and owns Sansea Design/Consulting.

A Balcony Deck Built to Last

■ BY MICHAEL MAINES

If decks and patios are outdoor living rooms, balcony decks are more like small, private nooks. Just because they're little, though, doesn't make them simple. The fact that balconies don't touch the ground makes them complex and challenging to build. The balcony featured here faces the ocean, which adds another design challenge: stability and durability in the face of hurricane-force winds. In fact, while we were running exterior trim on this house in Maine, two nearby houses were swept off their foundations and into the ocean during a severe storm.

You can support a balcony by using wooden knee braces angled back to the house or by cantilevering the interior floor joists through the wall. The problem with the former method is that wood-to-wood structural connections are rot-prone. The problem with the latter method is that it eventually channels rot into the house.

This railing won't hide the view. As a finishing touch to a bedroom hideaway, this cable railing is strong and durable. Because it's see-through, it won't spoil the view.

Welded Stainless-Steel Connectors Anchor the Deck to the House

For this project, we decided that the best way to support the balcony was to create a sturdy pressure-treated wood frame that later would be wrapped in PVC trim. An architect in our office consulted with a structural engineer for a plan that would support the necessary loads, be assembled easily, and show off nice proportions.

We used custom-made stainless-steel framing connectors to reinforce the major bracket-and-beam assembly and to tie it to the house framing. It's important to use stainless-steel fasteners on the coast, but it's even more critical when working with ACQ pressure-treated lumber, which is highly corrosive to plain and galvanized steel.

The metal framing connectors were all TIG-welded by a certified welder using 304 stainless steel, which is strong, corrosion-resistant, and easily obtainable. The brackets are strong and durable, but expensive: around $1,500 for the set.

I wanted to through-bolt the brackets to a built-up post inside the wall, but our engineer calculated that more support was needed. For the lower connector, he specified a steel fin that would run through

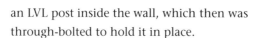

Framing members are cut to fit steel connectors. Sawkerfs are made with a circular saw, then cleaned out with a jigsaw so that the posts and ledger can slip over steel flanges and be bolted in place. The ledger and framing-connector posts are lag-screwed to solid-wall framing.

Concealed beneath decorative trim boards and rot-resistant framing lumber, custom-made stainless-steel connectors reinforce a pair of knee braces that support the deck and also anchor the framing to the house.

an LVL post inside the wall, which then was through-bolted to hold it in place.

Because we didn't have access to a timber framer's chain mortiser, the best way for us to make the slot for the lower connector's fin was to start the cut with a circular saw, then plunge-cut it with a chainsaw. Fortunately, the chain's thickness matched well with the fin's thickness. The most complicated framing connector is the top one. It connects the deck's horizontal and vertical framing members, and also has the job of keeping the balcony from pulling off the wall. If you imagine the bottom connector acting as a hinge, then the top one could be imagined as a latch.

Most decks are simply bolted to the rim joists of the house, but our deck could easily pull the OSB rim joist on our I-joist floor right out of the house. We could have added floor framing to fasten the connector to, but by the time this detail was figured out, the floor had been framed

Are the Hidden Heroes of This Balcony

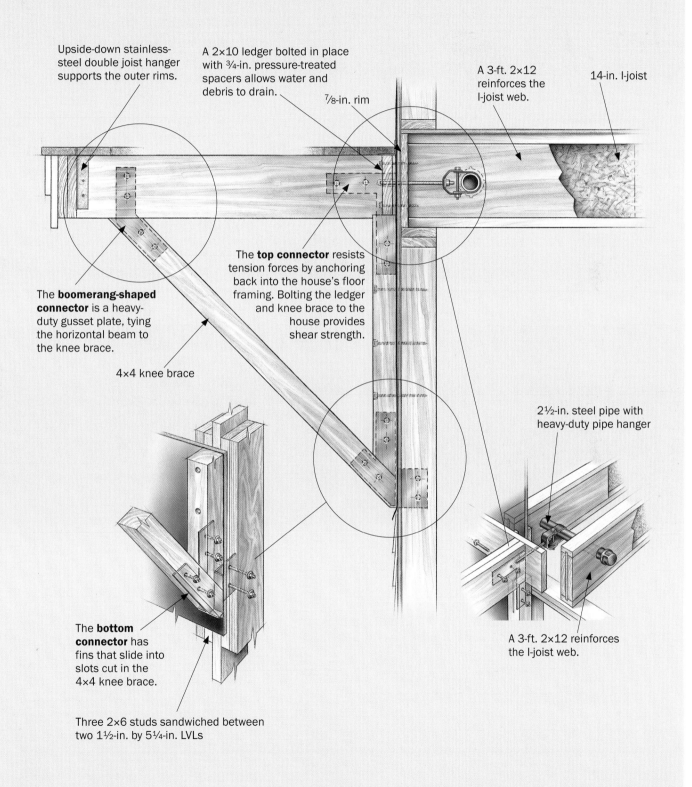

Upside-down stainless-steel double joist hanger supports the outer rims.

A 2×10 ledger bolted in place with ¾-in. pressure-treated spacers allows water and debris to drain.

⅞-in. rim

A 3-ft. 2×12 reinforces the I-joist web.

14-in. I-joist

The **boomerang-shaped connector** is a heavy-duty gusset plate, tying the horizontal beam to the knee brace.

The **top connector** resists tension forces by anchoring back into the house's floor framing. Bolting the ledger and knee brace to the house provides shear strength.

4×4 knee brace

2½-in. steel pipe with heavy-duty pipe hanger

The **bottom connector** has fins that slide into slots cut in the 4×4 knee brace.

A 3-ft. 2×12 reinforces the I-joist web.

Three 2×6 studs sandwiched between two 1½-in. by 5¼-in. LVLs

Framing Details Make a Bombproof Deck That Won't Rot

The materials and construction details have to protect this deck from hurricanes, windblown rain, and the risk of corrosion from being in a coastal location.

1. Spacers keep the ledger off the house, allowing water to drain away.

2. Diagonal blocking acts as a sway brace to solidify the deck in high winds.

3. Lead flashing directs water away from the upright post. Drain holes in the bottom of the posts allow water to escape if it finds a way in.

4. Gaps between doubled framing members allow water to drain through.

5. All framing connectors and fasteners are stainless steel for corrosion resistance.

and sheathed. Our engineer came up with a simple, cost-effective solution. With construction adhesive and nails, we scabbed 3 ft. of solid 2×2s to the webs of the I-joists, drilled through the ones adjacent to the connectors, and slipped 2½-in.-dia. steel pipe through the joists. As shown in the drawing on p. 169, we attached a heavy-duty pipe hanger, or stirrup, to the pipe, and we used a length of ½-in. threaded rod and a coupler to connect with the stainless-steel threaded rod that was welded to the framing connector.

Plan the Framing to Promote Drying

Another common weak spot in deck framing occurs when framing members are sandwiched together to create a built-up beam. Pressure-treated lumber can last for 20 years or more, but with good detailing, it can last a lot longer. The gap between deck boards lets in water, dirt, and other debris. That debris collects in the seam between framing members, eventually weakening the wood. I plan my decks with gaps between doubled members and easy pathways for water to drain.

The doubled 2×10s making up the balcony's horizontal beams are spaced the thickness of the steel framing connectors sandwiched between them. Two beams that extend from the upper framing connectors support an outer doubled beam, which is secured with upside-down stainless-steel joist hangers. This outer beam doesn't need to be spaced because it is covered by synthetic decking, which keeps water and debris out of the joint. The deck's floor joists are supported between the outer beam and the ledger with normally oriented stainless-steel joist hangers.

The ledger is connected to the house with stainless-steel through bolts and ¾-in. pressure-treated spacers behind the ledger to allow water and debris to drain.

Working with Plastic Trim

While plastic trim takes paint well and won't rot, there are some nuances to working with it. We have a love/hate relationship with this stuff: We hate the drawbacks, but we love the way our exterior-trim details look.

Don't back-bevel the miter joints. Because you need a solid gluing surface for the joints, you can't cut miters at 46 degrees rather than 45 degrees as you can with wood. The joints have to be perfect so that they can provide a big glue surface for when the Azek moves in response to temperature changes.

Support the stock. PVC is easy to bend, so it's easy to work with for curves. But it's also a pain in the neck. Tablesaws need long infeed and outfeed tables, miter saws need long extension wings, and carrying long pieces can be a two-person job.

Cut long. These plastic trim boards contract in the cold and expand when it's hot, so cut accordingly. In winter, we add between ⅛ in. and ¼ in. to the overall length, depending on temperature. In summer, we cut to the measured length or add just 1/16 in.

Durable Trim Dresses Up the Structure

The preassembled posts go up first

Furring strips flank these posts to keep the width consistent. The edges are mitered to accept the face, which is applied next (photo 1). We make a trammel out of a couple of strips of sheathing to cut a pattern for the sides of the curved knee braces (photo 2). With a bearing-guided router bit, we cut all the sides (photo 3). Each side has to be fine-tuned to fit perfectly (photo 4). When the sides fit perfectly, we assemble the curved knee braces. PVC trim makes this easy because it's so flexible (photo 5).

Plastic trim holds paint well and stands up to the salt air. We preassemble the trim boxes as much as possible, then fine-tune their fit. We apply the upright posts before installing the ceiling; then we fit the knee braces.

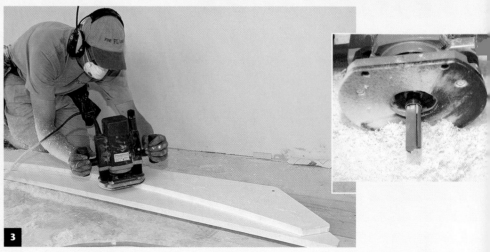

Details make the difference. We glue miter joints to minimize the effect of shrinkage in composite decking. We also like to round over the end cuts on deck boards to match the radius of their sides. The only visible fasteners are those securing the outer frame. The EB-TY hidden-fastener system uses plastic biscuits that fit into a slot along the length of the deck boards.

Over time, connections could loosen as the deck sways from high winds and heavy usage. To prevent this, we installed diagonal sway blocking into the floor system. In the rush of framing, we nearly forgot to add blocking for the top-mounted posts for the railing system.

The Materials Look Good and Last

We decided to use PVC trim for its low-maintenance features and because it would be easy to form to a curve on the bottom side of the knee braces. The homeowner also wanted synthetic decking for low maintenance and good looks. We used Trex Brasilia decking (www.trex.com) for its rich color and realistic grain pattern.

Because this balcony offers an ocean view from the master bedroom, we didn't want to use a clunky railing. We settled on a Feeney cable-rail system (www.cablerail.com). Feeney offers powder-coated heavy-duty aluminum posts and rails that work together as a system, and they also have pretty good technical support for optimizing the design. The system went together without a hitch.

Assemble the Trim Ahead of Time

Working high in the air—or even a few feet above a deck, as we were here—is never as efficient as working at bench height. We assembled as many of the trim components as we could on the ground. The vertical posts were wrapped and capped with a PVC "box." The corners were mitered and the three pieces assembled with Azek glue (PVC cement specially made for Azek trim; www.azek.com) and stainless-steel screws. We have tried regular plumbers' PVC cement, but the set time is too quick for us.

After the last two pieces of the upright were glued and screwed and the floor framing wrapped with a fascia, we installed the ceiling boards under the balcony. We wanted to hide the framing but allow water and debris to drain through, so we spaced the chamfered 1×6 PVC boards about ⅜ in. apart. After the ceiling was up, we wrapped the brackets by assembling three sides of the curved brace. We made a pattern for the side of the curved brace using a router with a trammel arm, then used the pattern with a flush-trim bit to make the remaining sides.

It was more complicated than the average deck, but this balcony does its job well. It provides a place to watch the sunrise over the ocean, it looks like it belongs on the house, and it won't require much effort to keep looking good. Most important, it is never going anywhere.

Michael Maines designs, builds, and remodels homes (and balconies) along the Maine coast (Harborside Design, Freeport, Maine, www.harborsidedesign.com).

An Elegant Border for Your Deck

■ BY JOHN MICHAEL DAVIS

There are a lot of parts in a deck, but in the end, it's the decking that everyone notices. One thing I've learned building decks in New Orleans's brutal climate is that of all a deck's parts, the decking also takes the most serious beating.

My default method for fastening deck boards is to use stainless-steel screws run in such dead-straight lines that they become part of the design. On this project, however, the homeowners wanted ipé decking, so I decided to upgrade to a hidden fastening system to showcase the wood. I speculated that the time and material expense for using hidden fasteners would not be much costlier or labor intensive than screws.

At the time, everything I knew about hidden fasteners came from a *Fine Homebuilding* article (see "Deck Fastener Options" on p. 54). I remember being impressed by the EB-TY system (www.ebty.com), so I decided to give it a try on this project.

EB-TY fasteners come in different sizes for various thicknesses and types of decking. Here, I used the EBE004, which has a built-in spacer of 3/32 in. and is specified for the 5/4 ipé I was installing. I made some jigs and took a production-minded approach to installation that kept labor time similar to screwing down the boards. The EB-TY system cost about twice what screws would have, but to me, it's a good value. There are no fasteners visible, so the deck looks clean and elegant. Also, the top surface remains unbroken, which makes for a more durable board.

Use Butt Joints Outside

During the design, I decided to wrap the rim joists with a 1×10 pressure-treated clear-and-better southern-yellow-pine fascia board. Given the anatomy of this deck, I knew that some lags, screws, and nails would be visible in various places around the rim joist.

Because I would need to use stainless-steel fasteners and take extra time installing them so that they looked like part of the design, a fascia board that would hide the fasteners seemed like a logical option. This tack turned out to be of dubious economic value when compared with the price of stainless-steel fasteners, but it does dress things up.

I also decided to create a border with three courses of deck boards. Framing the perimeter with a border isn't a new concept, but corners are typically done with mitered joints. In my experience, mitered joints in exterior applications don't fare well. Wood moves across the grain, so miters are prone to opening. I was wary of this fact even with ipé, which doesn't move much, and especially with the southern-yellow-pine 1× fascia.

With wood movement in mind, I stuck to square cuts and butt joints for the decking and the fascia. I ran the border around a field of deck boards and, instead of miters, made a herringbone design in the corners. The fascia boards die into corner blocks, which I incorporated into the design (see the drawing on p. 178).

Clean, Shape, and Seal Every Board

Although the ipé showed up on the job site in good condition, I took the time to clean and dress up the boards. After choosing the best side, I sanded it lightly with 80-grit paper on a random-orbit sander to remove surface flaws. Next, I put a ¼-in. radius on the two top edges with a roundover bit and router. Later, when the boards were cut to length, I rounded over the ends, too.

Once the boards were prepped, I cleaned them with naphtha, then laid them out across the joists, where I applied a coat of Flood's CWF-UV Clear Wood Finish (www. flood.com) to the tops. This brought out the wood's true glow. Once the deck was complete, I applied a second coat for further protection.

The dense ipé soaked up the sealer in varying amounts, which left some boards darker than others. I sorted the boards into a pleasing arrangement, taking into account grain pattern and direction, and placed the most beautiful boards where they would be most visible. Then I numbered each for sequence on the bottom and drew an arrow for direction.

Start with the Border

This deck is fairly large, about 17 ft. wide by 15 ft. deep, and is broken up into three sections. I treated each section separately, starting with the first course of border boards, then the second, then the third. Once the border was established for each section, I filled in the field boards, working from one side of the deck to the other.

The key when laying the border was to establish a square corner. If I had been using screws and plugs to start the border, this process would have been tedious. But I used biscuits, so I was able to rely on the groove they run in (see the inset drawing on p. 178). The groove parallels the edge of the deck board and locks into the fascia, which is attached directly to the square framing.

The Border Starts with Two Boards in One Square Corner

Three courses of deck boards weave together in the corners to form the herringbone pattern. Boards are held in place by EB-TY fasteners, which fit into slots and attach to the joists. Blocking beneath the joints supports the pattern and fasteners. The perimeter boards get two grooves (see the inset drawing below). The inner groove receives biscuits that run along the fascia and help to start things off square. The outer groove acts as a drip edge to keep water out of the biscuited joint. Fascia boards terminate into corner blocks in lieu of miter joints.

Biscuits replace screws. Instead of using screws and plugs through the face of the perimeter boards, the author chose to biscuit them to the fascia. Run the starter board long; it will be cut after the field is laid. Dry-fit the starter board with the biscuits in place. After applying glue to the biscuit slots, the biscuits, and the groove, reapply the board and clamp it in place.

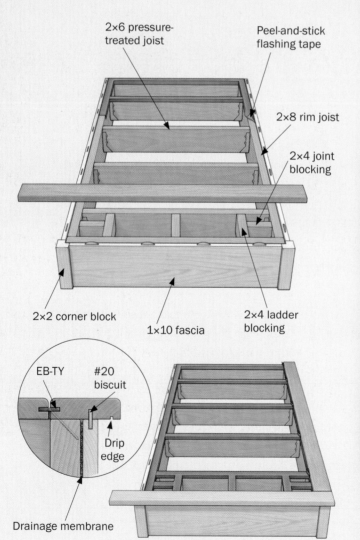

2×6 pressure-treated joist

Peel-and-stick flashing tape

2×8 rim joist

2×4 joint blocking

2×2 corner block

1×10 fascia

2×4 ladder blocking

EB-TY   #20 biscuit

Drip edge

Drainage membrane

Slot the first board in place. After gluing and clamping the first board, determine where the second board will intersect and where the third board will end. Cut the slots using a router outfitted with a slot-cutting bit. Bending over the board to make a cut like this is dangerous, so use caution. Using a biscuit joiner before the board is installed is another option.

The perimeter also had to be established first to determine the length of the field boards, so I completed a corner with all three courses. This corner became a reference point for determining the length of the field boards. I cut them all to the same length so that each would hang over the rear rim joist equally.

Lay the Field Production Style

Installing the corner boards took some time. I glued and clamped the outer boards, then cut the EB-TY slots in place with a router. Then I dry-fit the next two courses, marked the joist layout directly on them, and cut the slots. This was the best way to make sure I got the herringbone corner joints exactly where I wanted them. There were more than 1,000 slots to cut in the field boards, though, which could have been a daunting task. So I built a site-made slot-cutting jig with the materials I had on hand (see the photo at right).

The two boards that were to be laid last became the base for the jig. A stop block screwed into one end aligned each board to layout lines marked on the jig's base. Then I placed the first board upside down on top of the fixture boards and locked it in place with cleats. Now it was merely a matter of placing each board in the fixture in the correct direction and sighting the layout lines with the biscuit joiner, which made a tedious task fast, accurate, and easy.

Finally, I found out quickly that it was easier and faster to do everything I could while the boards were in the fixture. Therefore, once the slots were cut, I installed the EB-TYs and drilled pilot holes for the screws. Drilling pilot holes is mandatory with ipé and a good idea with pine. The self-drilling screw tips might let you slide when using pine, but the screw would probably run with the grain in some spots, causing splits.

John Michael Davis is a restoration carpenter in New Orleans.

Fastener Feedback

An EB-TY, which looks like a plastic biscuit with legs, slips into a slot cut in the edge of the board directly over each joist. The legs, or splines, hold the fastener off the joist and create a $3/32$-in. gap between deck boards (other sizes are available for 2× decking). A stainless-steel trim-head screw goes through the EB-TY and deck board at a 45-degree angle into the joist.

- While I erred on the side of "dead-on" when aligning the slot center with the joist center, I learned quickly that there is about $3/8$ in. of wiggle room from side to side.

- The EB-TY itself has about the same amount of built-in "slop" in the slot as a wooden biscuit, which gives you a slight amount of additional play. I figure that just sighting the jig's layout lines with the joiner, rather than marking the board for every slot, produced around a plus or minus tolerance of $1/8$ in., which is fine if everything else is also that close.

- Once fastened, the EB-TYs were pleasantly forgiving when accepting the next board's slot. It is possible to torque the outer flange over by cinching down too much on the screw. But I quickly got a feel for just right by putting a finger under the flange as I drove in the screw. There was also a slight click when the screwhead seated into the EB-TY's hole.

- Once I figured out the jig arrangement for cutting slots, the process went quickly, considering the huge amount of repetitive motion. I appreciated that the gap spacing is automatically built into the system, which helped both in consistency and in labor time savings.

- The $3/32$-in. gap between boards is too narrow to be practical; it won't let plant debris fall through. But much of this deck is covered, so the gap seemed acceptable.

Finish the Corner, and Fill the Field

Cut all field boards, then install them production style.

Move from the corner out. Once the first herringbone corner is complete, install the field. Cut the field boards the same size and use a biscuit joiner to slot both edges of the board at each joist location. Each board interlocks with the previous one. Move in this fashion until there are only three boards left to install.

Cut, Slot, and Weave to Finish

Cut the front boards in place. Before installing the last two boards, cut the innermost border board in line with the edge of the last field board. Start the cut with a circular saw, ideally a 4½-in. trim saw. Trim saws are easier to control and create a thinner kerf. Fein's® Multi-Master (below left) is the best tool for finishing the cut because its flush cut blade eliminates the possibility of cutting into the next board. It's also possible to use a jigsaw outfitted with a short blade, a Japanese finishing saw, or a sharp chisel. Ease the edge of the cut end with a ¼-in. roundover bit, then slot the end and its mating board to receive an EB-TY. Slot only one edge on the last board; then glue, biscuit, and clamp it in place.

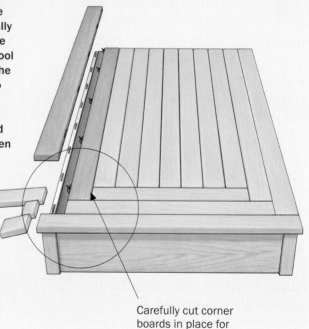

Carefully cut corner boards in place for precise reveals.

A Grade-A Deck

■ BY SCOTT GRICE

My clients were frustrated with their house, a 1960s-style ranch that had just been renovated. Once this long process was over, they quickly realized two things: First, having the kids play outside meant that a little bit of yard rode in on their feet every time they entered the house (this is Portland, Ore.); and second, the two doors opening to the backyard weren't leading to a welcoming destination.

Even when the renovation got under way, there had been talk of a deck in the backyard, but those discussions were sidelined in the push to get back into the house. Now the homeowners knew they needed to structure the yard both to mitigate the dirt entering the house and to create an inviting outdoor space. Because I had done the

renovation, I had a good sense of both the house and their needs. Dirt mitigation is easy enough, but "inviting" provided more of a challenge.

I ended up building a long wraparound deck positioned to catch the most sun on this forested site. The largest section adjoins the public part of the house, with a smaller platform off the master bedroom. The two sections are connected by a narrower strip of decking that runs along the side of the bedroom wing.

One Deck with Multiple Details

Linking the two sections gave me the opportunity to build in a few features that would

make this simple, on-grade deck stand out. To start, I wanted a picture-frame border. Picture-framing is a clean way of hiding the visible ends of the deck boards by running a long deck board perpendicular to those ends, giving them something to die into. Because the deck turns a corner and wraps partway around the house, I faced having a field of deck boards running at right angles to each other. This would be a perfect spot to run a herringbone weave; 45-degree miters only open over time, and having a stark junction of perpendicular boards interrupts the flow of a deck.

The homeowners also requested an opening with removable panels in the deck to accommodate a small tree. Because this tree was to be installed after I completed the project, I had to frame the opening in a way that would support removable deck panels that went around the tree and also would allow the landscapers to remove enough of the deck frame so that they could plant the tree.

Although the appeal of each of these features is primarily visual, modifying the framing is the first step in constructing each of them, and what I'll focus on here.

Scott Grice *is a builder in Portland, Oregon.*

Solutions for Tight Spots

The Lowdown on Working on Grade

The house sits low to the ground. I had about 14 in. from the ground to the kitchen door's threshold and 12 in. at the family-room door. That left enough room to bring the top of the deck in just under the house's cedar skirtboard. I planned to have a ledger to pick up the deck's load at the house and to run beams to carry the leading edge of the deck.

I cut spacers from ¾-in. pressure-treated plywood to allow drainage between the ledger and the foundation. Before installing the ledger boards, I cut them to length, tacked them in place with regular concrete screws, and temporarily placed the 4×8 beams that would carry the other end of the deck. I strung lines around the deck's perimeter and marked the footings.

Once the footing holes were dug, I cut the beams to length. I then temporarily placed the first beam and determined the joist layout. Because the deck sat so low to the ground, I took the ledger down and attached all the hangers for the joists with the ledger boards and beams on sawhorses. With the hardware installed, I bolted the ledger boards to the foundation with ⅝-in. by 6-in. concrete lag bolts (see the inset photo on the facing page), then set the beams.

With the deck so close to the ground, the beams sat right in the post bases. I put the bases on the beam first and then, using a stringline, a laser level, and some stakes, set the beams for final placement. With the beams in place, I filled the footings. While the concrete cured, I measured and cut the joists, returning the next day to install them.

Held fast. The ledger boards are bolted to the foundation. Angle-top spacers allow drainage and prevent rot.

Although most of the joist system was straightforward, I made slight modifications for the picture-frame border. When creating this type of border, I find it's a good idea to leave a drainage gap in the framing below the line where the deck boards meet the border so that water won't pool there. The framing also has to provide enough support to the border, which cantilevers off the edge of the deck by 1¼ in.

My answer was a triple 2×8 joist with ¾-in. shims (angled on top so that water will shed off them) placed between the second and third 2×8s (photo 1).

The double joist sits under the border. The single joist catches the end of the deck boards dying into the border, and the spacers allow water to drain. I left the rim board of this tripler long so that I could through-screw it into the end beam (photo 2).

Installing the frame boards requires marking where the board will sit on the structure, snapping that line, and face-screwing the piece to the line. Hidden fasteners can't be used here because the boards sit over a 4×8 beam. Because I didn't want the screws visible, I used a ¼-in. Forstner bit to recess the screw 5/16 in. so that I could fill the hole later with an ipé plug. After making the hole for the future plug, I drilled pilot holes and then used stainless-steel trim-head screws to fasten the board in place.

Because frame boards overhang the deck's skirtboard, the board can move a bit to remain parallel to the house or to true up a corner. With the frame boards in place, the field boards could be cut and installed. Before I did that, though, I put a ⅛-in. roundover bit in my router and used it on the cut ends of the deck boards to give them a more finished look (photo 3).

When Hardwood Meets Hidden Fasteners

For this deck, I used Deckmaster hidden fasteners. I've tried several hidden-fastener systems, but none has performed as well as Deckmaster. Ipé is a strong wood, and if it decides to move—which some ipé deck boards do—I have found that screws are the only things that hold fast.

Ipé is beautiful wood, but it is rarely straight and is difficult to make straight. Before installation, I take some scrap ipé and cut a bunch of shims the thickness of the gaps between the deck boards. I cut a lot and all at the same time for consistency. With my bag of shims and sized deck boards, I begin installation. As indicated in the photo below, I use pipe clamps to get the board where I want it; then I use two drills, one to make a pilot hole, the other to install the screws. Here's more on the challenges of working with ipé and hidden-fastener systems.

Mounting the hardware is the easy part. Deckmaster brackets mount on alternate sides of the joist. Having the ends overlap slightly ensures that a bracket is always available.

Pipe-clamp persuasion. Deck boards are rarely perfectly straight, and ipé is no different. The difference is how much force you need to straighten them. Use bar clamps: They can span almost any distance, allow a great deal of precision, and by reversing the heads can be made to push instead of pull. Use scraps or spacers to maintain a uniform gap.

Ipé needs pilot holes. Use a drill bit slightly smaller than the diameter of the screw. Use a stop collar to prevent drilling all the way through the deck board. Many drills now come equipped with headlights, which are helpful for this type of work.

Bad for the back. Be forewarned: While this system is easy to install on the joists, installing the screws through the brackets and into the bottom of the boards when the only access is from above will have deleterious effects on knees and backs.

Crafting a Herringbone Corner

Because the deck turns a corner and wraps partway around the house, I faced having a field of deck boards running at right angles to each other—a perfect spot for a herringbone weave. This, too, required a minor alteration to the framing: To support the corner, I had to run a double joist at a 45-degree angle into that corner (see the top photo below). This allowed me to keep my regular joist layout and catch the ends of the boards where they meet together in the weave. The double joist consists of two 2×8s with ¾-in. spacers sandwiched between.

With the boundaries of the herringbone set, I measured all the boards in the corner and cut and detailed the ends. I then used spacers to lay them all in place to see if any adjustments were necessary to make the deck boards parallel to the house (see the bottom photo below).

Everything was square in this case, but had the corner been slightly off, I've found that playing with the reveal between the boards will erase most discrepancies. Once I knew that the layout worked, I started with the longest board and worked my way to the corner.

Turning a corner. The finished weave lets the deck turn the inside corner without interrupting the flow.

Frame the opening

My approach to building the removable panels to accommodate the small tree my clients wanted to plant in the corner of their deck was basically the same as my approach to the picture-frame border. Like the border, the deck boards would die into the frame of the panels.

I used normal joist layout to determine one side of the box. From there, I laid out the dimensions of the box on the surrounding joists and built the frame of the box.

The side and header joists have to carry extra weight, so they are doubled.

I also extended the ledger board to the header to help tie everything together. I built triplers to support the panels and to allow for drainage. In this case, I left the framing loose in the hangers so that the landscapers could remove the framing when it came time to plant the tree.

I ran the deck boards around the box so that I could be certain that the layout of the boards in the panels matched the layout of the surrounding deck, and that I would have only full boards in the panels, not ripped pieces.

Tie one header into the ledger.

Double the side and header joists.

Set removable supports.

Shop-built panels are detailed and fitted on-site

I built the removable panels in my shop. The two panels were actually built as one unit and then cut down the middle to form the two units. This helps to ensure that everything is aligned.

I started by using a compass to mark the hole for the tree. Then I cut the two side rails and clamped them in position on my workbench. I then measured and cut the infill pieces.

Using spacers and clamps, I laid out the whole thing face down. Once it was laid out, I marked where I wanted to cut the dadoes for the 3/8-in. by 3/4-in. ipé stretchers that hold the panels together.

With everything marked, I cut the grooves and dadoes on a tablesaw, put the whole puzzle together again, then glued and screwed the stretchers in place. After the glue dried, I cut the panel in two and used a jigsaw to trim the middle stretcher flush with the

panel's edge. Later, on the deck, I used a router with a roundover bit to put the finishing touches on the tree hole.

The finished panels have framing support on all sides except where they meet in the middle. Where the two panels meet, I screwed a 1×2 on the bottom side of one panel to support the other panel.

Mark center hole for tree trunk.

Use spacers to lay out panels.

Glue stretchers in place.

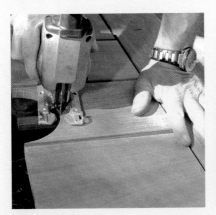

Trim middle stretchers.

Finish edges of panels.

Attach center supports.

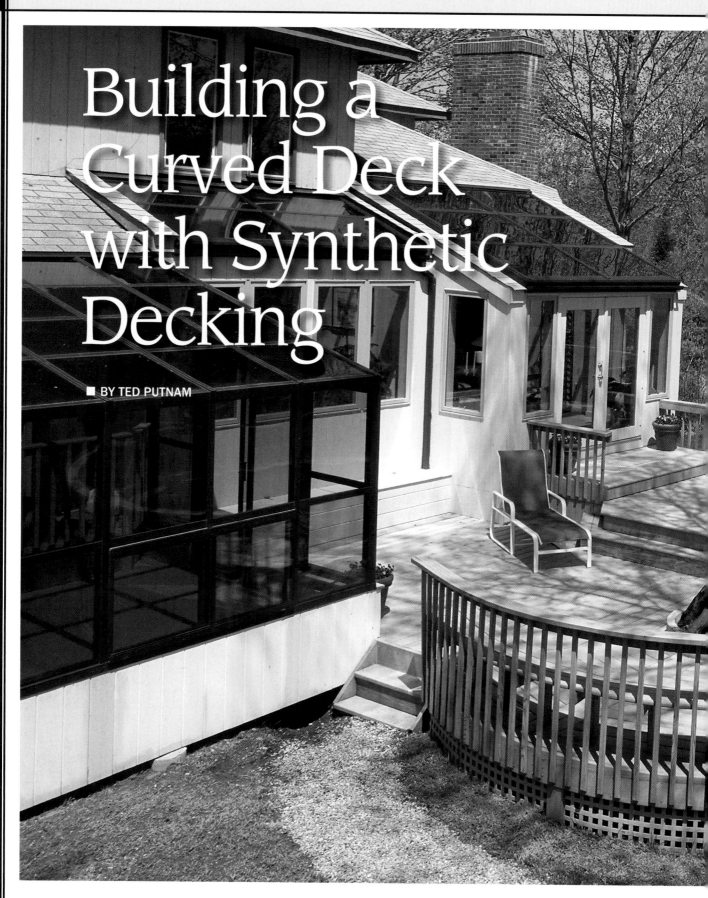

Building a Curved Deck with Synthetic Decking

■ BY TED PUTNAM

Prebending synthetic decking can be as easy as walking. Because Trex is made from a composite of high-density polyethelyne and wood chips, it has little lateral stiffness and can be bent easily. Once bent, the material keeps its shape for some time without reinforcement.

Curved Decks Start with a Rectangle

I framed this curved deck as I do many rectangular decks, with several doubled 2×8 beams to support the 16-in. on-center joists. However, I let all the joists run beyond the beams to extend past the perimeter of the finished deck (see the photo on the facing page).

With the joists run long, I was ready to lay out the circles with a rudimentary trammel. I tacked a piece of ¾-in. plywood roughly in the center of the joists on the upper deck and then measured and marked the exact center of a circle on the plywood. My trammel consisted of a 1×3 with a nail in one end, which was driven into the plywood at the centerpoint. I then cut the 1×3 to the circle's radius minus 3⅜ in. (1½ in. for the skirtboard, ⅜ in. for the lattice, and 1½ in. for the plywood band joist).

I pressed a fine-point felt-tip pen against the end of the trammel and swung it over the tops of the joists to mark the curve. Using a framing square, I transferred plumb lines to the joists and cut the joists 2 in. to 3 in. beyond the line.

To make the curved blocking that would support the plywood band joist, I trimmed the joist offcuts to fit between the joists. After nailing the blocking flush to the top, I redrew the arc and cut to the line with a circular saw (see the top photo on p. 194). The blocking for the bottom was traced from the top blocking, cut, and nailed into place flush with the bottom of the joists and the plumb line. I then trimmed the joist ends flush with a reciprocating saw.

To make the band joist, I ripped ½-in. pressure-treated CDX plywood into 7½-in.-wide strips and laminated three layers together across the joist ends. I clamped one end to the starting point and slowly began to glue, clamp, and nail, using construction adhesive and 8d hot-dipped galvanized box nails (see the bottom right photo on p. 194). I was generous with the glue and let the

I don't often get to build a curved deck, so when my clients asked for a deck to take advantage of the views across the salt marsh and estuary in their backyard, I suggested a stacked semicircular creation with a bricked fire pit on the lower level. Although I used pressure-treated material for the framing, wooden lumber on other parts of the deck would have required steam-bending for the curves. Instead, I chose Trex (www.trex.com), a wood-polymer decking, because it bends easily and stands up well to salty air and harsh winters.

A Barbecue Pit Requires Innovation

The ledgers, piers, and posts were straight-forward, but figuring out a way to support the raised fire pit was trickier. I ended up purchasing a 42-in.-dia. wire-mesh reinforced-concrete tube (normally used to house utilities underground) and setting it on a concrete footing. Filled with rubble and concrete, the tower supports a shallow pit lined with firebrick.

ends of the plywood fall without regard to the joist ends. However, I was careful to stagger the joints on each layer. When the band-joist lamination was complete, I cut the doubled 2×8 support beams flush with the plywood.

The lower-deck framing was identical to its upper neighbor with one exception: The curving band joist would run parallel to the framing along one side of the deck and would not be supported by the joists. Rather than fill in the void with short blocks, I nailed a length of pressure-treated 2×8 horizontally to the top of the last joist (see the bottom left photo on p. 194). After scribing and cutting the arc, I traced it onto a second piece of pressure-treated 2×8 that would serve as bottom blocking. The plywood band joist secures the blocking, and vice versa.

Bending Composites Is a Breeze

The skirtboard is 2×10 Trex. (Trex now makes very pliable 1×12 and 1×8 boards for this purpose.) Bending the 2×10 (see the photo on the facing page) was a cinch after leaving the board in the sun for a few hours.

I've found through experience that scribe-fitting the decking to the rim yields a more precise joint than installing the decking first. Scrap 5/4 decking established the height of the skirtboard above the rim, and with a helper, I screwed the skirtboard to the band joist. Joints were glued with PVC cement, and gaps were filled with a mixture of PVC cement and sawdust.

Dramatic shapes begin with a straightforward frame. To build a two-level curved deck, the author framed a large rectangle and let the joists extend beyond the deck's outline (above) so that he could cut the joists' curves and blocking at once. Trex decking, a composite of recycled polyethylene and wood, bends easily (facing page), so it's a good choice for curved decks.

Curved Deck Framing

Blocking makes it rigid. Blocking between the joists is nailed to the top of the joists first and then cut to the line. The upper blocking serves as a template for the lower pieces and is positioned tight to the plumb line. A reciprocating saw completes the plumb cut started with a circular saw.

Creative blocking strengthens the lower deck. Where the curve runs parallel to the joists, the author nailed a 2×8 to the top of the joist. A 1×3 trammel traced the curve onto the blocking. After the piece was cut, another just like it was nailed to the bottom of the joist, and the two were tied together with a laminated band joist.

Laminating thin layers of plywood is an easy wood-bending technique. To form the tightly curved rim joist, three layers of ½-in. pressure-treated plywood were glued, clamped, and then nailed to the blocking.

Scribe-fitting the decking ensures a precise fit. Using scrap pieces of decking to set the height, the author screwed the skirtboard in place first and then installed the decking so that he could cut and fit each piece individually.

Decorative patterns mean more blocking. Because many composite materials have poor lateral strength, a radial-spoke layout like this one requires enough blocking to ensure that each plank is supported at least every 16 in.

Curved Deck Rail

Balusters screwed to the rim joist serve as a bending form for the railing top. After spacing and securing the lower ends of the balusters, the author used bar clamps to bend the curve of the 2×4 vertical railing face. By ripping the Trex into thin strips and reassembling it with PVC cement and screws, he was able to follow the railing's radius for the top of the T-shaped railing.

Decking Is Scribed to the Skirtboard

On the upper level, the decking ran straight across the joists. I scribed the decking to the skirtboard and cut the decking to length with a jigsaw, trimming the butt ends with a block plane as needed.

The bottom level wasn't so easy. To bring a visual focus to the fire pit, the decking radiates out from it like the spokes in a wheel. This detail required a significant amount of additional blocking to support the diagonal runs of decking (see the bottom photo on p. 195).

Bent Railings Are as Solid as a Rock

With the decking complete, I turned to the railing construction. The balusters served as a form for the curved top rail. After drilling the top and bottom of each baluster, I plumbed them and screwed the lower ends into the skirtboard.

To bend the vertical face of the railings, the Trex 2×4 was clamped to the inside perimeter of the balusters (see the top photo on the facing page). After bending, Trex holds its basic shape for quite a while, so it was easy to move the 2×4 to the top of the railing, clamp it, and screw it in place. Getting the joints tight between 2×4s was difficult because of the curve, so I used as few boards as possible.

The top of the railing was a new challenge. I tried bending a Trex 2×6 on edge but could not get the radius required, so I ripped Trex 2×6s into 1⅜-in. strips for a laminated rail.

The first strip was glued with PVC cement and screwed to the top of the vertical 2×4; this served as the form. I then glued, clamped, and screwed successive strips into place (see the bottom photo on the facing page), staggering the seams as I went. Any irregularities were subsequently removed with a belt sander.

The final task was a bench for the lower level of the deck. Right-angle pressure-treated 2×4 supports were secured to every fourth baluster and to the deck, providing a finished seat height of 19 in. After tying the supports together with a vertical Trex 2×4 as a facing, I ripped, bent, glued, and then screwed 5/4×6 Trex for the bench seat as I had for the railing.

Ted Putnam is a custom builder and deck specialist in Connecticut.

Is Your Deck Safe?

■ BY MIKE GUERTIN

With 40 million decks in the United States that are more than 20 years old, there are plenty of families whose outdoor fun is resting on a shaky foundation. At least 30 people died as a direct result of deck collapses between 2000 and 2008, according to the North American Deck and Railing Association, and every year, many more are injured in deck-related accidents, many of which could be prevented. An annual deck inspection takes less than an hour and could head off a catastrophe. Here's what to look for.

Mike Guertin is a remodeling contractor in East Greenwich, Rhode Island, and the editorial adviser to Fine Homebuilding. His Web site is www.mikeguertin.com.

1. Ledger Boards

The ledger board, where the deck attaches to the house, is a common site for deck failure. Check the connection between the ledger and the house, especially if your deck is more than 3 ft. off the ground, in which case a collapse could lead to serious injuries. Ledger boards must be bolted or screwed securely to the house, not just nailed, because nails tend to pull out. The 2009 International Residential Code (IRC) has a prescriptive lag-screw and bolting chart that gives some guidance for adequate fastening and fastener locations. For example, the code calls for a 12-ft.-deep deck to be attached with ½-in. lag screws spaced 15 in. apart or ½-in. through bolts 29 in. apart.

Also, look for rot in the ledger board (see "Framing Lumber" on p. 200) and the wall behind the ledger. Water often leaks behind the ledger board due to improperly sized or

**BAD:
LOOSE LEDGER**

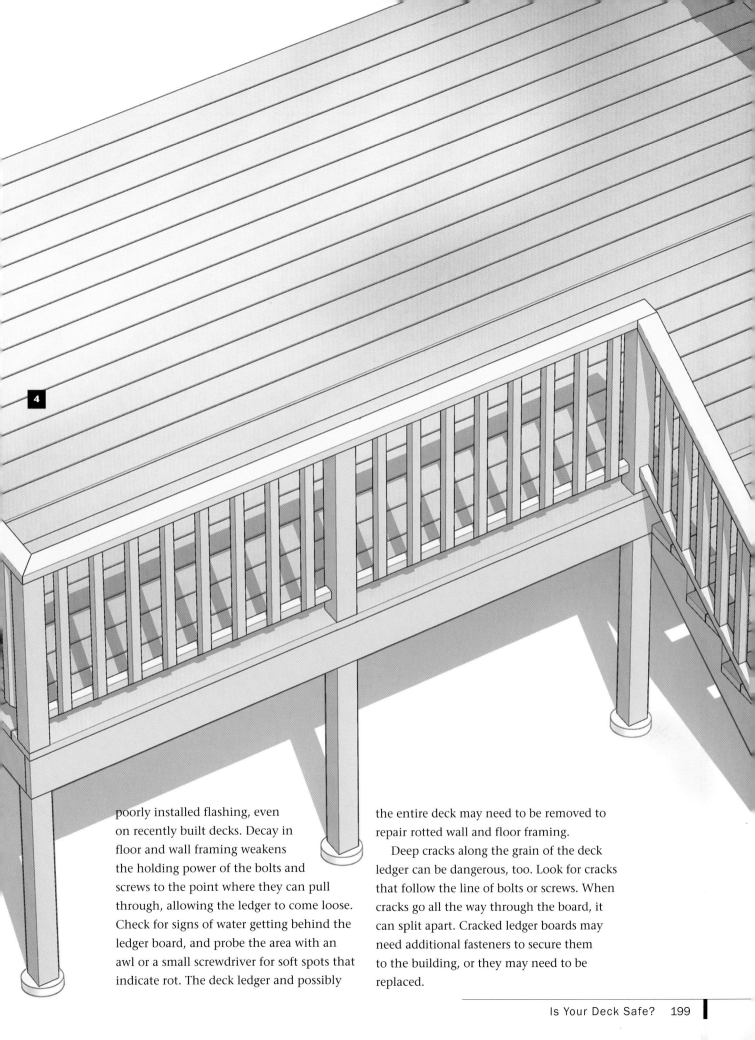

4

poorly installed flashing, even
on recently built decks. Decay in
floor and wall framing weakens
the holding power of the bolts and
screws to the point where they can pull
through, allowing the ledger to come loose.
Check for signs of water getting behind the
ledger board, and probe the area with an
awl or a small screwdriver for soft spots that
indicate rot. The deck ledger and possibly

the entire deck may need to be removed to
repair rotted wall and floor framing.

Deep cracks along the grain of the deck
ledger can be dangerous, too. Look for cracks
that follow the line of bolts or screws. When
cracks go all the way through the board, it
can split apart. Cracked ledger boards may
need additional fasteners to secure them
to the building, or they may need to be
replaced.

**BAD:
CORRODED HARDWARE**

2. Fasteners, Hangers, and Anchors

Fasteners—including nails, screws, bolts, metal hangers, and anchors—play a critical role in the integrity of a deck. It's important to tighten or replace any fastener that has become loose or excessively corroded. Old deck frames may be assembled without joist hangers securing the joists to the ledger or beams. The nails securing these decks are hard to inspect, can rust away unnoticed, and often come loose. Joist hangers can be added to joists when there's access to the underside of the deck; if that's not possible, a few deck boards can be pulled up for hanger installation from the top of the deck.

Nails or screws that fasten the deck boards themselves also can loosen or rust. Check for loose deck boards, and refasten them with new screws if needed. Stainless-steel and specially coated screws generally resist corrosion better than galvanized screws in pressure-treated lumber. Scan the deck's surface for proud nails or screws, which are a hazard for bare feet.

3. Framing Lumber

Decks built before the mid-1970s often were framed with untreated lumber, which decays more quickly than pressure-treated lumber. Check joists, beams, posts, stairs, railings, and decking to be sure wood is still in good condition. Pay special attention to areas that remain damp or are regularly exposed to water. Use an awl or a small screwdriver to test the wood. If the wood is soft and spongy, it's likely starting to decay and should be replaced. Also, inspect for insect damage and fungus growth, which are indicators of decay.

GOOD: END-GRAIN PROTECTION

Even pressure-treated lumber isn't immune from rot. Treatment chemicals rarely penetrate more than ½ in. into incised hem-fir lumber, leaving untreated cores. And although southern yellow pine has better treatment penetration, the centers and cut ends still can be susceptible to decay over time. Look for joists, posts, beams, and ledgers with splits and checked ends where water can enter and decay can take hold. Replace deck lumber that appears to have begun decaying, and treat splits and end checks with a copper-naphthenate solution (such as Green Termin-8; www.homaxproducts.com) to stave off future rot.

BAD: ROT

4. Deck Boards

One of the benefits of synthetic decking is that there are no splinters. Wood grain, on the other hand, can separate and lift when exposed to the elements. Deck sealants can reduce the likelihood that wood grain will lift in the first place, so regular treatments can head off problems. Check wooden deck boards, railings, handrails, and balusters for splinters. You probably can't halt the splintering process on older decks, but you can carve off splintering spots and sand problem areas to minimize the hazard. When there's a particularly problematic board, the best solution is to replace it.

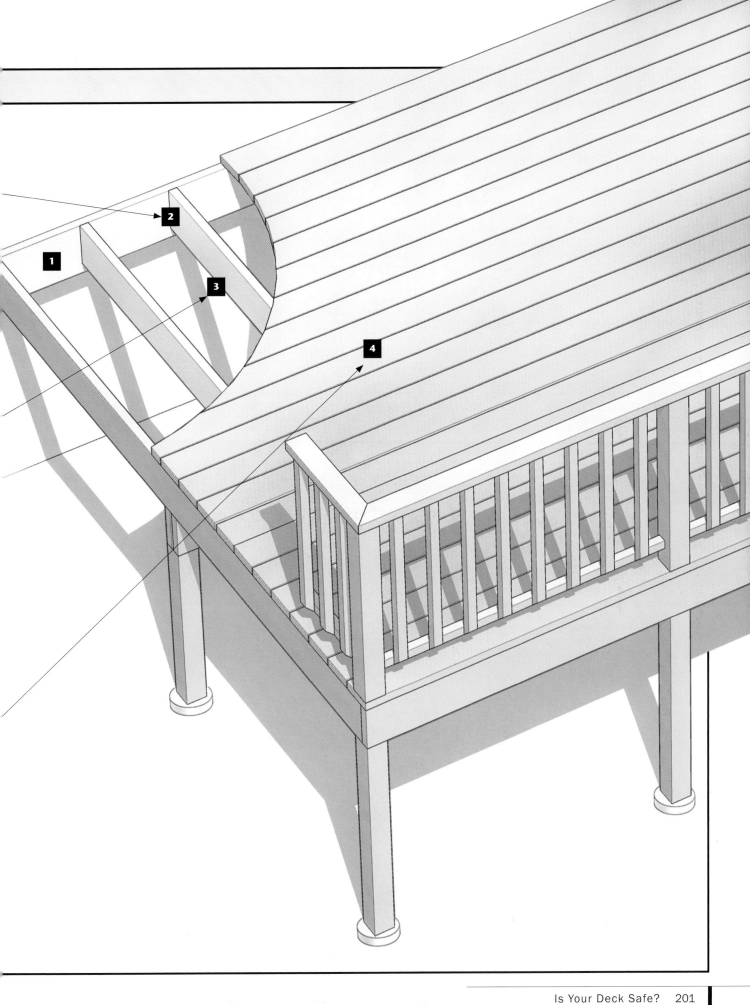

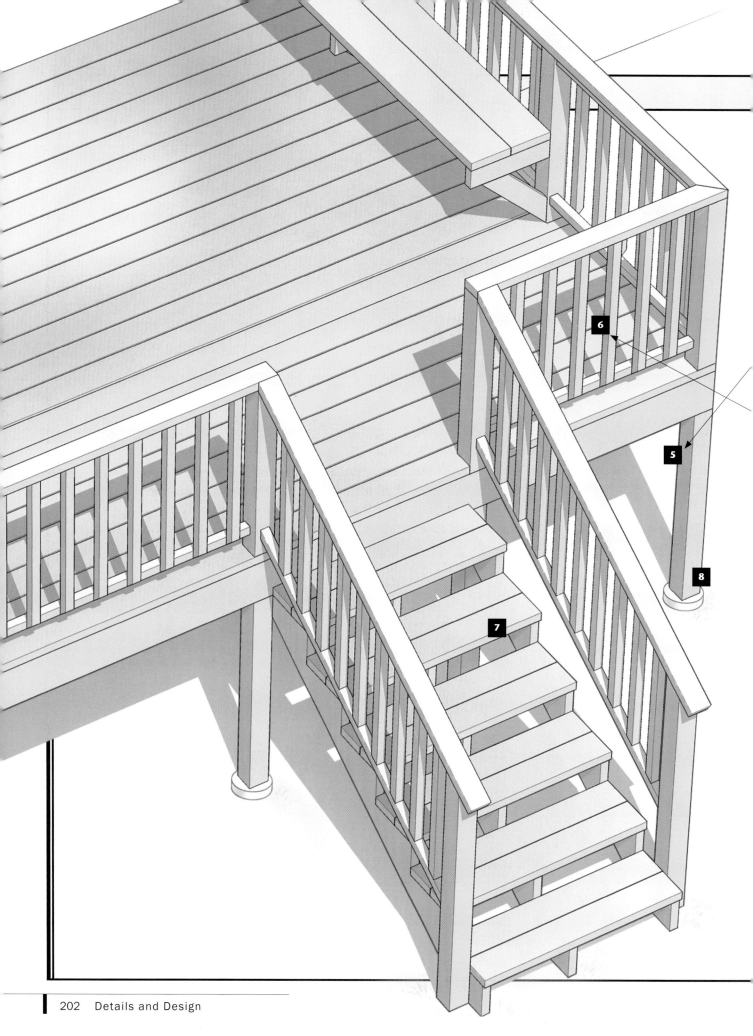

5. Post Bracing

Posts supporting decks 2 ft. or higher off the ground need to be braced laterally. Without bracing, decks can sway as people walk on them, which is not only unsettling but also potentially dangerous. Diagonal braces reaching 2 ft. down the post height and 2 ft. out to the deck frame should be added. Lateral bracing also can be incorporated into the deck frame itself, but before you try this solution, get verification from a structural engineer.

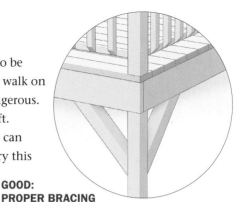

GOOD: PROPER BRACING

6. Railings and Balusters

BAD: BALUSTERS OUTSIDE

GOOD: BALUSTERS INSIDE

The railing system on a deck is a big safety concern, especially when the deck is 3 ft. or more off the ground. Guests tend to congregate and lean on railings, and children like to climb on them. Railings, structural posts, and balusters loosen over time, especially those that are nailed rather than screwed or bolted together. Push firmly on each part of the railing system to be sure it's secure. If your deck has balusters attached on the outside of the railing structure rather than the inside, consider reversing them so that they're less likely to be pushed off. If railing parts are fastened with nails, secure them with screws.

Current building codes call for railings on all decks higher than 30 in. off the ground. The top of the railings must be at least 36 in. above the deck surface and any built-in benches or seating. Built-in benches along the perimeter of a deck can be a hazard for small children who could stand on the benches and topple over the handrail. Under the new code, built-in benches must have 36-in.-high railings measured from bench level when the top of the bench is more than 30 in. off the ground. Regardless of a deck's height, railings are a good idea to prevent someone from inadvertently stepping off the edge.

The space between balusters should be no greater than 4 in. to prevent small children from crawling through. Older decks often have wide spaces between balusters or horizontal rails. Additional balusters, latticework, or other barriers (glass, polycarbonate, or wire cables, for example) can be used to reduce open spaces.

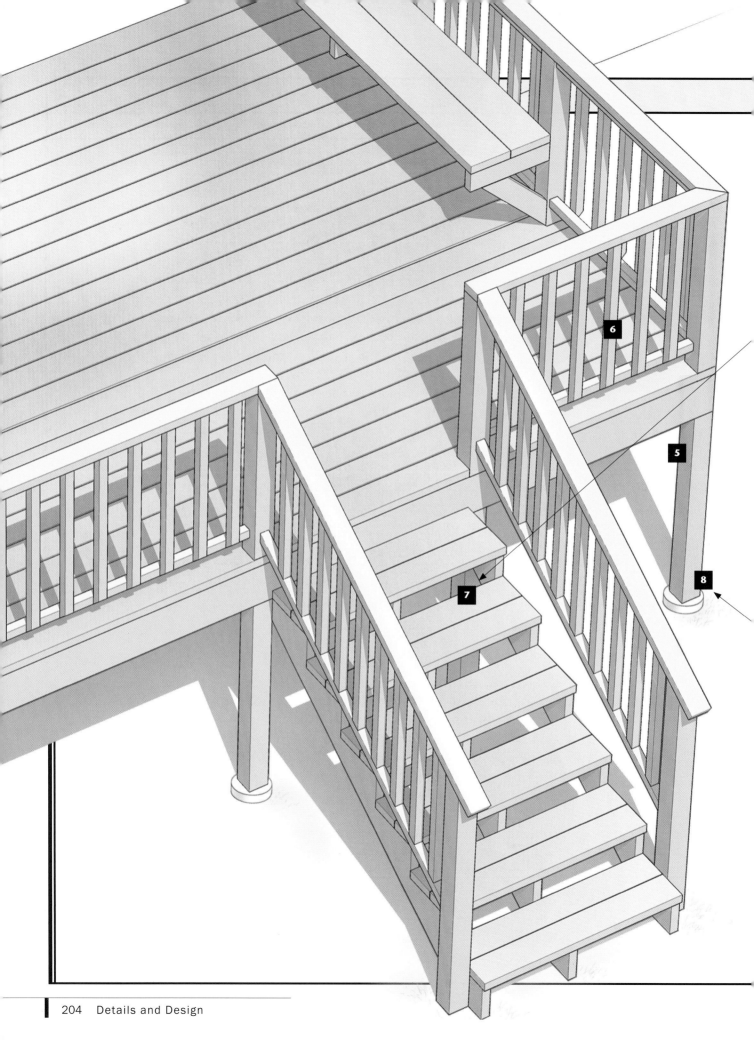

7. Stairs

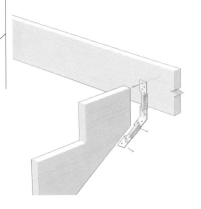

GOOD: PROPER HARDWARE

Stairs are another critical component where failures can lead to injuries. Check stair railings to be sure they are attached firmly, and inspect the risers, treads, and stringers to be certain they are attached securely and are not decayed. Look especially closely at the structural connections where the top of the stairs mounts to the deck framing and intermediate landings. Many deck-stair installations rely on nails through the back side of the stringers and may be subject to pulling out; other systems rely on toenails or metal hardware like angle brackets or straps used in a fashion they were not intended for. Stringer-mounting hardware from major manufacturers became available only in 2009. If you are concerned that the stringer-to-deck-frame connection is inadequate, consider installing this new hardware for a secure mount.

Make sure the landing at the bottom of the stairs is level and does not present a trip hazard. Current building codes call for at least 3 ft. of solid travel surface leading away from the bottom step. Stairs that end on earth rather than a solid landing pose a trip hazard. The earth level can change over time, making the rise to the first step greater or less than the common rise along the stair flight. The bottom of the stair stringers should be secured to the landing with metal hardware.

While you're inspecting the stairs, be on the lookout for unsafe handrails. Stair railings are often built with framing lumber, which does not offer a good grip. A grippable handrail with terminating ends at top and bottom can be added alongside the stair guardrail with handrail brackets.

8. Footings

Deck-support posts must be mounted to solid concrete footings. Often, footings are too shallow and/or too small to support a deck, making it unstable. Footings must be a minimum of 12 in. deep in the earth and extend past the local frost line. The footings must be sized to support the load of the deck while also taking into account the bearing capacity of the local soil. Consult your local building department if the footings seem inadequate. Footings can be replaced or added to an existing deck.

Posts embedded in concrete footings or buried in earth are prone to rotting even if they are pressure-treated. Embedded or buried posts can be trimmed at the ground/footing surface and secured to the footing with proper metal post bases. Where footings don't reach grade, new ones should be installed beneath the posts.

BAD: UNSECURED POST

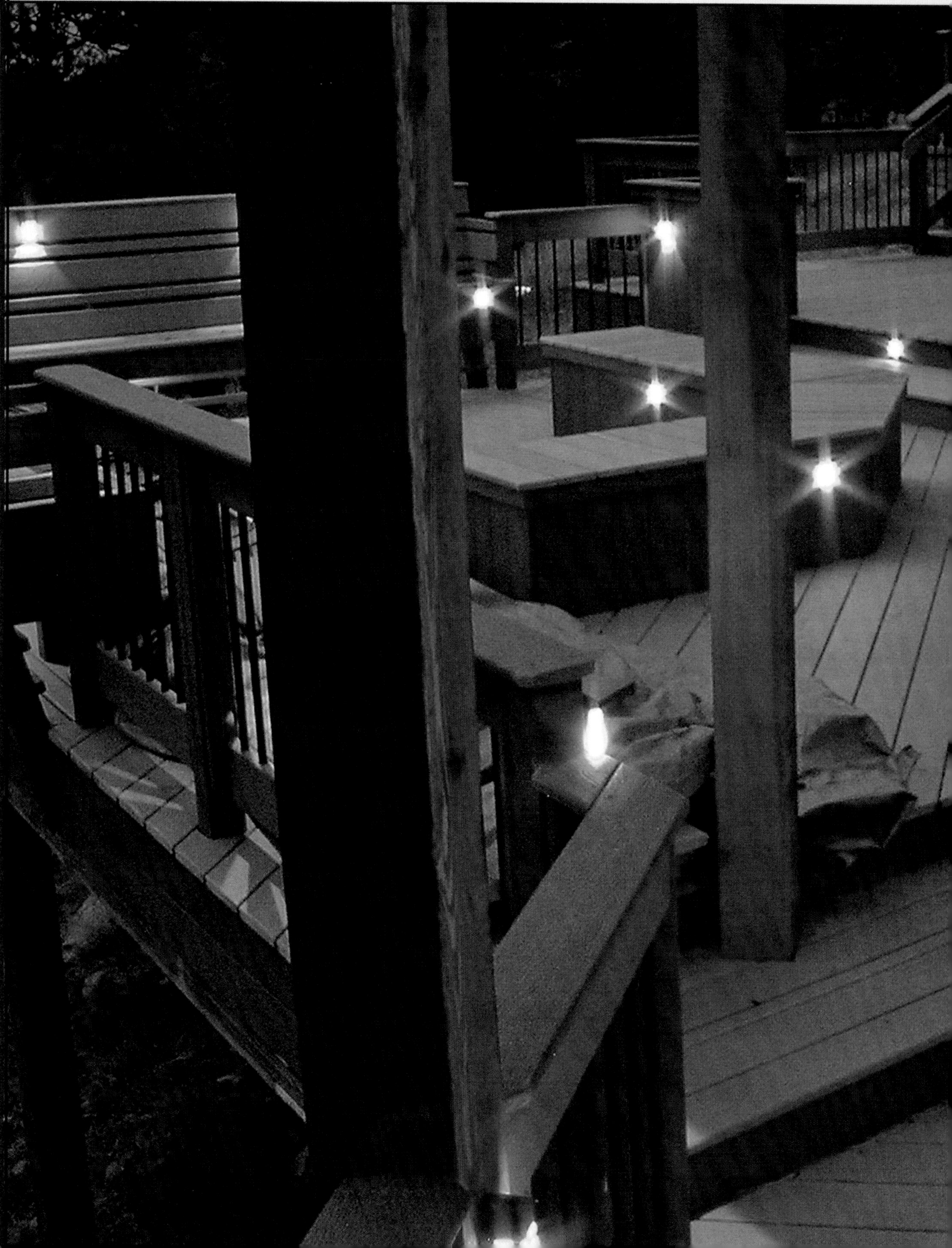

Accent Your Deck with Light

■ BY JUSTIN FINK

From a purely functional point of view, a deck-lighting scheme should serve a few different needs. Safety lighting lets you walk around after dark without tripping over a chaise longue. Task lighting enables you to see if the burgers on the grill are ready. Security lighting casts off the inky blackness on the other side of a sliding-glass door. But unless you plan to be interrogating intruders in your backyard, installing one or two wall-mounted floodlights to serve all these needs isn't the classiest solution.

Accent lighting can help answer safety, task, and security requirements, but its primary purpose is aesthetic. Rather than flooding deck areas with simulated sunlight, accent lighting integrates with posts, railings, stair risers, and other deck elements to create an inviting after-dark atmosphere. By taking advantage of the variety of accent lights available, you can create a lightscape that establishes edges, defines areas or elevations, and even highlights pathways or destinations.

Justin Fink is senior editor at Fine Homebuilding.

Power Sources: Low, Line, or Solar?

Low-voltage lights require a transformer. It converts 120v line power to safer 12v.

The type of power source that you choose is dictated by lots of different factors, and each factor has upsides and downsides.

Low-voltage lights are the most common type of accent lighting. They are a safer alternative to line voltage wiring, pose almost no threat of shock, and have simpler connections. One downside is that low-voltage lights require a transformer (above right); another is that unless the fixtures are divided into more than one run of wiring, they share the same 12v of power, which can lead to dim lights.

The installation of line-voltage fixtures is enforced more strictly. All connections must be made in an approved electrical box, and cables run in the open must be enclosed in

Solar-powered deck lights rely completely on sunlight. No additional power source or wiring is required.

proper conduit, such as schedule-80 PVC pipe. Also, most areas won't allow you to install line-voltage deck lighting unless you have an electrical license.

Solar-powered deck lights require no electrical connections, timers, or light switches. You don't need to drill routing holes, run wires, or make connections. But you do need to install the fixtures where there is steady exposure to sunlight, typically six hours a day. Each solar light has a photo cell that charges a set of nickel-cadmium (NiCd) batteries during the day, then uses the batteries to power the light after dark. This reliance on sun typically limits deck applications to post-cap fixtures, but recessed solar fixtures are also available. Unfortunately, the amount of energy collected is limited by the size of the photovoltaic panel (which is typically small on a deck fixture) and is dependent on the location of the fixture. Also, the NiCd batteries eventually need to be replaced, which is generally as simple as changing the batteries in your television remote.

Low-Voltage Wire Connectors: Disk, Snap, Barrel, or Wire Nuts

Many deck-lighting packages rely on quick-connect fittings to tie each fixture to the main supply cable that runs from the transformer. Designs differ, but most quick connectors, like the Quic-Disc (see the top left photo below) are designed to pierce the sheathing of the supply cable with two sharp prongs to create a connection. According to Gerry DeLaVega, president of TerraDek® Lighting (www.terradek.com), "Disk connectors can allow water to get into the system, and are susceptible to loosening up over time." Silicone-filled snap connectors (www.3m.com) are a better choice for weather resistance, and their small size and ability to join wires without stripping off the sheathing are both big bonuses. You just slide the wires into the holes of the connector, and snap down the tab with a pair of pliers. The trouble is that they are compatible only with solid wires, and stranded cable is used for many deck-lighting applications.

If you're wary of all quick-connect systems, wire nuts are still a great choice, as long as they are weather-resistant. The trouble with wire nuts is that they create what DeLaVega calls "bunny ears," which sometimes don't stay hidden when you're trying to run wire under a railing. For these situations, consider barrel connectors (www.nightscaping .com). These connectors allow two wires to be joined together, end to end, and then covered with a weather-resistant heat-shrink tube. They lie flatter than wire nuts or quick connectors and are great for spots where hidden connections are necessary.

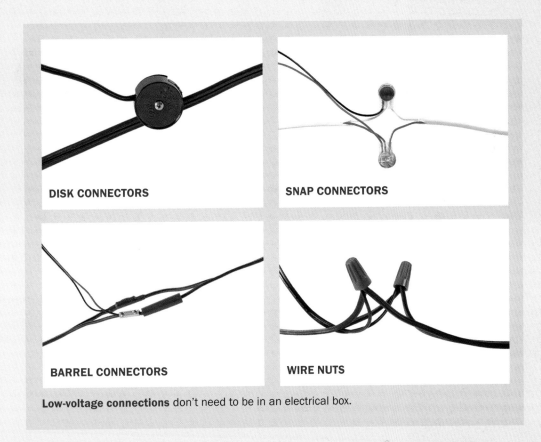

DISK CONNECTORS

SNAP CONNECTORS

BARREL CONNECTORS

WIRE NUTS

Low-voltage connections don't need to be in an electrical box.

Post-cap lights are the largest, most-prominent fixtures in the accent deck-lighting category. They highlight the posts at the top and bottom of stairways or deck entrances, or act as markers for intermediate posts along the perimeter of a deck. Fixtures are typically made to fit over 4×4 or 6×6 posts, but some are designed to fit both.

Custom sizes are available from some lighting manufacturers.

Lights are often available in several different colors and materials so that they can complement the look of a deck. Many manufacturers also make unlighted "dummy" post caps to match post-cap lights; this way, all posts look the same.

Lower the Beam: Side-Mount Lights

Many deck-lighting manufacturers suggest that the light from post-cap fixtures is too close to eye level when you're sitting on a deck chair or bench. Instead, these companies recommend that you consider lowering fixtures to the sides of the deck posts, about 32 in. to 34 in. from the deck surface.

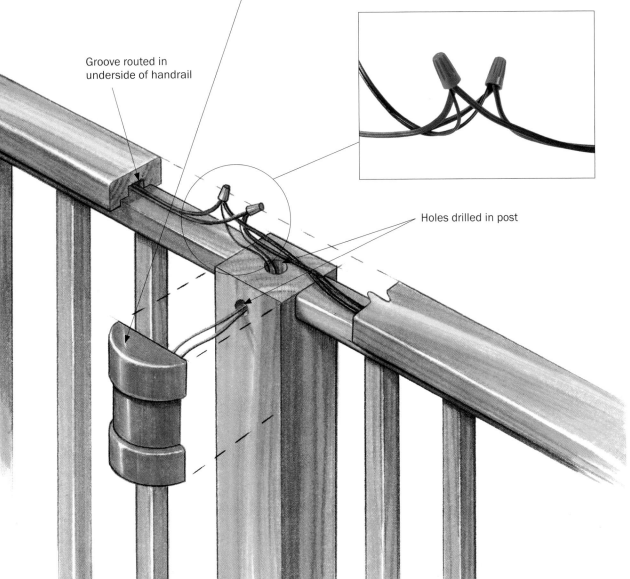

Groove routed in underside of handrail

Holes drilled in post

Recessed lights are the perfect example of how to accent a deck without overlighting it. They also offer the best chance at concealment during daylight. These light fixtures are available with either LED or incandescent bulbs, and each has a slightly different effect.

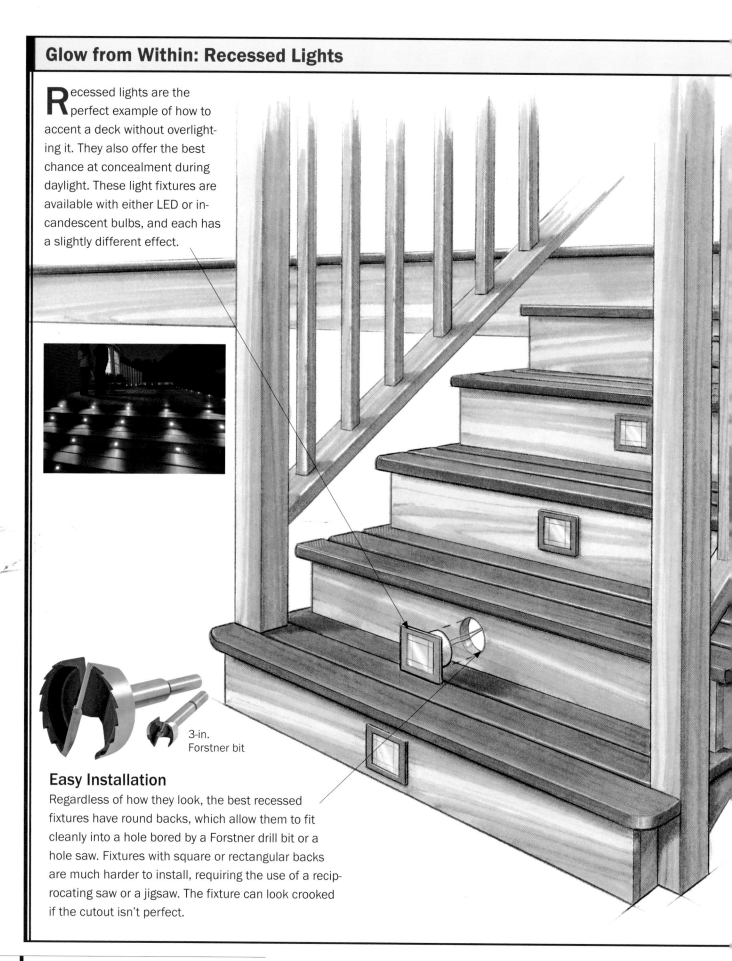

3-in.
Forstner bit

Easy Installation

Regardless of how they look, the best recessed fixtures have round backs, which allow them to fit cleanly into a hole bored by a Forstner drill bit or a hole saw. Fixtures with square or rectangular backs are much harder to install, requiring the use of a reciprocating saw or a jigsaw. The fixture can look crooked if the cutout isn't perfect.

Tips for Lighting Deck Stairs

Lighting exterior stairs is a delicate process, so don't install fixtures willy-nilly and hope for the best. In some ways, stairs with poor lighting can be more dangerous than stairs with no lighting at all. As a rule, you want to avoid creating shadows that can lead to uncertain footing, but you also don't want to flood the area with light and blind someone climbing the stairs. Remember that light-colored stair materials, or treads and risers built from contrasting materials, require less illumination than dark stair materials. Also, unless beams of light overlap, avoid positioning fixtures on alternating sides of a staircase.

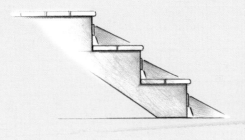

When mounting light fixtures on stair risers, select recessed fixtures to avoid trip hazards. Shaded or louvered fixtures direct light down rather than straight out and won't distract people ascending the stairs.

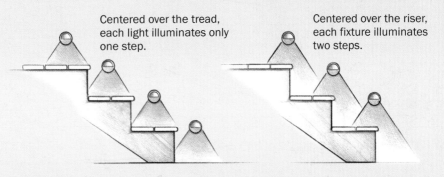

Centered over the tread, each light illuminates only one step.

Centered over the riser, each fixture illuminates two steps.

When mounting light fixtures on stair stringers or near the bottom of stair railings, consider their height and placement in relation to the treads. If space allows, place the fixture higher to cast light over a wider area.

Bulb Types: Incandescent or LED?

The world of exterior accent lighting is dominated by incandescent bulbs and LEDs. Incandescent technology is well-established, and the bulbs are widely available in several different shapes and wattages for only a few bucks apiece, making replacement quick and easy. They cast a softer, warmer light (right) than LEDs, but are inefficient because 95 percent of the energy they consume is emitted as heat. Also, incandescent bulbs have a relatively short life span of 1,000 to 2,000 hours of use.

LEDs (below) are more expensive because you are paying not just for the bulb, but also for the housing and the circuitry that go with it. The life span of LEDs is longer—from 10,000 to 100,000 hours of use, depending on the quality of the unit—and they produce little heat. Also, rather than burning out like ordinary bulbs, LEDs dim slowly over time. The trade-off is that unless mirrors or reflective surfaces are used, the light output is focused narrowly in only one direction and can be harsh on the eyes in contrast with a dark backyard.

Obscure the bulb. According to John Davis, owner of Highpoint Deck Lighting, "No matter which type of light you choose, it should always be shaded by a louver or softened by frosted, swirled, or coated glass. You should never see the bulb."

A versatile LED cap. De-Kor post caps use LEDs rather than incandescents, and they are sold in five different configurations, so you can choose how many sides of the cap will cast light.

Sources

Post-Cap Lights

Aurora Deck Lighting
www.auroradecklighting
.com
800-603-3520
(4) Sirius deck light
(9) Quasar path light

**Highpoint® Deck
Lighting**
www.hpdlighting.com
888-582-5850
(2) HP-801C (5) HP-570P
(7) HP-571P

Kichler® Lighting
www.kichler.com
866-558-5706
(8) 150470Z

Maine Ornamental
www.postcaps.com
866-780-3507
*(3) Tiffany-style sunflower
solar glass post cap*

Moonlight Decks
www.moonlightdecks.com
913-638-1685
*(1) Copper vein smooth
post cap*

Rockler® Hardware
www.rockler.com
800-279-4441
(6) Rectangular deck light

Sea Gull Lighting®
www.seagulllighting.com
800-347-5483
*(10) 92067-834 single-
light landscape deck light*

Recessed Lights

De-Kor Lighting
www.de-kor.com
303-991-2285
(6) LED downlights

Garden Sun Light
www.gardensunlight.com
909-594-6611
(7) ST212AC

**Highpoint Deck
Lighting**
www.hpdlighting.com
888-582-5850
(3) HP-770R
(4) HP-744R
(5) HP-740R

Hinkley® Lighting
www.hinkleylighting.com
800-446-5539
(1) 1546CO

Rockler Hardware
www.rockler.com
800-279-4441
(2) Deck/Dock light

A Complete Guide to Building Your Own Deck

■ BY RICK ARNOLD

To me, deck building has always been one of the most rewarding jobs. In just a few days, you've added a significant amount of finished square footage to a home. But deck building has dramatically changed since I started 25 years ago. Not only are there many more material choices, but there have been critical code changes that reflect the importance of proper design and construction. So while deck building remains one of the easier and more rewarding outdoor projects, it's crucial to adhere to codes and manufacturers' recommendations to ensure a safe and long-lasting deck.

The deck I'll describe here is medium-size, with two sets of stairs to easily access both sides of the yard. It is framed with pressure-treated lumber, and the decking, railing, and trim are synthetic products. A double border accents the deck's perimeter. A ledger attaches the deck to the house on two sides; its weight is supported from below by two beams resting on eight 4×4 posts centered on concrete piers.

Rick Arnold *is a contributing editor to* Fine Homebuilding.

From Footings to Finish

1. Pier locations

2. Ledgers

3. Main beam and posts

4. Joists and newels

5. Decking

6. Stairs

7. Trim and rails

Mark the Perimeter

To start, I measure and mark the edges of the deck's 20-ft. length on the house (photo 1). Then I plumb down to the foundation, measure out the width of the deck (in this case also 20 ft.) from each point, and drive in a stake at each corner (see photo 2 and the drawing on the facing page). Next, I adjust the stakes so that they are exactly 20 ft. apart. To make sure the deck perimeter is square, I take diagonal measurements in both directions (photo 3). If one diagonal is longer than the other, I adjust the corner locations until the diagonals are equal, making sure to maintain the 20-ft. distance between the two. I use string to outline the perimeter of the deck from the house, around the stakes, and back to the house (photo 4).

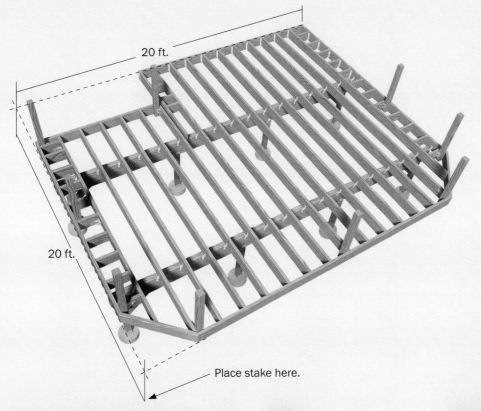

20 ft.

20 ft.

Place stake here.

3

4

Dig the Piers

Next, I string up a reference line to help me position the piers directly below where the beams will be. For this deck, I measured back exactly 3 ft. 6 in. from the perimeter to the center of the beam. To establish the center of the second beam, I measured 5 ft. from the house. To make adjustments easier, I use a batterboard, which allows me to fine-tune the string placement without moving the stakes.

You can purchase metal batterboards (above right) or make them with scrap wood on site (above).

I mark the locations of the piers, which are 6 ft. 9 in. apart, with surveyor's paint. I mark the center first, then roughly locate the perimeter of the hole. Now the strings can be removed and the holes dug.

Planning the Piers

Concrete piers transfer the weight of the deck to solid ground. To do so effectively, they must extend below the frost line and any backfill that has been used for grading. The typical pier consists of a cardboard form, concrete, and an anchor bolt.

Three things affect the number and the size of the piers you use: how you frame the deck, the weight the deck is designed for, and the load-bearing capacity of the soil. The deck we built here called for eight piers measuring 10 in. dia. to support the two doubled 2×10 beams supporting the deck. When calculating the size and number of piers I need, I use the International Residential Code's (IRC) design load for decks, which is 50 lb. per sq. ft., or psf (40 psf live load—the weight of people, furniture, etc.—and 10 psf dead load, or the weight of the deck components). Different soils have different bearing capacities, measured in psf; if you're unsure of your soil, contact your local building department for the bearing capacity of soils in your area.

EXAMPLE
Size of tubes: 10 in.
Number of tubes: 8
Average depth
per tube: 4 ft.
0.8 (8 x 4) = 26 bags

How much concrete do I need?

To pour the piers for an average-size deck, I use 80-lb. bags of concrete and an electric mixer, which rents for about $45 a day or sells for $250 or so. For major pours, I have a concrete truck deliver a 2,500-lb. mix. Either way, the basic formulas below will help you to estimate the number of bags or cubic yards of concrete required based on pier size and depth.

Tube size	Number of 80-lb. bags per ft.	Cubic yards per ft.
8 in.	0.53 bag	0.013 cu. yd.
10 in.	0.8 bag	0.02 cu. yd.
12 in.	1.2 bags	0.03 cu. yd.
14 in.	1.6 bags	0.04 cu. yd.

Position and Pour the Piers

Builder's tubes, or pier forms, come in diameters from 8 in. to 24 in. or more. The cardboard forms can be cut with a circular saw or a handsaw. Once the holes are dug, the tubes can be set in place and filled with concrete.

The top of the piers need to be only roughly the same height. After the concrete is poured, level and smooth it with a block of wood until the "cream" comes to the top and the aggregate settles. As the concrete sets, I backfill the holes and rake away any lumps.

Stop, Inspect, and Repair

If you're replacing an old deck, remove the existing ledger and inspect behind it for rot or decay. Nine times out of 10, you'll find some damage. In these situations, the most important thing is to identify the source of moisture infiltration and correct it before repairing the damage. If you find significant damage, address that before continuing to build your deck.

In this case, I removed the old deck to find that both the sheathing and the rim joist beneath it were damaged.

After repairing the rim joist, I used ½-in. construction-grade plywood to replace the rotten sheathing, butting it into the old sheathing and letting it hang down about 2 in. over the foundation. To prevent moisture migration in such places, I make sure the sheathing doesn't actually come in contact with the foundation.

Check✓Code

Check with your local building department to see that replaced sheathing and the nailing schedule conform to local building codes.

WALL STUD

BOTTOM PLATE

RIM JOIST

SILL PLATE

NEW SHEATHING

Before nailing the new sheathing in place, I snap a chalkline to mark the sill and the bottom plate to make sure the nails hit the bottom plate and the sill without going into any wiring. It's also important to make sure the surface underneath the ledger lies flat and tight to the framing.

Fasten the Ledger

Before attaching the ledger board, I apply a self-adhesive flashing to protect the sheathing from any moisture that might migrate behind the ledger and cause rot. Several types are available; I use Grace roofing membrane, which comes in 12-in. and 18-in. widths. It readily sticks to the wall and is easy to work with. I like to use the roofing membrane because it's thicker and has a less aggressive adhesive than the decking membrane. As with any flashing, the top edge of the membrane should lap under any housewrap or flashing above it.

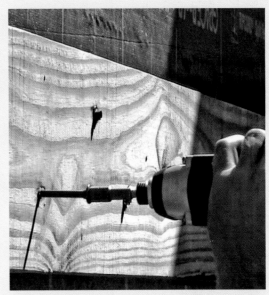

I use a laser transit to mark the height of the top of the ledger. I want the top of the ledger to be about 4 in. below the sliding door threshold to allow plenty of room for the decking as well as for ice and snow buildup. After marking the location on the house, I snap chalklines to indicate where to install the top of the ledger board.

I tack the ledger board in place with nails initially, but the ledger must be secured with code-approved hardware. On this deck, I used 3⅝-in. by ¼-in. LedgerLok fasteners (see the photo on p. 227) driven home with an impact driver.

Over the top edge of the ledger, I apply another layer of self-adhesive membrane, and over that, a strip of copper flashing purchased from a local roofing contractor who bent it to match the ledger detail. To ensure moisture is directed away from the house, I tuck the top edge of the copper under another strip of adhesive flashing and the housewrap above it.

Flashing the Ledger

Correct flashing is critical to prevent moisture damage to the house framing. Copper flashing, housewrap, and siding are the traditional choices for flashing the ledger. Self-adhesive membrane is also used to protect metal connectors from the corrosive chemicals used in pressure-treated lumber. For the best protection, this flashing is used in six locations:

- Behind the ledger
- On top of the ledger
- Above the copper flashing
- Behind the joist hangers
- Around the joist ends
- On the top edge of the joists

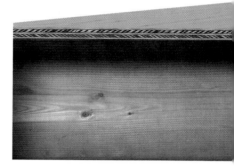

A joist hanger secures a joist to the ledger and rim joist (www.strongtie.com).

Check Code

Recent changes to the International Residential Code require the installation of additional hardware to increase the strength of the deck-ledger connection. Please consult your local code official to determine how the code applies in your area. Visit www.finehomebuilding.com for additional information on code issues.

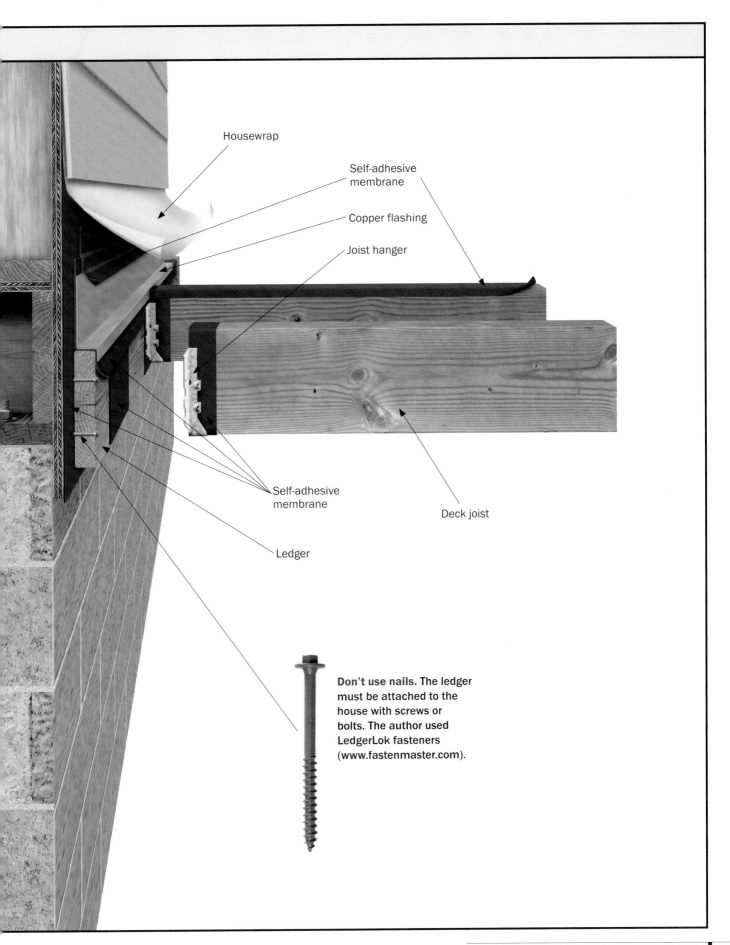

Housewrap

Self-adhesive
membrane

Copper flashing

Joist hanger

Self-adhesive
membrane

Deck joist

Ledger

**Don't use nails. The ledger
must be attached to the
house with screws or
bolts. The author used
LedgerLok fasteners
(www.fastenmaster.com).**

Assemble the Beams

The beams for this deck were too long for a single piece of lumber to span the entire length, so I assembled them from a series of 2×10s fastened together with 3½-in. stainless-steel framing nails. By assembling the beams directly on top of the piers (I already stripped the cardboard off the tops), I could ensure that the joints were positioned directly over the posts. When nailing beam sections together, I drive the nails at an angle so that they don't protrude out the other side; driving a few in the opposite direction locks the lumber together. Clipping the outside corner dresses it up a little and prevents crew members from giving themselves a headache.

I snap a line over the piers to locate the center and position the screw that holds down the post base, then I use a hammer drill to make the hole (photo left). In this project, I used Titen HD screws, which can be placed after the piers have hardened (photo right), unlike anchor bolts, which must be set when the concrete is wet.

With the posts plumb and in place but not yet attached, I use a laser level to mark them to length relative to the bottom of the ledger plus the double 2×10 beam underneath. For this project, I used a rotary laser from Stabila (www.stabila.com). A low-tech alternative would be a long 2×4 and a bubble level. Hold the 2×4 to the bottom of the ledger, level it, then mark the post. Measure down the depth of the beam for the cut-line. Once the posts are marked, you can take them down to cut them more easily.

Next, I plumb the trimmed posts and nail them to the post bracket. Do not use a standard nailer; use one with a tip specifically designed to locate nail holes in connecting hardware. I then set the caps on top of the posts.

With the posts firmly anchored to the piers, the first beam is lifted into place and the post caps are nailed secure.

As the support framing goes up, I check it for plumb, level, and square, and I attach temporary braces to keep it from moving. Later, I'll install permanent knee braces to increase the stability of the finished deck.

I follow with the second beam, again checking it for plumb, level, and square, and using temporary braces to hold it in place.

Post to Pier

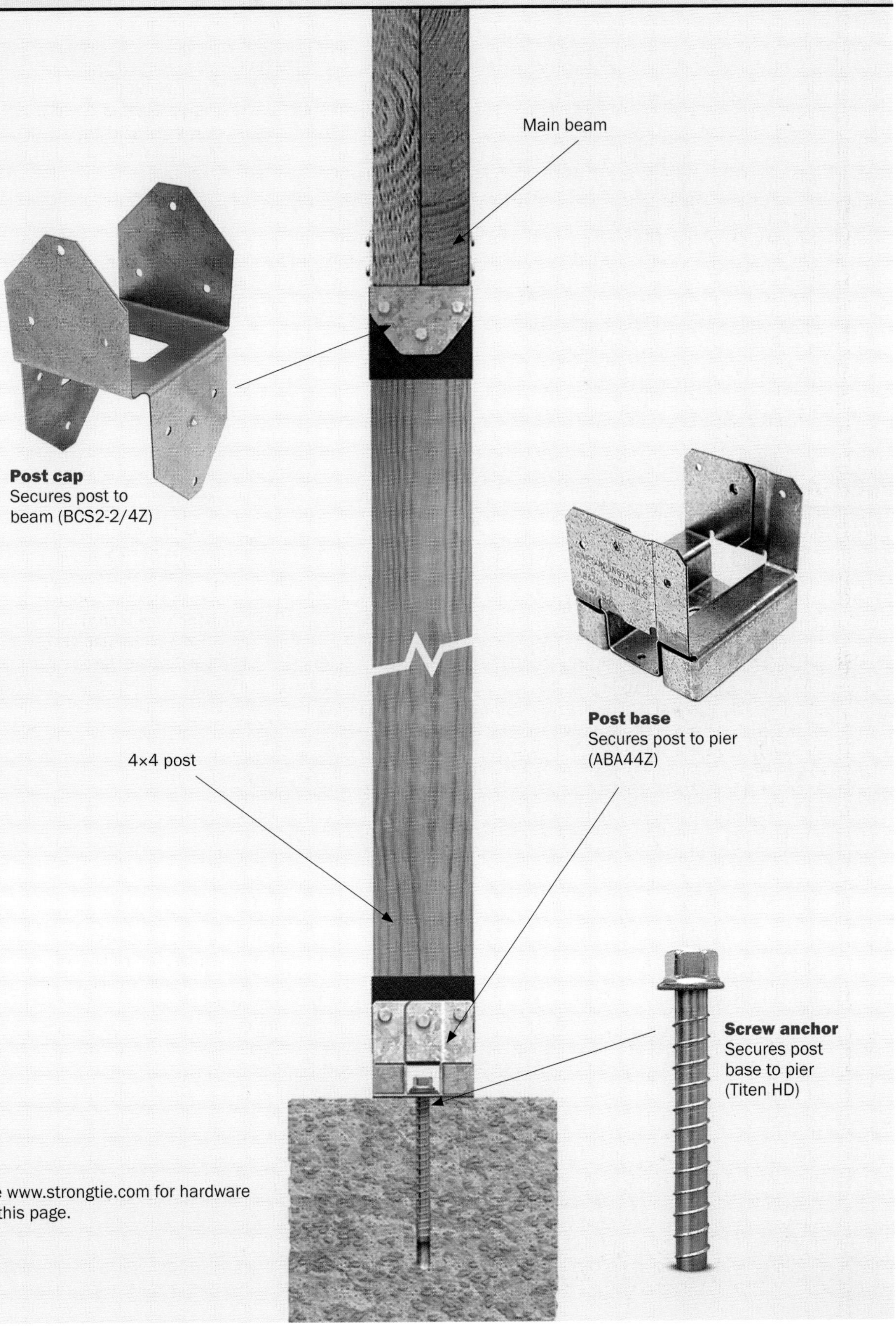
Main beam
Post cap
Secures post to beam (BCS2-2/4Z)
Post base
Secures post to pier (ABA44Z)
4×4 post
Screw anchor
Secures post base to pier (Titen HD)

See www.strongtie.com for hardware on this page.

Install the Joists, Rim Joist, and Posts

1

On this deck, the ledger against one side of the house doubles as the first joist. To be sure it's straight, I string a line 2 in. off the joist and measure back to it along the string. Where the board veers off, I hammer it into alignment. Once it's straight, I tack it in place by toenailing it to the beam.

2

The deck plans I'm using call for 2×8 joists that are spaced 16 in. on center. Before I install them, I need to mark the joist layout on the ledger and on the beams. I mark the center of the deck on the ledger and on the outside beam, then snap a line between them. I use that line as a reference to mark all the joist locations along both beams.

6

To cut the joists to length, I snap a chalkline, then square that line along the side of the joists with a Speed Square. I cut the joists with a circular saw.

7

I'm dressing up this deck with clipped corners, so I've cut both the rim and the side rim pieces to fall short of the corners by the same distance. I position the rim (the ends do not necessarily line up flush with a joist); then I nail it to the joists.

8

To create the angled corner, I string a chalkline across the inside points and snap it on the inside joist, draw the line down, and cut on the back side of it with the saw set at 45 degrees. I finish the corner with a section of rim joist with 45-degree bevel cuts in both ends. The cuts abut the square-cut rim joists.

3

After wrapping the joist ends, I attach hangers to the joists with a pneumatic nailer. There's more room to maneuver the nailer working off the stack than when the joists are in place against the ledger. Fastening a hanger to a joist first also makes it easier to align the joist flush with the top of the ledger.

4

With the hangers attached, the joists can be positioned according to the layout markings and nailed to the ledger. For now, I let the far ends run long.

5

The beams must be straight before I attach the joists. I run a string line, with ¾-in. blocks to hold the string off the beam at each end. Sliding a third ¾-in. block between the beam and the string reveals bends in the beam. A few whacks with a hammer usually set it straight. I then can secure the joists to the beam with right-angle brackets.

9

10

The outside posts are nailed in place using a level to plumb them in both directions (photo 9). Then I string a dry line from one to the other along the top. The inner posts are aligned with the string and then nailed (photo 10). Posts are permanently secured with through bolts and an angle bracket (see the bottom right drawing on p. 235).

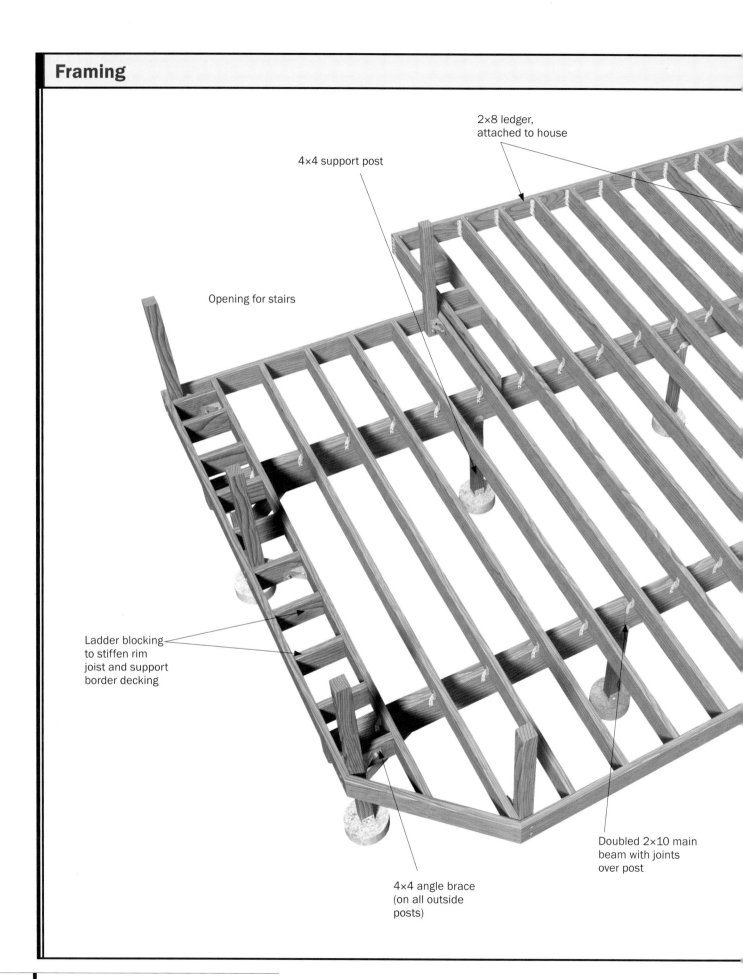

2×8 ledger,
attached to house

4×4 support post

Opening for stairs

Ladder blocking
to stiffen rim
joist and support
border decking

4×4 angle brace
(on all outside
posts)

Doubled 2×10 main
beam with joints
over post

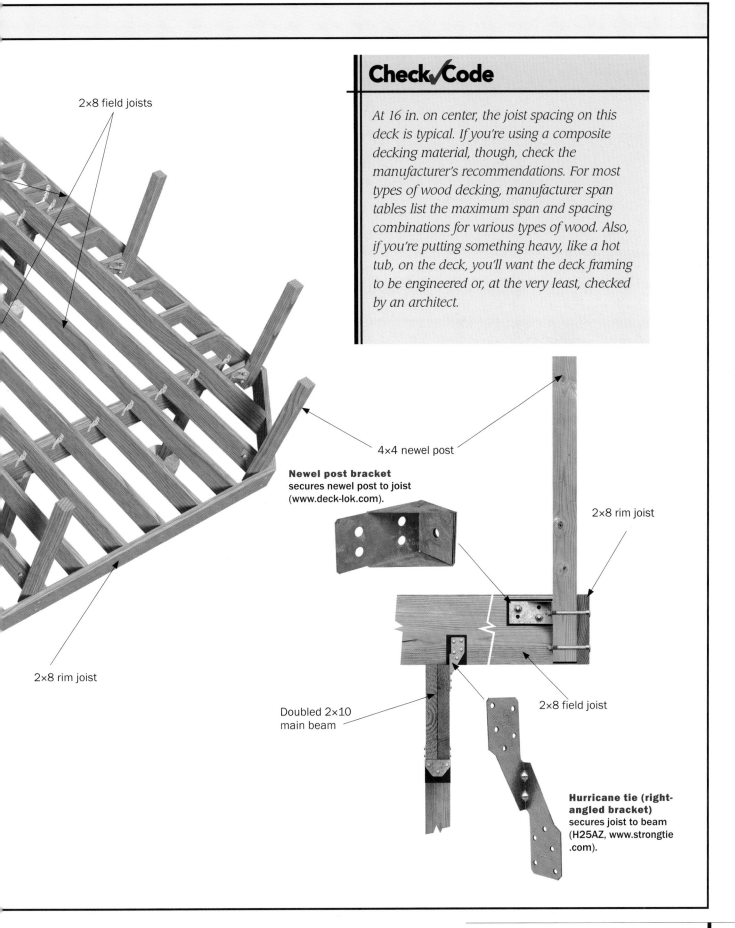

2×8 field joists

4×4 newel post

Newel post bracket secures newel post to joist (www.deck-lok.com).

2×8 rim joist

2×8 field joist

2×8 rim joist

Doubled 2×10 main beam

Hurricane tie (right-angled bracket) secures joist to beam (H25AZ, www.strongtie .com).

Lay Down the Decking

I start the decking with the border under the sliding glass door so that I can notch the first board to the wall of the house (photo 1). This allows me to create the 1½-in. overhang that I want around the entire rim. A second board parallel to this one creates a doubled-up border that runs all around the deck like a picture frame. The frame pieces are scribed around the deck posts (a decorative sleeve and collar hide up to a ½-in. gap here) and mitered at 22.5 degrees at each corner (photo 2).

I base the field decking layout on the stair opening, where I want a full board with a proper overhang on the highly visible edge. This means I must rip 1 in. off the board closest to the house and make another adjustment at the rim joist (see the drawing on p. 238).

4

I install the field decking first by butting the ends to the border, leaving a gap in accordance with the manufacturer's recommendations, and letting the far end run long. When the field is down, I cut it to length in place to install the border on that side.

5

For the final border, I snap a line the appropriate distance back from the edge and cut along it with a circular saw (adjust the blade depth so it doesn't cut into the framing). Additional blocking is added as needed to support board ends that don't land on the ladder blocking installed earlier.

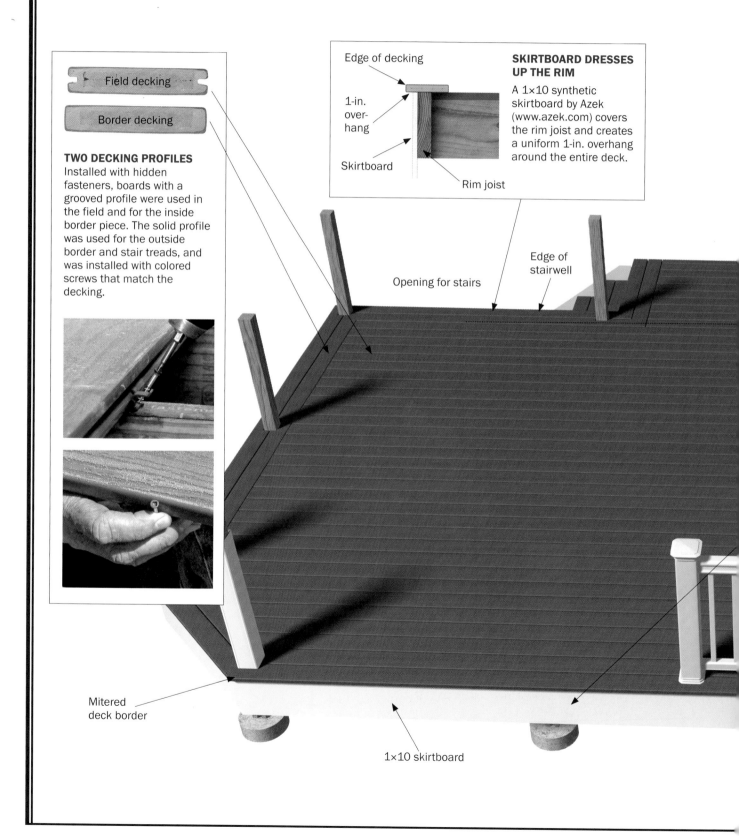

Field decking

Border decking

TWO DECKING PROFILES
Installed with hidden fasteners, boards with a grooved profile were used in the field and for the inside border piece. The solid profile was used for the outside border and stair treads, and was installed with colored screws that match the decking.

Edge of decking

1-in. over-hang

Skirtboard

Rim joist

SKIRTBOARD DRESSES UP THE RIM

A 1×10 synthetic skirtboard by Azek (www.azek.com) covers the rim joist and creates a uniform 1-in. overhang around the entire deck.

Opening for stairs

Edge of stairwell

Mitered deck border

1×10 skirtboard

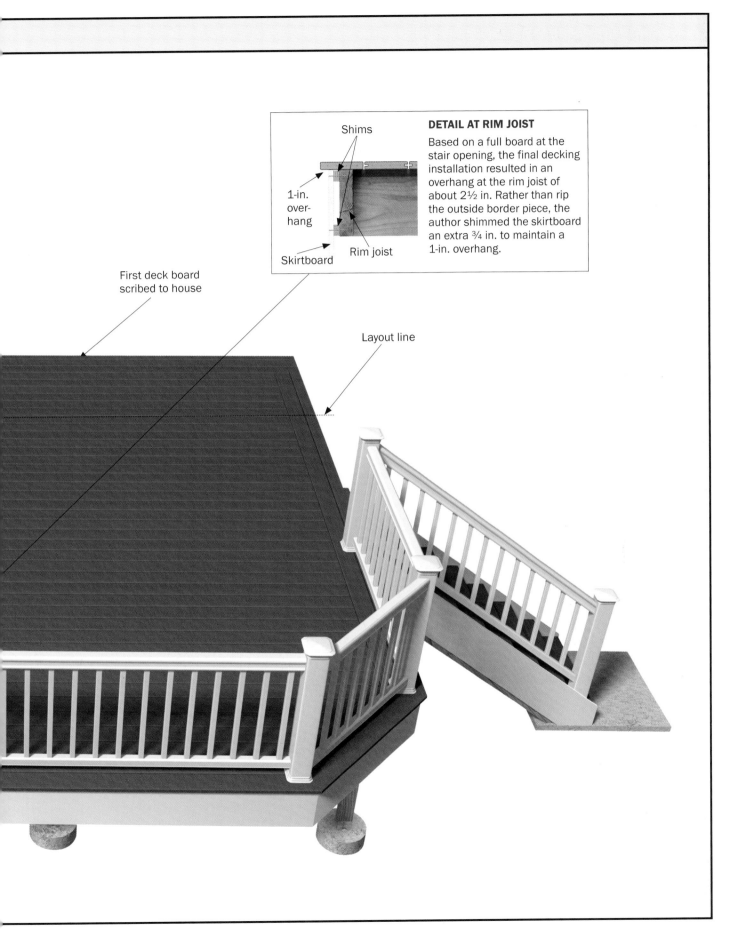

DETAIL AT RIM JOIST

Based on a full board at the stair opening, the final decking installation resulted in an overhang at the rim joist of about 2½ in. Rather than rip the outside border piece, the author shimmed the skirtboard an extra ¾ in. to maintain a 1-in. overhang.

Shims

1-in. over-hang

Skirtboard

Rim joist

First deck board scribed to house

Layout line

Build Sturdy Stairs

I start by placing concrete blocks as a temporary pad where I think the stairs will land. With a long level, I measure from the top of the deck down to the blocks (photo 1). This is the total rise, and it enables me to calculate the number of steps and the riser height of the stairs (see the facing page). I use two clamps and a piece of wood to transfer these measurements to a framing square (photo 2); this simple jig lets me mark the stringer board. Before cutting the stringers, I remove 1 in. (the depth of a tread) off the bottom so the rise there matches the rise of the other treads. Then I cut the stringer with a circular saw (photo 3), finishing the corners with a reciprocating saw to avoid overcuts. I trace the pattern on the other stringers (photo 4), and cut them the same way.

Check✓Code

The maximum recommended height for deck-stair risers is 7¾ in., according to the International Residential Code, which dictates other limits as well with regard to deck-stair construction. Be sure to consult the code or your local code official before designing stairs.

LANDING AND NEWEL POST
The temporary blocks are replaced with a 12-in.-deep concrete slab that provides a secure landing for the stringers. The concrete also anchors the newel post, which extends even deeper into the ground and is covered with a protective layer of waterproof membrane.

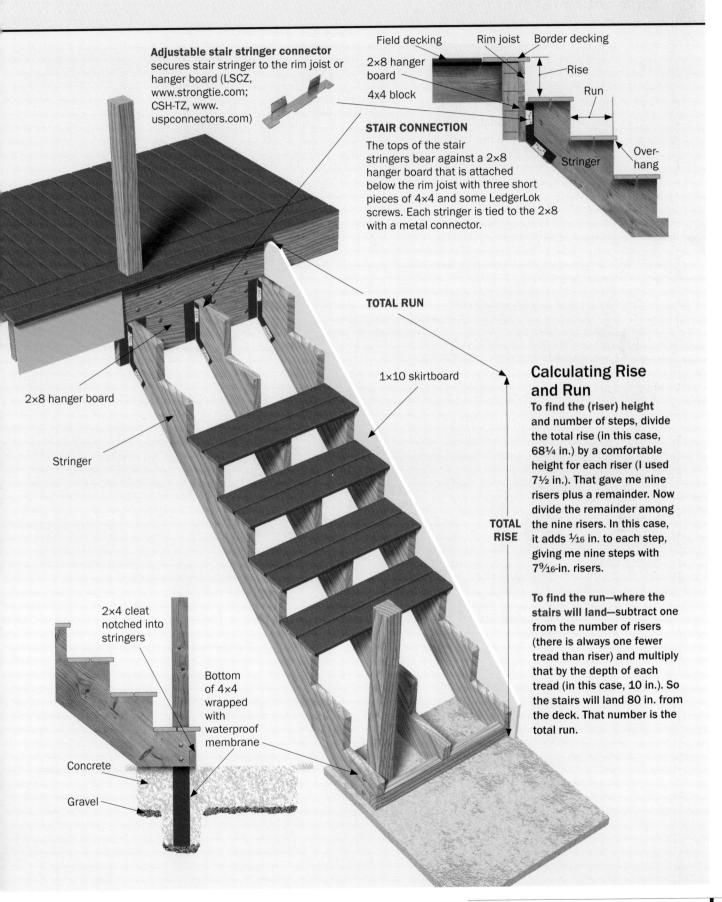

Adjustable stair stringer connector secures stair stringer to the rim joist or hanger board (LSCZ, www.strongtie.com; CSH-TZ, www. uspconnectors.com)

Field decking Rim joist Border decking

2×8 hanger board

4×4 block

Rise

Run

STAIR CONNECTION

The tops of the stair stringers bear against a 2×8 hanger board that is attached below the rim joist with three short pieces of 4×4 and some LedgerLok screws. Each stringer is tied to the 2×8 with a metal connector.

Stringer

Over-hang

TOTAL RUN

2×8 hanger board

Stringer

1×10 skirtboard

2×4 cleat notched into stringers

Bottom of 4×4 wrapped with waterproof membrane

Concrete

Gravel

TOTAL RISE

Calculating Rise and Run

To find the (riser) height and number of steps, divide the total rise (in this case, 68¼ in.) by a comfortable height for each riser (I used 7½ in.). That gave me nine risers plus a remainder. Now divide the remainder among the nine risers. In this case, it adds ¹⁄₁₆ in. to each step, giving me nine steps with 7⁹⁄₁₆-in. risers.

To find the run—where the stairs will land—subtract one from the number of risers (there is always one fewer tread than riser) and multiply that by the depth of each tread (in this case, 10 in.). So the stairs will land 80 in. from the deck. That number is the total run.

Finish with Rails and Trim

Like the decking, the trim elements of this deck are made of synthetic materials. I start with a 1×10 trim board to cover the rim joists. Getting the corner bevels tight can be difficult, so here's one trick to do this precisely: First, cut two short pieces of trim—I made these 4 in.—and bevel one edge on each at 22.5 degrees (photo 1). Fit them together precisely at the corner (photo 2), and draw a line on both sides to mark their position (photo 3). Then measure from the end of the last piece of trim (or in this case, the edge of the stair) to that line, and add the lengths together. That gives me the total length from the end of the last piece to the tip of the bevel at the corner. I tack up the skirtboards with a nail gun and permanently affix them with stainless-steel screws. I apply bonding glue at the miter joints to help hold the PVC corners together (photo 4).

Baluster assemblies fit over bottom rails I've installed. At the top, they attach with a bracket that fastens to the post sleeve. At the corners, the ends of the baluster assemblies are cut so that they fit centered on the post sleeves. As a final step, I fit decorative post caps on top.

Composite sleeves fit over the pressure-treated posts I installed earlier. I shim them plumb, then slip a decorative collar over the sleeve to dress up the base and cover the gap at the bottom.

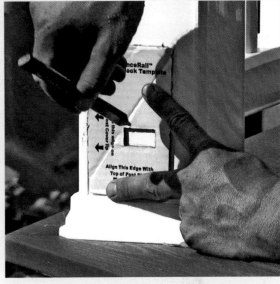

To install the railing, I attach brackets that accept a bottom rail that the baluster assembly clips over. Because they are prepainted, it's a good idea to take time to mark, cut, and fit the pieces carefully to make sure the finish isn't damaged.

The manufactured railing system on this deck, like most, has balusters spaced 4 in. apart as dictated by code. The pieces simply screw in place into predrilled holes. I start from the middle and work my way out, adjusting at the ends so that the balusters are close to 4 in. apart.

CREDITS

All photos are courtesy of *Fine Homebuilding* magazine (*FHb*) © The Taunton Press, Inc., except as noted below:

p. v: Photo courtesy © Scott Fleming; p. vi: (left photo) by Christopher Ermides (*FHb*), (right photo) by Roe A. Osborn (*FHb*); p. vii: (left photo) courtesy © www.advantagelumber.com, (right photo) by Krysta S. Doerfler (*FHb*); p. viii: (left photo) by Daniel S. Morrison (*FHb*), (right photo) courtesy © Scott Fleming; p. 1 (left photo) courtesy © Ted Putnam (right photo) courtesy © Highpoint Deck Lighting; p. 2: courtesy © Wentworth Construction.

p. 4: A Solid Deck Begins with Concrete Piers by Rick Arnold, issue 180. All photos by Christopher Ermides (*FHb*) except inset photo on p. 11 courtesy © Ardisma Inc.; Drawings by Dan Thorton (*FHb*).

p. 14: Get Your Deck Off to a Good Start by Scott Grice, issue 164. Photos by Daniel S. Morrison (*FHb*); Drawings courtesy © Bob La Pointe.

p. 18: Smart Deck-Framing Strategies by Mike Guertin, issue 196. All photos by Charles Bickford (*FHb*) except top photo on p. 20 by Krysta S. Doerfler (*FHb*), bottom photo on p. 20 and top photos on p. 21 courtesy © Mike Guertin; Drawings by Martha Garstang Hill Lockhart (*FHb*).

p. 28: Better Ways to Frame a Deck by John Spier, issue 172. Photos by Roe A. Osborn (*FHb*); Drawings courtesy © Vince Babak.

p. 36: In Pursuit of the Perfect Plank by Jefferson Kolle, issue SIP 21. Photo on pp. 36–37 courtesy © Fiberon; p. 38 courtesy © TimberSIL; photo on p. 39 by John Ross (*FHb*); photos on pp. 40–41 and top photos on p. 45 by Dan Thorton (*FHb*); photo on p. 43 courtesy © www.advantagelumber.com; bottom photo on p. 45 courtesy © LockDry

p. 46: Deck Boards Done Right by Mike Guertin, issue 202. All photos by Charles Bickford (*FHb*) except bottom photos on p. 52 by Krysta S. Doerfler (*FHb*); Drawings by John Hartman (*FHb*).

p. 54: Deck Fastener Options by Justin Fink, issue 178. All photos by Scott Phillips (*FHb*) except photo on p. 55 courtesy © Wentworth Construction; bottom right photo on p. 57 courtesy © FastenMaster; Drawings by Chuck Lockhart (*FHb*).

p. 62: Putting the Fast in Fastener by Mike Guertin, issue SIP 21. All photos by Dan Thorton (*FHb*) except photo on p. 64 courtesy © HIDfast, Inc.

p. 66: An Explosion of Decking Choices by Chris Green, Scott Gibson, Daniel S. Morrison, and Rob Yagid, issue 132. All photos by Scott Phillips (*FHb*) except photo on p. 67 courtesy © CPI Plastics Group Ltd.; top left photo on p.68 courtesy © Epoch Composite products Inc.; large photo on pp. 70–71 courtesy © California Redwood Association; large photo on p. 72–73 courtesy © Brian Vanden Brink, top photo on p. 75 by Krysta S. Doerfler (*FHb*), large photo on pp. 76–77 courtesy © Arch Wood Protection Inc.

p. 78: The Care and Feeding of Wooden Decks, by Jon Tobey, issue 138. All photos by Tom O'Brien (*FHb*).

p. 86: Start Your Railing Right by Mike Guertin, issue 212. All photos by Charles Bickford (*FHb*).

p. 90: Deck Railings Grow Up by Scott Gibson, issue 181. All photos by Krysta S. Doerfler (*FHb*) except photo on p. 92 by Scott Gibson (*FHb*); top right photo on p. 94 courtesy © Rob Anderson; left photo on p. 95 courtesy © CertainTeed.

p. 100: Deck Railings That Stand Up to the Weather by Arthur Chenoweth, issue 146. Photos by Roe A. Osborn (*FHb*); Drawing by Dan Thorton (*FHb*).

p. 106: Deck Railings by Andrew Wormer, issue SIP04. Photo on p. 107 by Jeff Beneke (*FHb*); top photo on p. 109 courtesy © Anton Grasslin; bottom photo on p. 109 courtesy © Jacek Bogucki; photo on p. 110 courtesy © Dean Della Ventura; photos on pp. 112 and 114 by Andrew Wormer (*FHb*); Drawings by Christopher Clapp (*FHb*).

p. 116: Railing Against the Elements by Scott McBride, issue 70. All photos and drawings courtesy © Scott McBride.

p. 122: Deck-Stair Basics by Scott Schuttner, issue SIP21. All photos courtesy © Jim Hallin except bottom right photo on p. 122 by Tim O'Brien (*FHb*); Drawing courtesy © Ron Carboni.

p. 124: Durable Deck Stairs by Scott Grice, issue 198. Photos by John Ross (*FHb*); Drawings by Dan Thorton (*FHb*).

p. 134: Curved Deck Stairs by Mike Guertin, issue 162. All photos courtesy © Mike Guertin except photo on p. 135 by Charles Bickford (*FHb*); Drawings courtesy © Bob LaPointe.

p. 142: Fantail Deck Stairs by José L. Floresca, issue 83. All photos and drawings courtesy © José L. Floresca.

p. 146: Custom Details Make a Better Deck by Michael Ayers, issue 188. Photos by Dan Morrison (*FHb*); Drawing by Dan Thorton (*FHb*).

p. 155: A Comfortable Outdoor Bench by David Bright, issue 82. Photos and drawing courtesy © David Bright.

p. 158: A Furniture-Grade Deck by Scott Fleming, issue 106. Photos and drawing courtesy © Scott Fleming.

p. 166: A Balcony Deck Built to Last by Michael Maines, issue 193. Photos by Daniel S. Morrison (*FHb*); Drawings courtesy © Dan Mannes.

p. 176: An Elegent Border for Your Deck by John Michael Davis, issue 204. All photos by Chris Ermides (*FHb*) except top right photo on p. 180 by Dan Thorton (*FHb*); Drawings courtesy © Christopher Mills.

p. 181: A Grade-A Deck by Scott Grice, issue SIP21. All photos by John Ross (*FHb*).

p. 190: Building a Curved Deck with Synthetic Decking by Ted Putnum, issue 111. All photos courtesy © Ted Putnum except photo on pp. 190–191 by Charles Bickford (*FHb*).

p. 198: Is Your Deck Safe? by Mike Guertin, issue SIP21. All photos by Debra Silber (*FHb*) except bottom left photo on p. 200 courtesy © Bob Falk, © Kent McDonald, © Jerry Winandy, © Steve Schmieding, and © Jim Vargo; bottom right photo on p. 205 by Brian Pontolilo (*FHb*). Drawings by Dan Thorton (*FHb*).

p. 206: Accent Your Deck with Light by Justin Fink, issue 189. All photos by Krysta S. Doerfler (*FHb*) except photos on pp. 206–207, top left photo on p. 208, top right photo on p. 211 courtesy © Highpoint Deck Lighting; top photo on p. 210 courtesy © Aurora Deck Lighting; bottom photos on p. 214 courtesy © De-Kor Lighting. Drawings Courtesy © Bob LaPoint.

p. 216: A Complete Guide to Building Your Own Deck by Rick Arnold, issue SIP21. All photos by John Ross (*FHb*) except bottom right photo on p. 227and top left photo on p. 235 by Krysta S. Doerfler (*FHb*), photos on p. 226 (bottom left), p. 231 (top left, right middle and right bottom), p. 235 (bottom right), p. 241 (top left) courtesy © Simpson Strong-Tie. Drawings courtesy ©Toby Welles/WowHouse.net.

INDEX